IN THE BORDERLANDS

LEARNING TO TEACH IN PRISONS
AND
ALTERNATIVE SETTINGS

THIRD EDITION

EDITED, AND WITH AN INTRODUCTION AND CONCLUSION,

BY

RANDALL WRIGHT, PH.D.

Published by

CALIFORNIA STATE UNIVERSITY
SAN BERNARDINO

CALIFORNIA STATE UNIVERSITY
SAN BERNARDINO

Published in San Bernardino, California,
by California State University, San Bernardino.

Image credits

Photos of Auburn Prison, Walnut Street Jail, Auburn Prison Mutual Welfare League, and panopticon prison are from the special collection at the Center for the Study of Correctional Education, California State University, San Bernardino. Images of CYA classroom, the bench, and Gehring and Eggleston courtesy California State University, San Bernardino Academic Computing and Media, photos by Robert Whitehead, alterations by Scott Rennie, used with permission of Sid Robinson. Photos of Council of Europe, Mountjoy Prison and Kilmainham Goal from Wikipedia Commons. Incarceration rate table, 1980-2006 retrieved February 13, 2008 from http://www.ojp.usdoj.gov/bjs/glance/incrt.htm. Photo of Millhaven Institution retrieved February 13, 2008, from http://www.csc-scc.gc.ca/text/facilit/institutprofiles/millhaven-eng.shtml. Images of Prison Education Service playing cards used by permission of Kevin Warner and the Prison Education Service of Ireland.

Cover images: We gratefully appreciate Ms. Veronica Hoen and the Irish Prison Service for their permission to use "Landing, Portlaoise Prison." Background photo and back cover photo of Kilmainham Gaol, Ireland by Dr. Randall Wright.

Printed in the United States of America by
Wirz & Company Printing
444 Colton Avenue
Colton, CA 92324

ISBN 978-0-9776008-4-7

This book is printed on permanent/durable paper.

ACKNOWLEDGEMENTS

I am grateful to all my generous colleagues who kindly volunteered their knowledge and encouragement to see this project to completion. I am inspired by them all.

I would particularly like to thank Drs. Eggleston and Gehring for their constant inspiration as colleagues and friends. They have charted a constant course in the field of correctional education; this book attests to their guidance in a difficult profession where many need a hand to find the way.

Every labor of love exacts a price. I want to thank my wife Patricia and my children Kevin and Christina for their patience—they always seem to be waiting for mew to complete "another project." Thanks for waiting.

"Life fills space" Bill Muth

CONTENTS

ॐ

WHAT TO PUT ON MY TAX FORM?

By Carolyn Eggleston

"When he was asked, 'How can you immure yourself of so dreary a place, and among such a class of men?' Curtis guessed the inquirer had 'yet to learn what is the richest luxury that a benevolent heart can enjoy.'"

Jared Curtis, Boston Prison Discipline Society, 1830

Although the above quote was written a long time ago, it remains relevant to our work in correctional and alternative education today. Curtis was working in Auburn Prison in New York and was speaking about one of the best kept secrets in our field—that it can be the most rewarding, most important work in which to participate. Veteran correctional educators, who have made it through all the challenges facing new teachers in prison, understand how great this work can be. There is an enormous distance between starting prison teaching and getting to this point. This book addresses that distance, and how a number of correctional educators have successfully made the journey.

New York State's Auburn Prison front entrance, 1906.

As you read about the paths the authors have taken in their prison work, you may be struck with the common themes woven throughout their narratives. Although their stories differ and the authors did not access each other's chapters, there are some common threads. One of these is each person's lack of training upon entering the prison. These teachers truly felt unprepared for the challenges. Yet they discovered some truths along the way that helped them cope and learn.

Correctional educators come from very diverse professional backgrounds. In mainstream education, teachers are prepared for the work they will actually be doing. They know the major contributors in the field, they know the current paradigm and they have been trained in relevant curriculum and pedagogy. Correctional educators may have backgrounds that include reading instruction, special education or vocational education. Some have no educational background. This adds to the problems facing the novice teacher.

The authors in this book describe, in various ways, their feelings of a profound lack of preparation. This is exacerbated by the fact that they never planned to teach in a prison in the first place. As most say, "We fell into it." Both women and men experience difficulty adjusting to prison teaching, although the experiences are likely to be different. Several of the women authors in this work articulate the difficulties with teaching in prison and Jane Penwell expresses the unique dynamics of teaching women prisoners. For women teachers, restrictive views on the stereotypes of women (mother or whore) must be addressed in some way before teaching/learning can take place.

In addition, the authors experienced adjustment problems associated with the physical plant in which they found themselves. The loud, heavy door clanging shut was a common image, well remembered by everyone who experienced it.

Some of the settings in which we teach are generously labeled "classrooms." I once taught in the visiting room, which was loud, dirty and heavily trafficked; another time in a converted broom closet. The prison setting is actually anti-educational, not pro-educational. As teachers in these settings we are truly in "the borderland," as several have stated. We must negotiate many kinds of people and agendas to be successful teachers.

Several authors articulated problems with reconciling their initial expectations of the school and students. Invariably these expectations were wrong. Before coming into the prison, most relied on what had been hawked by the media and entertainment industries.

As correctional educators, we enter with our own social and political views of the prisoner, which affect how we interact. We can over- or under-identify with the prison or with the prison staff. This in turn helps determine what and how we teach our subjects. As Steve Duguid stated, our belief systems determine these areas. (In a speech Duguid once said he did not consider himself particularly more moral than his students, but that he did not commit crime because he did not want to mess up his retirement. He had something to lose, unlike many of our students.)

Randall Wright calls the "acculturation" process one of the major issues facing the novice teacher. The dedicated, energetic teacher can face such challenges that burnout closely follows. That same teacher may have access only to long-tenured, disenchanted colleagues and find that the path of least resistance is adopting similar characteristics. Alternatively, the new teacher can engage in behavior that gets him/her in trouble with prison authorities. Removal from the position is then a likely result.

Several authors, including Jane Penwell, mention the struggle with content relevance. English grammar or the multiplication table may not seem the most important content for someone who knows what faces her or him upon release from prison. There is also a "transformational imperative," articulated by Thom Gehring, about how correctional educators must bring meaning to the content for prison students. The grammar or multiplication subject might be the vehicle for teaching, but the lesson must address greater issues. The lack of academic skills is not the reason for incarceration. Still, this may be the last opportunity for formal education for our students and we must make the best of it.

There is discussion in several chapters about what working in prisons and alternative settings does to us as people. Cormac Behan expresses the view that prison damages people, including prisoner, teacher and guard. Muth, Guttman and Penwell all say in some way that prison teaching changes us. We are as affected by the experience as any one. This, I believe, leads to the transformational imperative for us, not just for our students. We must be on a path to improvement as well. The model taught to many of us—the teacher as the font of all knowledge—is insufficient in these settings. It is just plain wrong. Correctional educators themselves have an obligation to continue to learn and grow. It makes us better teachers. It makes us better people. This is captured by the phrase, "teacher as student, and student as teacher." Although some of the life experiences our students have had could curl the hair, we can learn from their wisdom.

Madeline Kiser describes ways to bring the community into the prison, which provides for more appropriate release planning. I have always pondered the practice of removing someone from society, making all his/her decisions for a period of years and then expecting the person to magically do better once released. Zebulon Brockway, who opened Elmira Reformatory in 1876, stated that the "best behaved prisoner is often the worst citizen." We must make our educational efforts relevant and useful to prisoners. Bringing together the best of the basic and marketable skills approaches in North America, and the developmental, holistic approach aspired to in Western Europe, may give us the foundation for doing this.

However, even in the model proposed by the Irish system and the *European Prison Rules*, Costelloe, Warner and Behan express concern about trends in their systems. The *European Prison Rules* articulate standards for prison systems in Europe, and reflect the highest and best standard we have as a field. Even so, their systems are increasingly being pressured to offer only courses that can be proven to reduce recidivism. This trend is the wrong direction for correctional education, but it is pervasive in most of our systems. It reflects the social and political realities of today, but does little to improve our programs.

Correctional educators have more of an imperative to study and learn about their field than perhaps any other discipline of education. Some teaching strategies are relevant to all practitioners. Good teaching is good teaching, no matter what the setting. However, correctional education is also the "last frontier" in education and it requires teachers with unique skills and characteristics. We have a responsibility to develop a professional identity as correctional and alternative educators. We must recognize what in our field is different from, and the same as, other disciplines of education. We have to study and read. As I have often said, I knew I identified as a correctional educator when I wrote, "correctional educator" as my profession on my tax form.

The things that make it so hard to work in correctional facilities—the lock downs, the not always subtle disincentives to programming, the poor funding and setting—make it more important that we stay current, continue learning and continue growing. We have an imperative to transform ourselves as well as our students. I believe this book will help us in that mission.

INTRODUCTION

CULTURE SHOCK AND TEACHER PRACTICAL WISDOM IN THE BORDERLANDS

by Randall Wright

Most prison teachers do not intend to teach in prison or alternative settings such as juvenile halls. They landed there by accident. They did not have the benefit of a university program that provided them with a sequenced, mediated, pre-service professional development program (Geraci, 2002; Eggleston, 1991; Wright, 2002). Once inside, novice teachers discover that teaching is a "totally different" experience and prison is a "foreign place." The mainstream, stereotypical images of criminals and prisons disseminated in the media do little to dispel the confusion. Lacking the cultural maps (Geraci, 2002) to understand this foreign school and prison culture, teachers have to "work by the seat of their pants" (Wright, 2002) to make sense of their experience. Learning to teach this way is confusing, disquieting, unsettling and "dangerous and frustrating" (Eggleston, 1991, p.16). Without pre-service programs teachers are more susceptible to stress and burnout" (Wright, 2005b, p. 49). Without mentoring programs and/or professional pre- and in-services, teachers often experience profound culture shock as they experience the stages of acculturation and the identities that accompany these stages (Wright, 2005). All the while they feel isolated and powerless in a world that appears confusing or even meaningless. These experiences mark their identities and limit their professional growth, sometimes permanently.

Schools and prisons are cultural landscapes where values, beliefs and preferences are embedded and reproduced in patterns and punctuation of time, the bounding of physical space, methods of discipline and control, connections to the outside world and, most importantly, relations between inhabitants and staff. Organizational cultures are tacit, taken for granted assumptions about "the way things are done around here."

Prison cultures infuse teaching cultures in prisons, not totally absorbing them, but transforming them sufficiently so as to create culture shock for the novice teacher. Prison teaching cultures are hybrid, syncretic cultures—a blend of "home" and "host" world teaching behaviors, experiences and identities. School cultures sometimes appear as countercultures of resistance to the prison organizational culture. This culture is militaristic, authoritarian, vigilant, strategic, hierarchical, status-ridden and grounded in divisive practices entrenching a rigorous taxonomy that distinguishes "Us" from "Them"— even among the inmates or wards. Schismatic struggles and contradictions abound. These confinement cultures are generally grounded in strategic rules and processes oriented toward administratively incorporating inmates (and teachers?) easily and effectively into the system to uphold institutional order (Goffman, 1970). The issue of control and power is omnipresent (Wright, 2004).

Caught on these cultural borders, many teachers take up marginal identities such as tourists, sojourners, strangers, translators (between insides and outsides) while they simultaneously face institutional demands for them to be police officers, gatekeepers and double agents or covert operators for the good order of the institution. They experience the tension that comes from knowing their students as human beings—subjects who share the need for love, acceptance and hope and who grieve and feel remorse—and the treatment of them as objects that must be kept at a social distance. Teachers struggle to find the right professional distance, or "relational mean," between student and teacher. So they find themselves on the ethical and social borders in their interactions with students as subjects and objects. They are caught too on the borders between insides and outsides, so that when teachers describe their jobs to community members some are quick to ask, "Why would you want to teach THEM, in THERE?"

Teachers become suspicious OTHERS to those on the outside and feel obliged to plead their cause, hoping others will agree their work is worthwhile and that yes, they are "real" teachers. Teachers find themselves on the social-cultural borders between the school and the prison; here, too, they become suspicious OTHERS to prison staff and must often prove their worth. Borders are everywhere—formed in the social, physical (and even temporal) edges of teachers and inmate/student; the school and the prison; and, the prison and the community. Everywhere teachers experience the divisive practices that separate "Us" from "Them." Along these edges in these spaces they must, to be successful, sustain the ambiguity that I argue shapes our professional identity. Learning to teach in prisons and other institutional settings is a phenomenon of the borderlands:

> Borderlands are a kind of space, social as much as physical or geographical, which are co-inhabited by people of different cultures, classes, ethnicities, religions, languages, as well as sexualities and genders and politics. A borderland is a contested zone. (Stanley, in Wright, 2005, p. 36)

The teachers' dislocation is a rich source of professional knowledge and practical wisdom: "The borderland is potentially, an introspective and perspectival place where teachers experience the collision of cultures and the deeply embedded assumptions in them" (Wright, 2005, p. 37). In the borderlands teachers encounter enigmatic students with lives and experiences at the margins of social life. They confront their beliefs about good and evil. They must negotiate anew their pedagogical relations with students both young and old. They are challenged with regard to their pedagogical outcomes. They question their curricular knowledge to see if it makes sense in these settings. Teachers must not only cross the social and cultural borders to reach their students. They must also invite students to cross these borders to understand their worlds and the worlds of others. Giroux uses the term *border pedagogy* to suggest how teachers provide students with "the opportunity to engage the multiple references that constitute different cultural codes, experiences, and languages" (Giroux, 1997, p. 147).

In these essays, the practical wisdom of prison teachers unfolds as they narrate professional dilemmas and concerns that arise as they experience "frictions in the machine" (Wright, 2003). This anthology shares teachers' experiences of teaching to ease the novice teacher's transition into alternative school settings such as prisons and juvenile halls and enable veteran teachers to reflect upon and perhaps even reconsider past experiences. Unfortunately, teacher professional development is often narrowly defined as a technical activity rather than "in terms of genuine developmental change" (Arlin, 1999, p. 13). The essays in this volume share experiences of teachers' trial and error that led to innovation, reflection and, I would argue, to genuine developmental change. The aim of this book is to contribute to the development of wise prison teachers. According to Arlin (1999):

> Wise teachers possess: (a) rich factual knowledge about teaching and about their subject matter; (b) rich procedural knowledge about teaching strategies and the practical knowledge of how and when to use them; (c) a sense of the context of instruction and the context in which the students are being instructed; (d) an awareness of the relativism associated with variations in values and priorities of both their peers and their students; and (e) an uncertainty about the effects of specific teaching decisions coupled with a willingness to take risk and to try a variety of ways to actively participate with the students in the learning process. (p. 13)

Certainly some teachers arrive at the prison gates as mature, wise educators—flexible, sensitive to context, prepared to live with uncertainty— while others embark on a personal and professional journey on the inside that is insightful and transformative. These essays illustrate the accumulated practical wisdom of teachers. At the heart of their stories is their struggle to shape a professional identity behind bars, in the contested borderlands. Their stories do not prescribe the proper pedagogical course of action for the reader. They are stories about professional dilemmas that hopefully evoke personal, practical, professional and philosophical reflection from readers.

Pauline Geraci reflects on the prison context by examining the relationship between organizations, their cultures and identities: "I now realize that an understanding of culture is important and necessary to correctional educators, but so too is a thorough understanding of professional, personal and organizational identity." She notes how prison is a place of contradictions: "If we do not reconcile these contradictions, we will be victims of ongoing changing circumstances." She quotes one correctional educator who says, "You have to be on the same page and know what the organization wants. If you don't, you create friction and are not really part of the organization. But you also have to be careful not to lose part of yourself in the process." She asks how we can live authentically as professionals in these settings.

Bill Muth finds it useful to use the stages of acculturation and experience of culture shock explored by Wright (2005) to reflect on experiences he recorded in his journal more than two decades ago. In the initial phases of his prison teaching, Bill feels "exposed" and vulnerable—afraid that he doesn't know how to teach. His vulnerability provokes a backlash as he finds himself angry at his students, colleagues and the prison system. This is the initial, disintegration and frustration phase of the cultural shock experience. He worries that the unexpressed anger and frustration in the classroom will haunt his relationship with his son, so that he must build borders around his work and home life.

A borderland is a contested zone marked by the struggle for power, knowledge and authority, and identity. In his work, border skirmishes with his students for power, status and authority are evident. This theme comes home as he expresses the professional dilemmas he faces with the prisoner-tutor in his classroom. Tutors frequently believe they have more status and power than the other students they teach and so they often become a challenge to the teacher's authority. Bill faces professional dilemmas as he realizes he must solicit their help but, at the same time, keep control of his classroom and them. After all, they are "just" prisoners whose status as tutors is conferred on them by him.

His work gives us personal and practical examples of what sociologists describe as "role strain," because prison teachers sometimes have to cross the school-prison border to enforce the good order of the institution—as guards. Bill describes his transformation of identities when he had to shave his beard so the gas mask would fit better on his face when he was called to join the riot squad. Teachers often experience re-identification processes (and crises) in the practical situations they encounter.

Bill's journey illustrates how teaching in prison is full of uncertainties and how, as prison teachers, we cannot be overly daunted by them—we must be willing to take professional risks, knowing that the outcomes of these decisions are not always predictable. He becomes tolerant of this uncertainty and, out of this uncertainty, comes practical wisdom.

David Werner shares with us his early experiences as a prison teacher and helps us understand the tactile, aesthetic sense of enclosure, isolation and, of course, the experience of a border crossing as he enters prison for the first time:

> Doors closing is actually many people's first impression of prison; the impression of finality, enclosure, of somebody locking you in. Doors in prison seem to weigh tons apiece. I've often thought

that they make doors in prison have the sound they have more for effect than actual need. Some years later we hired a man to teach in a prison who seemed to be perfectly suitable and even-tempered. He made it only as far as the inner sets of gates on his first day, then turned around and fled and we never saw him again. It turned out he had a severe case of claustrophobia.

On his first day of teaching, David's students ask him what he feels about teaching in prison. He is tempted to lie (prison teaching often raises ethical issues) and build borders between himself and his students. Their deceptively simple question is ultimately more complex because it raises ethical and pedagogical issues. They are really asking, "Do you respect us enough to tell us the truth?" David writes:

> Why do we set up the walls we do? Primarily, to "save face"— which is a pretty interesting term. I set up the walls I do to save the face I project to the world. I lie to protect myself, or to protect the image of myself that I project to the world.

How do and must prison teachers "prepare a face to meet the faces they meet"—as T.S. Eliot would have it? We know we cannot take our impression and classroom management strategies for granted in prisons. We must be cautious so as not to give students the impression that we are prepared to cross professional lines of propriety. Negotiating professional boundaries is both a personal and professional identity issue, and it is a practical issue: We must also scope out identities or presentations of self that meet the students' approval so we can teach them.

As I noted above, sometimes teachers in alternative settings deeply experience role strain or a deeply conflicted self—they perceive almost irreconcilable contrasts between the images they have of themselves in private moments of honest self-reflection and the self that they present to others. The struggle to sustain one's authentic professional identity in the face of a prescribed organizational identity is a product of the conflicting ideological orientations embedded in prison and teaching cultures. Some teachers cannot manage this ideological conflict and simply leave, frustrated, disillusioned and burned out (Wright, 2005b).

David Werner responds to his students' question with honesty. He tells them he is "scared shitless." These brief moments when teachers choose what to disclose to students are defining moments that speak to their assumptions about self, other, trust, power and authority, and professional boundaries. These fleeting questions become serious matters of navigating or achieving the right relational distance or proper professional boundaries with students. David initiates for us a conversation about ethical judgment in pedagogy; his answer suggests how he will negotiate his pedagogical relations with his students.

Like many of the other authors in this book, David crosses borders to explore his students' worlds. He overcomes the social stigma (constructed by those on the outside) that made his students into monstrous others and filled his mind with negative images before he got to know them as individuals: "We talked about how all of my being afraid had to do with something I expected to be there, and nothing to do with what was actually there."

Jane Guttman's essay, "Teaching in the Existential Village," describes her school in juvenile hall as a "reservoir of possibility." Her story reminds us that teaching in alternative environments is more often than not, a pedagogy of hope. (How else could teachers instruct students with so many disadvantages, in such oppressive environments?) In the juvenile hall, Jane undergoes a professional "stripping process." She realizes that to teach well, she must become a student again. Her experience with juvenile offenders/students "wakes her" out of her emotional and spiritual "slumber" and opens up her "heart and soul." Prison education is transformative, not only for students but also for teachers when they empathetically cross the border between self and other, in caring relationships.

Sensitive to context and nuances on the inside, she describes the symbolism of the bench in her facility. The bench, where wards of the state sit, is a divisive place where keepers reprimand, verbally abuse and discipline the kept. It is a physical point of transition, as wards wait for permission to move to other parts of the facility. She reshapes the meaning of this place, turning it into a place of encounters, connections and community for juveniles on their daily journeys in the institution. This is an important transgressive act because prison culture is embedded in meanings and symbols that signify and support the oppressive order. This redefinition of the situation opens up the world for her and her students and creates, in her words "a space of kindness." Like many border dwellers, she must deal with the local representatives of power and authority, and she brings them to the bench too, in efforts of reconciliation and restoration. And so she learns to champion border crossings among the school, prison and the world outside: Wise educators gain a practical knowledge of context and the ability to make meaningful and care-full judgments and choices within it.

Paul Ropp, an administrator in the Canadian prison school system, takes on the serious issue of professional boundaries in prison. It is difficult in prison to find the right social and psychological distance between teacher and student. This is especially poignant in prisons because teachers often care deeply for their students (Wright, 2004). Exercising sound pedagogical judgment in prisons is difficult. Identifying too closely with their students— crossing over into their social world—teachers endanger themselves and others. Paul identifies the reasons teachers sometimes forget where they are and as a result are set up by inmates. He cites lack of training, groupthink, isolation (The Mad Trapper Syndrome), the Maverick Mindset and personal vulnerabilities as characteristics that turn teachers into "rogue" correctional educators. Rogue teachers enjoy and flaunt living on edges of the professional distances between student and teacher—sometimes at their peril.

As I have suggested, without proper in-services, or professional support, teachers must learn to teach by the seat of their pants—they are generally unprepared for the work set out for them. Jane Penwell describes the feelings of culture shock in a newly constructed and somewhat threatening women's prison:

> In the beginning, we huddled together, finding comfort in numbers in this alien environment and clinging to our old routines—setting up our offices, arranging our furniture, booting up our computers and waiting—waiting for them to arrive and then one day, they came. But by the time hundreds of them came, we had learned the prison routine—we knew about chits and counts and chow, lock ups and lock downs, belly chains and cuffs. We had created our program and assigned ourselves duties, we had worked with the few women who were in the facility as cooks and clerks, we had taught mock classes and ordered more books—we were ready, or so we thought.

Her story briefly describes the rites of passage from traditional school teacher to teacher "on the inside." One of her greatest challenges is devising what Freire (1970) would describe as a "pedagogy of the oppressed"—a pedagogy that merges meaningfully with the students' lives. The students Jane imagined were not the students who appeared at her door; she is not ready at first, to cross the borders into their world:

> Instead, the women who filled the seats in my classes were introverted, unresponsive, angry, bitter and resistant to group activities (which I had thought would work quite well). These were not the wisecracking jokers from my high school classes or the bad boys who squirmed in their seats and loved it when I read to them. These were adult women whose lives had been ruined, whose children were with strangers, whose men had betrayed them and whose parents blamed them. These students, when asked to write an essay, wrote about rape and beatings and drug deals gone wrong in which people were killed or seriously wounded. They wrote about drive-by shootings and gangs—a world that I had read about in the newspaper or seen on TV but hadn't really understood existed. They accused me of using their stories to get attention at parties, of not caring about their traumas, of walking out at night and forgetting them and, worst of all, of trying to get them to learn something that just didn't matter in their lives.

Wise teachers understand the specific contexts and understandings of the learner in the classroom. Jane Penwell recognizes how her middle-class, taken-for-granted assumptions clash with the lives of "real incarcerated women." She recognizes how she and they have lived separate lives and this is the beginning of a more authentic curriculum and dialogue, where students are considered on their own terms. She begins to understand that prison teaching as a bordered pedagogy. Jane recognizes the need for what Arlin (1990) describes as a constructive classroom "where teachers and students negotiate as they attempt to construct shared meanings" (Cobb in Arlin, 1990, p. 82). She crosses the socially constructed border that constitutes the criminal as "Other" and learns from them the importance of teaching in a way that is meaningful to their lives; teaching becomes a conversation (Arlin, 1990). Shaken by her initial prison experience helps her become a wiser, more reflective teacher.

Her essay is also a cautionary tale about subtly trying to instill middle-class values in students whose very lives challenge her worldview with understandings they bring from their specific contexts. Critical theorists discuss how many lower class students lack "cultural capital"—or habits, ways of speaking and interacting valued by the middle class or the wealthy. Jane's work reminds us that juvenile halls and other institutions extend (and hence support) the power relations and social dynamics on the street; schools are contested sites for power and knowledge and teachers are often ideologues for middle class virtues and worldviews.

Within the classroom, she recognizes other power relations that suggest to us how difficult it is to empower students whose silences are strategic and necessary to their survival in prison. This is apparent when Jane discovers that students who choose to speak in class do so with impunity because they are connected to those with muscle on the outside, or simply because they know they can physically overpower others in the prison pods outside the school. This knowledge gives them liberty to speak their mind.

Madeline Kiser's essay, "In the Name of Liquidity and Flow," is also concerned with dissolving the socially constructed borders between the prison and the community that contribute to the social abandonment of her students. Like many of the authors in this text, she is challenged to recreate some form of community within the prison walls. And, like some of the authors in this book, bridging the outside and the inside with the principle of pedagogical "relevance" becomes an integral element in her curricular theorizing. As a teacher, she wonders what to do to facilitate a "kind of imagining" that opens up her students' world to the world of others in the community—those who do not only think in terms of money, prestige and power, but also about living richer, meaningful lives with others. She invites survivors of tragedy into the school to share their stories of resilience and care with students; they model the human capacity to transcend pain and loss to care deeply for others in the community:

> Narrative is everything; narrative, and stories. All of the visitors
> who spoke to us had two qualities in common: they had suffered
> a loss, a disease, some personal disaster or misfortune and
> subsequently live owning up to loss by working to lessen others'

suffering; and, they are capable of narrating this loss in a way that's engaging. Hearing these narratives, participating in them for a while, inmates were made to feel part of a community before leaving prison and not just part of any community: Part of a group of people who don't live predominantly for money. Surprising numbers of my students hadn't been exposed to these kinds of people. It's not that altruism doesn't exist for them; rather, it isn't dominant among the ethics and reality they've inhabited. "You work for HOW much?" they liked to ask, when I'd share my hourly rate. "Man, you're nuts," they would say and think. Then, I'd see them, changed from tan prison clothing to tennis shoes and jeans walking out through prison doors to the taxi, waiting to take them back to where they came from.

For Madeline, sharing others' stories of tragedy and resilience with students is one of the most important activities of the prison teacher because it helps them cross the restrictive, limiting emotional borders that circumscribe their abilities to care and identify with others.

Of course gender relations are another source of friction for teachers in alternative settings. Women working in prison often are doubly alienated; they are dislocated professionally from conventional schooling on the outside and they must also shape a professional identity in the predominantly male-dominated militaristic prison culture (Geraci, 2002; Wright, 2004). In these spaces, women are forced to retreat from their own identities—striving to be unmarked with regard to their sex by not wearing perfume, jewelry and provocative dress. Marginalized in the borderlands they may almost become invisible and their voices muted.

Thom Gehring describes his transition from practitioner to a theorist and author over three decades. Thom's work is one of the most salient examples of how practitioner/theorists, concerned with the democratic reorganization of prisons, can bring about change by blending theory with practice (praxis). This is a difficult position for many correctional educators to accept, as they often privilege practice over theory (Gehring & Wright, 2006). Correctional education, he argues, embroils us in issues of professional development, social justice, and institutional change. We can and must be social activists when it comes to the cause of education behind bars. His strategy to overcome the anti-educational, authoritarian biases of the prison system is to promote reflection and articulation of one's schools of thought; this professional armor will protect teachers as they assume the roles of what Giroux (2004) would describe as transformative intellectuals. One's school of thought can and should be supported by a historical and contemporary sense of the major contributors to the field of correctional education. Thom writes that for teachers, "this is a low cost, effective strategy to avoid being co-opted by the prison system and/or losing their sense of themselves as teachers rather than correctional officers."

Influenced by Ken Wilber's work, Thom proposes a different—"transrational"—way of thinking about the advancement of teaching in alternative settings. He believes teacher intuition and dedication to greater, just causes can "pull" us from the present state into a better future where prisons and other institutions are governed by democratic principles. He challenges the current scientific worldview that privileges antecedent forces—causes—that appear to "push" us forward from behind. This position detracts from our ability to act as agents of institutional and social change (and coincidently, feeds into alienated and burned out teachers' perceptions that their professional world is the result of causes "outside their control"). While not denying the constraining effects of the prison (the push), his essay is inspiring because of its utopian spirit. Like other authors, his correctional education philosophy is imbued with a sense of hope.

Teri Hollingsworth develops a philosophy of correctional education partially grounded in her previous personal experiences as a ward of the state. This experience informs her concern for the professional development of the "highly qualified correctional educator" who can relate to the unique needs of incarcerated students. Influenced in part by Gehring's work, she explores the issues of professionalism in correctional education, noting how the process constrains as well as invigorates a profession and its institutions. Conventional school cultures are perpetuated by public school teachers who teach the way they were taught (which can be either positive or negative). Correctional educators experience more freedom: Untrained for the job, educators are ideally positioned to adopt models of practice that emphasize innovation and transformation, if their professional development program underscores these principles. Informed by critical theory, which focuses on issues of power, Teri worries that the political and pedagogical voices of prison teachers and students will not be heard in traditional university credential programs and in-services monopolized by public school traditions. She recognizes the need for more specific professional development courses for teachers in these alternative environments and proposes a credentialing model for them that bridges their contextualized, local and practical knowledge—with theories of effective teaching and learning.

Like other authors in this anthology, she re-examines the conceptual underpinnings of correctional curricula, concluding that their behaviorist biases toward control of behavior do not meet the needs of the correctional student. She challenges the control or governance models implicit in the behaviorist curriculum, citing literature to demonstrate its ineffectiveness: Students only experience short-term learning in these programs to appease the authorities (as a "get out of jail card"). These curricula reduce teachers to technicians responsible for manipulating variables in their environment so as to elicit the appropriate stimulus and response from students. Instead, Teri proposes a constructivist framework that takes into consideration the meaning of education from the students' point of view, a position that illustrates again a trait of a wise teacher.

Duguid's account of his role as university teacher and administrator in a Canadian prison university program underscores the desire on the part of many theorists and practitioners to develop democratic communities in prison. His retrospective on his role in the provision of university courses in Canadian prisons speaks to his social justice model of prison education and his political, curricular and personal commitments. Influenced by Michael Foucault's (1977) work on prison discipline and punishment, he argues teachers must position themselves as insiders and outsiders simultaneously (in the borderlands, I would add) if they are to be effective. His essay describes how he managed to do this.

His philosophy of prison education is based on cognitive models of decision-making. He writes: "...most criminals are not helplessly 'driven' to crime by poverty, ignorance or illness. Choices involve decisions, which in turn engage both reason (critical thinking) and ethics (moral assessments)." This choice model is implied and realized in the cultural literacy program he developed for university students in Canada. Later on in Canada, the theme of choices was taken up by the Federal Correctional Service in their work with women offenders and the opening of the new prisons for women (Wright, 2004). David Warner takes up Duguid's work in his essay in this volume, to critique the inexorable ties between education and recidivism rates that flatten or hollow out educational programs. This chapter clearly demonstrates how his personal belief systems regarding criminality and his tacit assumptions about reducing crime underpinned his cultural literacy program.

Cormac Behan's critical-theoretical work examines prison education in Ireland. He believes the current prison education discourse is too narrowly focused on the goals of rehabilitation and skill development and neglects critical and transformative adult education practices. The current educative discourse (a discourse is a linguistic representation of reality that shapes and even determines what is noticed or forgotten) has silenced the critical discourse that would position inmates as potentially critical adults and citizens. He tries to expand the current education discourse by pointing out what seems to have been overlooked, citing pivotal policy documents such as Education in Prison (Council of Europe, 1990), The Management of Offenders (Department of Justice, 1994) and the Strategy Statement of the Prison Education Service 2003-2007 (Irish Prison Education Service, 2004). His work serves as a wonderful example of a teacher exploring the policy landscape to provide a foundation for a critical pedagogy that creates horizons of hope and possibility based on the self-realized needs of adult offenders. It also demonstrates how our professional identity (as transformative intellectuals) can be shaped by the literature in our field.

Looking to find local theories and practices in the margins that empower students, Cormac attempts to locate the social and physical spaces—the cracks in the system of surveillance and power—that might permit more authentic dialogue and social/institutional transformation in prison and on the outside.

His article in this book signals the turn toward a more critical and suspicious stance to prison education as a form of power. He writes how prison:

> ...damages people. It damages those who are committed there, those who send them there, those who guard them and those who work in the various social and educational services. Society suffers by using it as a method to punish some of those who have transgressed accepted norms. Those who enter prison will find an environment, architecture, regime and a stultifying atmosphere that is alien to the human condition. It is an unnatural place. It is a horrific institution, but one which society seems incapable of doing without.

Frequently now, prison educators turn to Goffman's (1970) analyses of total institutions such as prisons and mental institutions to gain theoretic appreciation of education in prisons. (See Richard Ashcroft's article in this anthology in this regard). Goffman's description of the total institution paints a gloomy picture of life entirely controlled and administered under one roof. In these institutions inmates are stripped of identities to facilitate their management and administration in "large batches."

Goffman has contributed to the recent spatializing trend in critical theory—where ethical, social, pedagogical "spaces" become the analytic terms to understand social interaction. Useful to critical theorists then is the way Goffman (1961/1997) fragments the social/physical spaces in total institutions. He identifies three distinct spaces: first there is the space that is off-limits or out-of-bounds; second there are surveillance spaces where inmates may be present but highly supervised; and, third there is the "space ruled by less than usual staff authority"—a "third space" that is "shielded from the eyes and ears of staff" (p. 324). In Goffman's terms, Cormac seeks out this "third" or "free space" (p. 326)—a physical and social-psychological, pedagogical space—to introduce adult-centered educational practices where the disciplinary tactics and power-full relations of the prison seem almost absent. Prison schools often can be, relatively speaking, the "back stages" of prison life and thus provide opportunities for different cultural norms, patterns of interactions and values to surface (Wright, 2003).

Cormac's project in these relatively unsupervised spaces is immense. It is none other than to use adult education to recover the "stolen humanity" of prisoners stripped away by their confinement in a total institution. Adult education, conceived holistically and transformationally, resists the identity politics of prisons that ignore the fact that inmates are both adults and citizens with basic rights. Mezirow's theory of transformational learning is inspirational in this regard because it challenges the teachers' and learners' assumptions about the world that limit our thinking and hence our possibilities for social justice.

Anne Costelloe and Kevin Warner, like Cormac, interrogate the current penal discourse in Ireland and abroad from a critical perspective informed by their European prison experience:

> It is our concern that education, like many other professions and activities in prison, is now expected to give priority attention to the new discourse and its advocacy of programs that are presumed to address directly the "criminogenic factors" in the prisoner. It would seem to us that the dominance of this discourse has shifted the ground rules. Prison education, like all other activities, must now defend itself primarily in response to the question: How is it addressing offending behavior? It is no longer deemed acceptable or apt to suggest that perhaps the question is itself misguided. As a result, evaluation of prison education tends to be based on whether its courses can be seen to reduce recidivism.

Stephen Duguid and others have identified this position as an endorsement of the "medical model" of programs (a term first used by Goffman) that presumes offenders are either mad or bad and in need of "fixing," thereby robbing them of their dimensionality and agency. I believe this deficit model confers on prison officials (including teachers) a therapeutic or pastoral power (Foucault, 1980)—the power exercised by priests, counselors and therapists to use techniques to draw out, scrutinize and discipline the inner worlds of their clients.

Kevin and Anne challenge the socially constituted borders between the inside and outside. Without the "liquidity and flow" of programs, social contacts and holistic, integrative curricula from the outside to the inside, the debilitating effects of the prison on the autonomy, dignity and agency of the prisoner will be keenly experienced. The democratic thrust of European policy statements that frames prison practice and education, if ignored by prison authorities and the public, will give prison officials full reign when it comes to perpetuating the negative, debilitating culture of the total institution. Anne and Kevin would have us turn prison education into a vehicle for border crossing that contributes to the "resettlement" of prisoners. They believe teachers must adopt identities as border guards so as to preserve the social and educative free spaces in schools and thereby protect prisoners from the damaging effects of the prison. Their position is consistent with objectives of European prison "rule number 65," which is:

> ...defensive, focused, quite properly, on recognizing and attempting to undo or minimize, the negative effects of imprisonments itself. This is a long way from the confidence of much offense-focused work, which asserts it can intervene and improve people while ignoring the counter-influences inherent in the prison system.

Instead of pathologizing prisoners and developing narrow programs to fix them, Anne and Kevin cite Duguid's research that indicates comprehensive education programs actually lower recidivism rates because prisoners become "interested in something else." It is easy to understand then, how contemporary constructivist theories of education such as those proposed by many authors in this anthology become a discourse of resistance to the current state of penal affairs.

Susan Yantz' introspective essay considers prison teachers' professional identity and practice as a borderland practice. Her work introduces us to a more recent (post-modern) ethnographic writing genre with different voices contributing to her narrative. Post-modern and ethnographic research is very concerned with the language(s) used to (re)present reality. This is because many post-modernist theorists adopt a strong or mild version of linguistic determinism where language or more broadly, symbols systems, create reality rather than simply represent it. Struggling with the politics of representation, Susan uses and provides us with some of the "data" she gathered to explore what it means to be a prison teacher. This consists of her journals, theories about prison teaching and borderland cultures, and interview transcripts conducted with a colleague (this author). She aptly uses the borderland as a metaphor to discuss the problems of shaping a professional identity behind bars:

> The borderland space of a prison classroom is a marginalized location that is full of obscure contradictions for the powerful and the powerless, for the insiders and the outsiders. It is a borderland also of dominant and subordinate identifications. To which group do correctional educators belong—insider or outsider? I wondered if I could belong to both groups at the same time? In my experience, I was both insider and outsider at once. I participated in both inside and outside worlds. My classroom consisted of complex and confusing interconnections between the prison and the outside world. The multiplicity of borders and border-crossings experienced by the prison educator take place not from some located place or space, but instead from within a borderland space in which borders and border crossings are difficult to name and claim.

Susan examines identity formation in a post-modern framework that underscores its socially constructed and highly negotiated quality. Her view and that of the post-modern school contrasts sharply with the Enlightenment view, which considers the self as an autonomous, self-contained, rational, monad possessing fixed and roughly unchangeable and essential characteristics. This is a liberating theoretical and practical position because it permits all of us to re-negotiate and repudiate our stereotypic or taken-for-granted identities based on gender, race and class.

How do researchers who are conscious that prisons turn prisoners into objects actively pursue research strategies that position the prisoner as subject? This is the issue of "giving voice to the voiceless" that Anne Costelloe takes up as a teacher and researcher in prison, and as a researcher/practitioner in her chapter.

Anne Costelloe calls attention to her borderland experience or "in-betweenness" as she struggles with her dual role as a researcher and teacher who is inside (the prison) and outside (the prisoner culture). Heavily schooled by the post-modern, critical tradition and qualitative research, she worries about (re)presenting her students' world in her research knowing that (re)presenting others is an issue of power because researchers (and teachers) have privileges or cultural capital (Bennett-deMarrais & LeCompte, 1999) to define truth, knowledge and, ultimately, reality. Anne writes:

> As a prison teacher carrying out academic research into prison education I was faced with a dilemma. On the one hand, I wanted my research findings to represent accurately my students' experiences and beliefs. On the other hand, I believe firmly in postmodernist research notions that there is no such thing as an accurate reflection of the truth. By this I am referring to views like those of Denzin and Lincoln, 2000, that there is "no clear window into the inner life of an individual, any gaze is always filtered through the lens of language, gender, social class, race, and ethnicity." (p. 19) My dilemma was compounded further because I concur also with the view that any research carried out on behalf of somebody else is ineffective: So what was I to do? How was I going to resolve these seemingly conflicting issues? In other words, how was I to realize my research objective of "giving voice to the voiceless" while simultaneously stressing that in any research project there is a world of difference between the text being collected and the text being created? In terms of research ethics, this was the major quandary I faced.

Richard Ashcroft's chapter offers us a comprehensive overview of personal and professional identity issues and provides the reader with opportunities to pursue further research on professional identity issues. Richard builds on his experiences as a correctional educator in a juvenile facility to describe how identities in alternative settings are subject to negotiations of status and power. Like others in the anthology, he uses Goffman's work to consider the implications of identity formation and creation of institutional orders in California juvenile facilities. Goffman's work illustrates how presentations of self are managed through one's attention to appearance (i.e., clothing), manner and setting. These appearances tell others what is expected in the interaction; these definitions of the situation create and perpetuate social order:

> "Do not wear denim," is a serious caution I gave to my SJSU graduate students when we visited youth prisons in California.

Denim clothing could have identified them as wards. In these total institutions denim is the "uniform" of the imprisoned. Prison guards wear uniforms that are similar in style to those worn by others in the "policing" professions. These uniforms clearly serve as "identifiers" of them and their role within the institutional context. The uniform signifies parameters, especially regarding communication. The communicative tone or register used when communicating "from" the role of uniformed guard "to" uniformed ward, is dramatically different than the reverse: the tone or register used when communicating "from" the role of uniformed ward "to" uniformed guard. Much of the institutional context is produced by this difference in vocal register.

Richard's work extends our discussion of teacher professional identity development by mining the social psychological literature on the formation of self by Cooley, Mead and others whose work confirms that the professional and personal self is socially constructed though interactions. The self is a communicative phenomenon.

It is my hope the reader will appreciate how these contributors, in their different ways, contribute to constructivist models of education that suggest a respectful dialogue with prisoners and promote the concept of prison and alternative education as the co-production of meaning:

> Wise educators are sensitive to the relativism associated with variations in the values and priorities of their peers, students, families and communities. They have an understanding of the values of the various groups with whom they interact and make a concerted effort to incorporate knowledge of and sensitivity to those values into all instructionally related decisions. (California State University, 2000, p. 3)

Constructivism as an educational stance promotes communities of learning because it underscores the ethical and practical position that both students and teachers are engaged in educational conversations. Constructivist pedagogy promotes learner inquiry and cooperative learning; provides room for multiple and transformative representations of reality and embeds education in real-world situations and authentic life experiences. A constructivist approach is a "defensive practice" against the dehumanizing effects of prisons. It creates free school spaces and prepares prisoners for "resettlement"—by making a place for them in the world. In prisons, the school is quite possibly an interior garden, where other ways of being and knowing are nurtured for both teachers and students.

I hope that readers will find much to ponder in these essays. If these stories facilitate reflection, cause consternation, provoke responses and suggest novel lines of inquiry and practice, then I will be satisfied that this book has supported the professional development of teachers and contributed to the collective wisdom of our craft.

Scott Rennie's contribution to this third edition takes a retrospective look at the field of correctional education. He reminds us that a historical consciousness—knowledge of the major contributors to the field—is necessary to better understand who we are and what we are capable of accomplishing as correctional educators. Without this knowledge, we are often imprisoned by a present mindedness and forced to reinvent ourselves as educators, perhaps needlessly.

Philadelphia's Walnut Street Jail, cradle of the modern penitentiary and birthplace of U.S. correctional education in 1787.

PROFESSIONAL, PERSONAL AND ORGANIZATIONAL IDENTITY IN A CORRECTIONAL EDUCATION SETTING: CAN WE BE OURSELVES?

by Pauline Geraci

Introduction

Many correctional educators lack a definition of who they are, what their mission is and how they fit in as professionals in a correctional setting. Teaching is a people-profession; our mission would be rather meaningless without our students. But these very same students are the ones that test who we really are. Teaching in a correctional setting becomes an exercise in understanding oneself in relationship to where and who we are. These ubiquitous issues in the process of understanding ourselves are personal and in need of close examination by all correctional educators. One of my challenges as a correctional educator for the past ten years has been the questioning and re-defining of my identity. I have had to teach while feeling a sense of imbalance and discomfort, but the introspection has been well worth it. My chapter describes the identity issues that confront teachers as they learn to teach on the inside.

In my book, *Teaching on the Inside*, I stated that knowledge of cultures is important to correctional educators. In prisons, we must have knowledge of correctional, inmate and educational cultures. All these cultures are separate at times, but in many cases they become multilayered. After some research (Evans, 2002; Gergen, 1991; Goodson & Cole, 1994; Lamb & Davidson, 2002; Magala, 2003; Marsh, 2003; Seifert, 2004; Wink & Wink, 2004), I now realize an understanding of culture is important and necessary to correctional educators, but so too is a thorough understanding of professional, personal and organizational identity.

This is not a new concept. You will find this need to understand personal, professional and organizational identity in any work setting. I stress the importance of negotiating often-conflicting identities in a correctional education setting because we put our jobs on the line. If we do not reconcile these contradictions, we will be victims of ongoing changing circumstance. As one correctional educator put it, "You have to be on the same page and know what the organization wants. If you don't, you create friction and are not really part of the organization. But you also have to be careful not to lose part of yourself in the process." It is only when we become more knowledgeable about professional, personal and organizational identities that we can reconcile the differences and contradictions we see ourselves enacting from one situation to the next.

Correctional educators raise *professional* identity issues when they ask questions such as: What is the correctional organization all about? What is my role and mission in a correctional context as a professional educator? How do I understand corrections? They raise *personal* identity issues when they ask: Who am I? How do I understand myself?

Personal identity theory is not the same as social identity theory. Basically, identity theory states that we are all made up of a collection of identities and each identity is based on roles we engage in at a particular time. For example, when we answer the question, "Who am I?" with "I am a correctional educator," we identify ourselves with that role. If we answer "a mother," then our answer reflects our personal identity. The identity we choose to be at any given time influences how much effort we put into playing that identity or role. We look at and respond to situations differently based on our particular role. But in a correctional setting, we should look first at the situation, then choose our role to help us navigate these situations rather than the other way around.

When first we enter the world of corrections as teachers, we bring with us a professional identity as an educator. We have diplomas and certification from the state, proclaiming we are educators. We belong to professional organizations that reinforce our identities as educators. We also bring our personal identities. We may identify with the role of mother, daughter, wife, husband, son, artist, writer, etc. In addition, we also take on an organizational identity. Sociologist Whyte has noted that "the workplace strongly influences our identities and self-preservation." Even organizations such as prisons have multiple identities. Magala, 2003, has suggested there are five facets of collective identity in a business organization. These are:

- *Professed* identity (clear mission statements, articulated claims that individuals believe in);

- *Projected* identity (mainly the use of managed media and symbols in corporate communications to the outside world, highly supervised);

- *Experienced* identity (conscious and unconscious impressions leading to some representations in individual minds);

- *Manifested* identity (historical identity of a given organization over some period of time); and,

- *Attributed* identity or how organization is experienced from the outside.

Just as organizations must look at how their identities mesh, we too need to look at the organizational attributed, manifested and projected identities in relation to our experienced and professed identity as teachers and find a way to make them fit, or else we need to move on.

2

In corrections we find ourselves asking, "What happens when the projected identity can no longer be reconciled with the experienced identity inside the organization?" (Soenen & Moingeon in Magala, 2002). We should also ask, "What happens when my personal identity no longer fits with the organizational identity?"

Other questions we should ask: Do I have a strong sense of personal identity and a good understanding of the correctional identity? Do I know if they can work together? How does my perception of organizational identity shape my self-reflections? What does it mean to be a teacher in a correctional setting? Asking ourselves these questions and others is part of the ongoing self-reflection of our personal identities.

This is not a simple task for correctional educators because there is a complex interrelationship among correctional organizations, individual teachers' attributes and teaching cultures. Teachers are faced with a variety of organizational norms. They are taught certain expectations at correctional academies, including that they be suspicious of inmates (trust no one), not take things "personally," be "firm, fair and consistent," and "follow the rules." One educator, who was told to follow the rules gives this account about her first few months on the job: "I was always looking around and making sure my back wasn't turned on an inmate, because that's what we were taught. I now realize that the students appreciate me for what I do and they aren't all trying to kill me."

Everyday we walk into a correctional setting with our professional educator identity, or Mask 1, and our personal identity, or Mask 2. Then we put on another mask called organizational identity, or Mask 3. There may even be other masks that we wear. The assortment of these identities is not a problem for some professionals, but it can become tiresome and stressful for correctional educators. We become weighed down by conflicting selves. We are challenged by the dichotomy between "real" emotion and external "fake" expressions. Our identities or roles may become blurred and result in confusion and anxiety about which role we should be playing at a particular time. At any given time, personal and professional identities may overlap. We are constantly walking a fine line between who we really are and who we are trying to be.

"It's very stressful balancing identities. I'm finally getting used to being two different people," stated a new educator.

Juggling identities is indeed stressful. It has also been described as "emotional labor." In the book *The Managed Heart* by A.R. Hochschild (1983), emotional labor is described as "the management of feeling to create a publicly observable facial and bodily display." According to A.B. Castro, a nurse and senior staff specialist for the American Nursing Association Center for Occupational Health and Safety, emotional labor:

...requires effort to create expressions or to change feelings to meet employer or job expectations, it's an occupational demand on workers and can alienate them from their own true feelings, creating a sense of inauthenticity. The energy needed to maintain emotional labor throughout one's career can lead to job stress, dissatisfaction, and burnout.

Correctional educators may not have to "create expressions or to change feelings to meet employer or job expectations," but we do have to reign in our emotions and feelings because of our students: "Teachers in prison struggle to care within institutionally prescribed prohibitions on relationships with inmates" (Wright, 2004). We have to maintain boundaries and constantly watch what we do. In training we are told not to forget "where we work."

Just think of the number of times you put on each of these masks or take on different roles. When you get up in the morning you wear one mask with your family or significant others. Another mask goes on when you enter the facility in which you work. If you happen to have some interaction with institutional staff you wear another mask and then when you are actually in the classroom, you put on another. All day long we are putting on or taking off masks. When we walk through the gates or enter into various roles, we are very conscious of ourselves changing to another mask. "Once you leave this place and walk out the gate, you come back to life and have to deal with outside problems once again like, 'Will I make it to my college class on time?'" commented one educator.

Changing our identities to fit roles may cause some educators conflict. We are caught in a spinning whirlwind of inner dialogue because we are experiencing such conflicting emotions. We tell ourselves:

> As an educator I'm in a helping profession and consider myself caring, yet I can't wear my emotions or feelings...I would like to provide a much needed activity for the class, but I am not allowed to do it...I would like to let the students know I am human, too, but I can't let them know too much about myself...How do I express myself vocationally?...I must maintain a professional demeanor at all times...I can't be myself when I want to be and consider myself inauthentic...I have to act like the organization expects me to act...I bring all of who I am to this job, yet I have to leave most of me behind.

In other words, how do I negotiate a sense of self?

In order to be a good teacher in a correctional setting, we know that we have to be ourselves, which actually means not to be our real selves. It means that we have to create another self and be that self. One teacher explained how he feels working in a correctional setting: "When I come in here and relate to staff and offenders I am completely different than when I am not working. I rarely think of my personal life while I am in here. I work very hard to do that."

Another said she coped with these multiple identities just by leaving one identity at the gate when she walked into a facility: "I leave who I am outside when I step inside. I just follow the rules and go by the book. When I get home, that is when I can be creative." Yet another educator commented:

You become selfless, because you are always trying to give something of yourself by exerting your identity on the students. You are constantly thinking of the needs of the students. You are so busy mentally, that you don't have time to sit down and think about your life on the outside. When I am back on the street, I think of myself as a student because I am still going to school and learning. When I get home I'm in a different environment and I act differently again.

Females in particular have to work at presenting themselves as someone different, especially in a correctional setting. They take great pains to act asexual in an attempt to avoid being seen as sexy. One female educator remarked:

I am very conscious of what I wear here. I feel I am on display, so I wear completely different stuff than I would in a public school. I try to dress casual, but not too casual as to play down the fact that I am a woman.

Another commented:

I've started wearing baggier and baggier clothes, stopped wearing makeup, and tried to act even more assertive than I already am. It doesn't work. Sometimes I wonder if I will ever be taken seriously as a professional in such a male-dominated field.

Even though we are similar to all prison staff as far as conforming to the overall institutional goals of security and management of prisoners, we view ourselves differently. In turn, we are also viewed differently:

Correctional officers are themselves troubled when they see medical providers, members of the clergy, teachers, and others come away from the prison feeling a greater affinity for the inmates than for the individuals on whom the safety and success of their visit depends. Reactions to this persistent stereotyping are undoubtedly implicated in work-related stress and job dissatisfaction. (Riley, 1998)

Often, we end up thinking of ourselves as "us *vs.* them" or "we *vs.* they." At other times we think of ourselves as "I *vs.* he/she" or "me *vs.* him/her." We need to quit pitting ourselves against others and look at who we are and how we need to fit in with the whole organization. We need to pay attention to how we present ourselves and ask if we can live with that image.

Correctional education professional identity: teachers or jailers?
Loyalty to institutions or to students?

CHAPTER II

WHAT I LEARNED IN PRISON

by David Werner

Introduction

The first class I ever taught was in a prison. This was not planned; only a fool, in fact, would plan something like that. But while I did not intend many of the things to happen the way they did in my life, that first prison classroom experience and the ensuing years of prison teaching changed me forever. I learned what it meant to teach by teaching in a prison. I came to realize over time that the lessons my inmate-students taught me were lessons for all teachers in all situations. These were lessons that all teachers need, but which many teachers never learn or take a very long time to learn. I decided I was fortunate to have first taught in prison, because I learned things about teaching there that I may not have learned otherwise or elsewhere. If you can appreciate the irony: Prison made me honest. I am a more honest teacher for having taught in prison.

Insofar as we are all the products of where we have been, "the past is prologue to the play we're in." I believe I am a good teacher and know that I am the teacher I am because I taught in prison.

How It Came About

In the fall of 1975 I was drifting through Claremont Graduate School in Southern California with a master's degree in English under my belt, working on my doctorate. For about a year previously, I had been working as a research assistant for a professor in the graduate school. By that fall, I was tired of it. I was weary of spending hours in the library looking up references in which I had no personal interest. So, I decided there must be some easier way of making money.

I decided I would apply for a teaching job.

Now note here that I had never taught—anything at all. (It is quite possible and even usual for someone to get all the way through a master's or a doctorate degree in a subject and never teach a single class.) Nor had I ever heard anything directly about teaching. While my professors had spoken of many things, they had never spoken really about what it was like to teach. Of course I had watched my various instructors and professors teach, but I was usually concentrating more on the subject matter (as one does in graduate school) than on the process of teaching, for the latter of which there was no immediate need. None of my professors had ever uttered a word about teaching as a process, as an occupation, as something one did with students. People going into grade school or high school instruction are taught how to teach, but colleges and universities leave it up to chance. So, I was a graduate student who knew nothing about teaching looking for a teaching job. What's more, I knew that I knew nothing about teaching.

But I still thought that teaching would be easier than what I was doing. There is no doubt a lesson in that—something about considering a vocation one *has not* done or experienced easier than something one *has* done or experienced. It is more complicated than the simple old saw about the grass always being greener. Yet, there it was. So, I began to send out applications.

Actually, I called three nearby schools. I remember at the time that seemed like quite a job, but in retrospect, it was not. In fact, I am surprised anything happened, because at the time (the middle 1970s), teaching jobs were pretty scarce. I was probably lazy, but I may have also unconsciously known that I didn't have the foggiest idea of what I was doing.

About a month later, I received a telephone call. A man named Bill Willoughby from the University of La Verne, a private college a few miles from my home, called and asked if I was still interested in teaching. I said that I was, and he asked me if I was interested in and able to teach a class in creative writing. In a previous life I had lived in San Francisco. During that time I had been writing a lot of poetry as many people had been doing in San Francisco in the heady days of the late 1960s. I had even thought of making a living as a poet. So, I said I would be happy to teach a creative writing course. He then told me the class was at the Youth Training School, a local State of California Youth Authority prison. "Great," I said. Later, I went to an interview at the University of La Verne, but I remember nothing about it. I must imagine that I was brilliant, because I cannot otherwise imagine what on earth I could have said since, (1) I knew nothing about teaching, (2) I knew nothing about teaching creative writing, and, (3) I knew absolutely nothing about prison.

I was hired in November, but the class was not scheduled to start until the beginning of January. I went to the prison for some sort of orientation and to pick up my identification card and acquire keys, but I remember little about the place, except for many large, heavy doors closing with a loud, deep, final clang.

Doors closing are actually many people's first impression of prison, the impression of finality, enclosure, of somebody locking you in. Doors in prison seem to weigh tons apiece. I've often thought that they make doors in prison have the sound they have more for effect than actual need. Some years later we hired a man to teach in a prison who seemed to be perfectly suitable and even-tempered. He made it only as far as the inner sets of gates on his first day, then turned around and fled and we never saw him again. It turned out he had a severe case of claustrophobia.

I wonder, now, if after whatever choice we make in life there is not behind us the sound of some heavy door closing.

8

So, I had a few months to think about things. Since I quickly realized that I knew nothing of prison or teaching or teaching creative writing, I reacted in the way that every true English major reacts to everything: I decided to read a book about it. (Somebody once said that if you give an English major a choice between going to heaven and reading a book about it, he or she will take the book.) At the time in the middle 1970s, the popular book on prisons was Eldridge Cleaver's *Soul On Ice*, so I got that and read it.

It was probably not the best idea. Cleaver was a founding member of the Black Panther Party, a politically radical, socially active group that had originated in Oakland, California in the 1960s. As a result of that politically unpopular affiliation, Cleaver spent much of his life in the custody of the State of California Department of Corrections, which *Soul On Ice* was about. In addition, Cleaver spent much of his time in what were termed the "gladiator prisons" of California—San Quentin, Duel Vocational Institution, and Folsom. *Soul On Ice* is about killing and shooting and shanking (stabbing). I read it and I got pretty nervous.

My First Day

January finally rolled around. I went to the university, filled out employment paperwork and stopped by the English Department office to pick up stuff. I mean here, really, "stuff," the accoutrements of teaching; the stuff we hang out with, the stuff that defines us. I picked up a blue grade book, a few yellow, lined tablets, some chalk in case the prison did not have any, a couple of pencils, some mimeograph forms (which tells you when *that* was) and some pens, and I was set to go. I already had a briefcase from my graduate student time. I was ready.

I drove to the prison, which was built in the middle of dairy fields just beyond the edge of urban Southern California about 15 miles from both the university and my house. Years later, in a book on prison teaching, I wrote about the psychological effect of the isolation of prisons (they are usually and intentionally built in the middle of nowhere) on the prospective prison teacher, but let that bide for a time. I drove up to the gate, showed my identification to security, parked my car, headed into the building, exchanged my identification for a set of keys, unlocked a few doors and headed to my classroom.

I unlocked the door to my classroom and looked around. It was the first time I had seen the room. It was the first time I had ever seen any classroom where I was going to be a teacher. The walls were concrete, there were metal windows with metal sashes, the floor was linoleum, and the room was basically filthy. Dirt lay on the sashes and the floor; the windows were streaked with grime. A large swamp cooler protruded through one window, and there was a large desk completely covered with papers in one corner. The student desks seemed odd; they were similar to student desks with an attached writing surface that I remembered from high school, but they were larger, in fact, quite a bit larger.

There was a lectern in the front of the class and on this I began to put my stuff. I took out my empty grade book, my blank folder and my freshly sharpened pencils and arranged them on the podium and the shelf underneath and waited for my students.

After about a half hour, they began to file in. The first thing that was completely obvious was they were all *huge*. Most prisoners, as it turns out, are pretty big and pretty muscular. I used to think it was the result of a macho thing about being in prison and maybe it is to some degree, but there are few ways to exercise in prison other than by lifting weights. (I mean, it's not like you can take up aerobics or pole-vaulting!) So the students filing in were enormous. Some seemed to have biceps the size of hams. Most were (or seemed) taller than I, and most of them were certainly in better shape. They were beefy, and they had cigarette packs (you could smoke in prison at that time) rolled up in the sleeves of their T-shirts, which further emphasized their Virginia-baked ham biceps. I started to worry.

The prison at the time had a security system that consisted of a telephone in the classroom. They said if I ever got into trouble, to "just pick up the phone and call Security and we'll come and rescue you." It doesn't take one long to discover the fundamental flaw in *that* logic. I imagined a riot breaking out in the classroom, desks flying, bodies hurtling through space and me saying, "Do you mind, just a minute, while I use the phone? I need to call Security." It didn't take long to realize that if I could get to the phone, the situation probably was not that bad. I figured out that if real "trouble" occurred, I couldn't get to the phone.

So the students began filing in—mostly Blacks, then Hispanic and Asian and a couple of white guys. I certainly did not consider myself to be prejudiced or racist, but this was a hell of a lot larger minority or ethnic population than any I had ever considered facing. It's probably a population that I would never have encountered if I had not taught in prison. It's probably a population most white teachers never see or think about seeing. Since most prison teachers are white, I imagine that is the situation with most of them—white folks going to teach in prison inhabited largely by minorities. My concern grew.

One guy walked up to the podium where I was taking roll and stood in front of it, watching me check off students' names as they walked in. He stood right in front of the podium, maybe even his belly touching it or lapping over it as he looked down at me. He was considerably taller than I was. He looked down at me and I looked up at him. He said nothing, but just stood there watching me for maybe ten or fifteen seconds and then went and sat at a desk.

The tension rose another notch.

In addition to the book about prison, I had also read a book about teaching creative writing. It was about the "story workshop" method of teaching creative writing, where you start by asking someone to "think of a time and place." Then you ask, "What do you see, what colors? What smells are there?" Stuff like that, designed to get people to start thinking creatively. So, I started to ask people to do that and they responded, and I managed to get the class going. I asked them questions and they answered.

And this started to trip me out, as we used to say back then. I would ask a student something and he would answer. Then I would ask another student something and he would answer, too. I would tap on someone and he would say something, and then I would tap on someone else and he would say something. It was like they were those bottles partly filled with water and I would tap on one and he would make a note and then I would tap on another and he would make another note.

It is the singularly most astounding thing about being a teacher, the thing they don't tell you and which you cannot imagine. It is the complete and utter thing that defines the difference between being a student and being a teacher, and it is the thing people rarely talk about. Teachers ask the questions. What we are talking about here is power. You call on little Mary or little Johnny, and little Mary or little Johnny says something. It is like you are some kind of symphony conductor, where you tap on someone and he or she makes music.

So, I am calling on guys and they're answering and I am just amazed by the whole thing. It seems as if part of me is calling on people and conducting (note the word) the class and part of me is watching that part of me and just blown away by the whole power thing and the control. I am calling on people and watching them respond and hugely enjoying the whole process. I mean, I have never experienced anything like this.

So we're really rolling along. I'm asking and they're answering and about an hour and a half goes by of a two-hour class when a guy in the back of the class raises his hand and I call on him. He says, "OK. You've had the class for quite a while. Now it's our turn. Now you tell us how you felt when we walked in today."

My heart stopped.

My first impulse was to lie.

Many people do in similar situations and I am sure I have in other situations. My first impulse was to say something like, "Oh, it's just another class, just like those I've had before." Why lie? Well, why do we in such situations? Why do we set up the walls we do? Primarily, "to save face"— which is a pretty interesting term. I set up the walls I do to save the face I project to the world. I lie to protect myself, or to protect the image of myself that I project to the world.

What actually saved me was poetry. As I said earlier, I had been living in San Francisco and writing a lot of poetry and I took it pretty seriously. I still take literature very seriously, as it is about truth and reality and telling truths about the world and people and life. I thought (and think) that literature has a responsibility to tell us the truths that we cannot learn in other ways. I thought (and think) that poetry is especially about that.

What saved me was that I figured if I was going to expect them to tell me anything significant, any truths about their lives, then I would have to do the same with them.

I said, absolutely literally, "I was scared shitless. And I still am."

I realized only much later that I was not giving them any information. I was not telling them anything they did not know. It took me some time (Weeks? Months? Years?) to realize that they did not ask me the question they did because they did not know the answer. They asked me what they did only to see what I would say.

The One Important Thing

I would like to stop here a minute and dwell on the implications of this point, because I think they are very important. This may be, in fact, the most important single thing I could ever say about being a teacher and it may do more to define you as a teacher than any other thing. How you respond when your students ask you that question or one like it will more than anything else define who you are and how you teach.

This is a particular problem for prison teachers. A lot of prison teachers lie to their students on a regular and consistent basis. That is because many prison teachers are afraid of their students. My real tendency here is to say "most." Most prison teachers lie most of the time. That is a pretty harsh thing to say, but I think it is important and defines more of the problems of prison education than any other single thing.

This dynamic defines much of what takes place in prison education. Think of all the talk about inmates "testing" teachers. In fact, most inmates test most teachers, but what they are most often testing is if you are going to tell them the truth or if you are going to lie to them. This is absolutely no different from what happens in every classroom everywhere with every group of students and with every group of teachers. All students test all teachers and many teachers respond by lying.

You will have to figure this one out for yourself, but how you respond to telling the truth as a teacher will define who you are as a person, and who you are as a teacher.

A Creed

So, I said, "I was scared shitless. And I still am," which they already knew. I even still remember who it was that asked me that question. I eventually knew him quite well afterwards and grew to like him a lot. Of course they knew that I was scared, and we talked together for the rest of the period about why that was, about why I was afraid of them when I did not know them or have any relationship with them. We talked about how my being afraid had to do with something I expected to be there and nothing to do with what was actually there. They were really curious about that, about what some white kid on the outside thought of them and of prison, and we carried that conversation on and off for most of the rest of the semester. I have found that people in prison are often very curious about how people on the outside view them. I think they have to be curious, since they are going to have to deal with those feelings and reactions of people on the outside once they get paroled. They are well aware that they will have to face people's preconceptions and prejudices once they hit the streets, and they well know that the attitudes of people on the streets will determine the direction and fate of their lives. Prisoners are curious about what people on the outside think of them; their survival once they leave prison depends on it.

It was also the only time teaching in prison that I have ever been afraid. It faded after that. I began to realize (although it took me quite a while to consciously formulate it), my prison teaching creed (or my teaching creed, you could say, since I really do not believe there is much difference between the two): *People respond to the way they are treated. People live up to or down to your expectations.*

This is really not rocket science, as my mother used to say. It is really just another formulation of the "do unto others" statement expressed by every major spiritual tradition. It is saying that if you expect someone to be a creep, then most of the time that person will conform to your expectation. If you expect someone to be stupid, then he or she will be, whereas if you expect someone to be intelligent, then that person will be that also. There is a sufficiency of research to support this, including a famous case in, I believe, Palo Alto, California, where teachers were told that classes of actually intelligent students were developmentally disabled. After some time the teachers and students were performing at the level of a developmentally disabled classroom.

Of course there are obvious physical qualifications to this creed, but you are always better off expecting more of your students than less. If you expect less of your students, then they will always live up to that expectation. But if you expect more, then who knows?

This creed has to take place in an atmosphere of truth. What matters here is what you truly believe about your students, not what you tell them. In fact, what you tell them does not really matter at all. If in your heart you think that your students are evil, stupid criminals, then what you tell them is not going to matter at all. This is why I said earlier that there is a lot of lying that goes on in prison education.

The Dilemma of Prison Education

All of this positive thinking is often very difficult to accomplish in a prison classroom. Maybe the real difference between public education and prison education is the enormous amount of baggage the prison teacher carries into that first classroom. We enter any classroom expecting certain things to happen, but we come into a prison classroom expecting much more. These expectations are mostly negative. Even the positive expectations can be just as harmful. I know quite a few people who have gone off to prison teaching with some sort of pseudo-liberal notion that they are going to bring the light of reason to poor, deprived individuals and many of those people have been seriously disappointed. But most people began as prison teachers with a whole cartload of negative baggage.

In my case I walked into my classroom carrying Cleaver's *Soul on Ice* as a suitcase. Cleaver was intelligent, politically savvy and creative, so at least I had that positive impression of a prisoner going for me as I walked into that classroom. In fact, that may be the other thing that saved me, although that was not what I really remembered from *Soul on Ice* when I first read it.

What I also came into that classroom with was what every white kid knows about prison, what every person on the street thinks they know about prison, what all of my campus students think they know about prison, and what many politicians (most politicians) think they know about the system, and that is nothing. At least, nothing useful. We all enter the prison pushing the baggage cart of popular culture. We all come carrying the luggage of "Eyewitness News at Eleven" or some headline or other from the local paper, or some article in *Time*, or show on TV (Oz), or film (maybe The Shawshank Redemption)—which is worthless. We come carrying the baggage of what, in short, popular culture tells us to expect when we get there. Some of us can work in that system for years and never drop the impression we had of the place before we ever walked through the door.

I know many people who teach in prisons who are afraid of teaching there, who wrap themselves around the security system and the comfortable notion that these people are "criminals" and that you can never trust them. I know a lot of people in prison education who I am sure think me naïve or wrongheaded for writing the kinds of things you are reading here. I know plenty of people in prison education who figure that I've just had it lucky, that I've been fortunate to have "nice" students, that most or their students in prison are not like mine.

The Dilemma of Expectations

This is a real dilemma. I attended a Correctional Education Association convention workshop a couple of years ago on teaching Shakespeare in prison. The basic feeling of the workshop leaders was that Shakespeare had a lot of good ideas that people in prison could understand, but that the text was too difficult for people in prison to read. Their solution was to create a parallel-text Shakespeare with the original on one side and the "translated" and simplified version on the other, so inmates could read the original if they wanted, but of course "most wouldn't be able to." In fact, they were especially proud of an inmate who had read the original text version.

By contrast, a friend and I have been teaching Shakespeare in prison for years, he in the high school program and I in the college program, and we both have always used original text Shakespeare and everything has been just fine. Neither of us would think of "dumbing it down."

Why is this? What accounts for the two different responses? Are our students smarter than theirs? I cannot prove it, but I truly do not think so. I think the difference is simply what we expect from our students.

This can account for a great deal of what goes on in prison education. It can even account for much of the more physical occurrences in the prison. For example, my university has run a college program in a youth prison for thirty-three years. We conduct about 10 classes per week or 520 or so per year. That would mean we have had more than 17,000 class meetings. During that time we have had five minor fights or incidents: No one was even slightly injured. I wonder, sometimes, if school classrooms on the streets can boast of such a record. All of this occurred in an institution noted as one of the roughest in the California Youth Authority. The institution has had many, many inmate assaults on staff.

A number of years ago, a teacher at the institution was assaulted by a ward (the state name for younger inmates) who broke the teacher's nose. For weeks afterward training sessions were held at the institution stressing how dangerous the wards were and how closely they needed to be watched.

The only problem was that the teacher was a person whose nose you would just love to break. I think you know what I mean by that. He was an authoritarian, genuinely unhappy and quite mean person. While you or I might just love to pop a person like that in the nose, we would not because, primarily, we have been acculturated not to do so. But take a ward who had not gone through a similar process of acculturation (as most in prison have not), put him in a similar situation and he winds up doing what you or I only think of doing.

Does that justify the ward breaking his nose? No, but it is something that needs to be taken into account if we are to understand our own behavior and the behavior of our inmate students and if we are to understand events that take place in prison.

It May All Be Attitude, or It May All Be About Truth

How I treat my students matters. If I consider them worthless and incapable of learning, they will certainly live up to that expectation. They will be the dolts I claim them to be and I will be proud of myself for being so insightful. How many teachers have you heard claim that students are not as intelligent as they used to be? What does that attitude do to one as a teacher? Even on college campuses it is becoming almost a mantra that students are not coming out of high school as well prepared as they once were. Colleges complain about the high schools, high schools complain about the grade schools, and grade schools complain about television and parents. All of these schools use all of these excuses to explain why they are not delivering quality education.

The point here is a peculiar one, but one I do not believe is at all subtle. I can neither guarantee my students' success nor failure, but the attitude I hold toward them can do much to push them in either direction. The important attitude will be the one I truly hold in my heart of hearts, not the one that I tell my students about.

In short, you have to tell the truth to your students. Maybe you also have to tell the truth because it is actually useless to lie to your students—they will catch you in it anyway. When a lie is foolish, tell the truth. When you think about it, this must be true for all human endeavor—children are as adept in knowing that their parents are lying as parents are adept in knowing the same about their children.

So, we have to tell the truth to our students. Beyond that, we need to be extremely careful about the assumptions we make about them and we can all use some work on our attitudes.

In Closing

There is much material out there to help you discover more about the prison system, teaching or your students. You could always try asking them, if you can manage to be noninvasive about it. And I do not mean asking them about the crimes they have committed, which you should never do uninvited, but asking them about who they are, about the lives they have lived and the experiences they have had. My most consistent piece of advice to beginning teachers I talk with on campus is, "Do not be afraid to ask your students."

16

CHAPTER III

TEACHING IN THE EXISTENTIAL VILLAGE

by Jane Guttman

Introduction

The door slams behind me and I enter the world of incarceration, rows of cold buildings housing children accused of often very serious transgressions and ruthless behaviors. Ranging in age from nine to nineteen, they spend much of their days and all of their nights in accommodations befitting wayward souls. My job: To join the ranks of educators charged with the task of imparting knowledge and wisdom, and awakening the stagnant spirit yet to embrace the glory of learning.

There is a song by R.E.M., *Everybody Hurts*, which serves as the theme song for my students' lives: Cramming too many sorrows into young lives amid deficiency upon deficiency, asking them to manage lives of frantic desperation without providing the necessary tools or life lessons.

My journey as their teacher, a mentor in a land of turmoil and despair, is shrouded in hope and steadfast in determination to find the formula for student success and healing.

My list of questions is still long and constant. The task at hand requires knowledge, persistence, tolerance and the willingness to release the outcome. It has not been easy to watch a student's failure to progress in the traditional manner of semesters and school years. Yet, I have come to understand the intrinsic reward of putting forth the instruction and guidance while releasing my attachment to the result. Valuing moments has taken on new meaning; that one or sometimes twenty hours I spend with students have been transformed into reservoirs of possibility. Five minutes are to be savored and carefully managed as a significant fraction of teaching and learning time. This personal lesson is shocking as I recall many moments in my life, unsavored and undesigned, when I thought I had time to spare. Now I know even a five-minute encounter with a student can make a difference, can change a life and can possibly alter the course for us all.

My thoughts turn to Columbine High School in Colorado, the scene of student slaughter and the course that is charted in a moment, the changes that result from every action, and I deepen my commitment to the moment at hand; to become all I can be, give all I can give in the hope of inspiring change, diverting disaster and opening doors for those destined to live on the fringe of the pursuit of happiness that is our birthright.

Where do I begin? Did the district orientation prepare me for the prison setting, the barbed wire and rose bushes that grow into statements of what we're about?

The first walk inside was surreal. As I was given a tour of the facility, I tried to take in rows of students walking solemnly, hands clasped behind their backs, looking grim, a silent shuffle of shame, hopelessness, fear or boredom moving toward the next destination, either class or unit, directions clear and waiting.

As I was escorted to my classroom, I wondered if and how I would acclimate to this setting. I recorded some impressions after some time had passed:

> *For the past several months, my teachers have been boys and girls, ages 12-18 in a juvenile detention facility. The lessons have stirred vast emotion, awakening a place of feeling and spirit that has long slumbered.*

> *What began as a return trip to the field of education has opened my heart and soul in ways I would not have expected or even understood. The journey of detention is unforgettable to both the detainees and those in charge. There are few moments when the students are not in my consciousness, even when they are out of sight and physical proximity. Their stories, their anguish and their plight capture my attention time and again, and I search deeply for answers to the complex questions that continue to bewilder and shock me.*

> *One of the insights I have acquired since beginning this experience has been the realization that all the world's children are ours. I have told the students, repeatedly, that we are all in this together. We are part of that essential and existential village and the outcome is up to us all.*

> *As one moves into the world of juvenile angst and hope, hearts may be rocked by the despair and, hopefully, lifted by the resiliency and evident purity of heart in children labeled criminals. I have met this innocence in the classroom, on the walkway to and from their living unit and on the hard bench in the hallway by the control station where students must wait in the choreography of movements. Hopefully it has been transformed into a bench of accomplishment and transformation.*

The bench: a divisive place Guttman was able to turn into a space of kindness.

The school day begins and ends with reflection. I ask these questions of myself as I begin each day:

- What can I do today to encourage a student to read, to develop a love of reading, to explore the path of lifelong learning?

- How can I shift attitudes, beliefs and behaviors in an instant, letting students know that books are empowering, meaningful and engaging?

- And how can I ensure that the spirits of my students will soar, even in a few minutes, an hour or a few days, amid the roaring and condemnation that is etched into unit protocol?

These questions led me to some core beliefs that sustain my work in this tense learning space:

- I discovered the essential tool, kindness, as a primary teaching modality.

- I quickly learned that a punitive and harsh probation setting was not conducive to sound learning practices.

- I would have to create a protocol that honored my students, knowing that they were separate from the behaviors that had brought them to incarceration. Learning about *the bench* was, for me, a true rite of passage.

Everything begins and ends on this bench. Referred to as "the hard bench," it becomes a place of reprimand, commands and, sometimes, verbal abuse and restriction. It could be the place to simply seat students as they wait to move to class or to other activities, but on many occasions it has been used to belittle and defile.

On my first visit to a unit, I assessed things quickly and decided to use this bench as a place to begin my community. To let this bench symbolize that we had begun our connection, established through handshakes, a smile and kind words, laying the groundwork for the classroom to follow in which each person, regardless of crime, could be addressed with dignity and compassion. Those first days I experienced discomfort initiating this bench work. I soon realized how vital it was to create a space of kindness—so foreign to the unit and their agenda—and that our humanity is fitting wherever we find ourselves engaged in educating and mentoring, even in a jail setting.

After a brief assignment with an all-male class, I worked in a classroom for female students, before moving to my current assignment as the library media teacher. As chance would dictate, a confrontation occurred. I struggled to keep my students safe and treat the offending student with dignity. Did I succeed?

We came very close, too close, to a violent outburst. Morris was at the edge, her anger flying across the room and startling all of us. Calling for help brought another shock, as I watched a recurrent staff walk from her unit to our classroom, in slow motion, seemingly unaware of the dangers within. I watched from my place in the classroom, horrified and bewildered as she strolled like a Sunday tourist to her destination. Finally arriving, I requested she escort the student back to the unit and, with shaking legs and a racing heart, I turned my attention to the students, who were seated and waiting with courtesy for direction.

We returned to the unit for lunch and I immediately sought the supervisor to express my dismay and outrage at staff error and delay in arriving at the classroom, after my specific request for immediate help. She was polite and shared her concern and frustration over issues of safety and security. I told her how hazardous such a delay could be and she instructed me to call for a "Code Red" in the future. This code would bring help, without delay. I struggled to know what was right, best, safest and warranted in each situation and as yet have not called for this form of back up.

I had to face the student. She was going home the next day and I wanted her to know how her actions affected the class, the world, and me...In a stream of chaos, I found myself face to face with her in the supervisor's office. Both the supervisor and another staff were present. The student was sitting, somewhat quieted by our numbers and acquiesced to our circle of authority. I didn't really think about what to say, I just began, letting her know that she could not return to the classroom in the afternoon. I explained that my responsibility to safety and security were both prerequisites to any teaching that followed. She listened to every word, giving me her perfect attention now that she was surrounded by officers, her teacher and pepper spray. We were ready for any incident and I could be brave, speaking my truth in the protection of those who were bolstered by handcuffs and spray, training and experience.

I continued, advising her that her actions and words would be costly in the midst of family members, school personnel and a prospective employer. How would she cope in the world, lashing out with her anger, rudeness, frustration and agitation? How would she manage to survive a school day, with outbursts of "attitude" and mutterings that create chaos and danger?

Obstacles to teaching and learning mar many school days in the form of codes, interruptions within the classroom, institutional schedules, student behavior and even resistance from institutional staff. Seasoned teachers adapt to these hardships, but for a novice teacher, the disruptions are harrowing. I have learned, thankfully, to move from moment to moment without the frustration of earlier times, remembering that we are housed in another land, the ultimate goal being a worthy and peaceful collaboration. After all, these professionals provide safety and support to all and our rapport is essential to the success of both our programs. Since my move to the library, I have taken a new view of our probation neighbors and have sought to find our similarities and common threads, building upon those shared goals and working as an agent of change through avenues of respect and cooperation. Although, in the past, my frustration and dismay clouded many a day:

> *The day began with hope and peace. Driving in from the desert refueled and lifted my spirits. I had a new chance for bringing sense to chaos and comfort to unmeasured pain, and offer the ultimate remedy: Education. As I readied the classroom for the day, I wondered what would transpire. Each day brings crisis in one form or another and I steadied myself for that day's fare.*

> *Watching the students play basketball revealed the tension between them. I realized the day would require extra vigilance, as if such a stance could safeguard against the unknown. I silently began to prepare for what I could not name, but only sense.*

The first two years witnessed many staff conflicts and sometimes harassment. Prison climate was a far cry from the educational setting as I knew it. To find myself in a space that formulated structure often in seemingly harsh ways, not conducive to reframing character or providing avenues for change, proved trying and irritating. In time I have discovered allies in Probation, like-minded professionals who care deeply for their charges and let a congruence of philosophy and practice emerge. Thankfully, a patience and calmness have transpired on my part regarding prison protocol, but this came slowly and with a willingness to see the world from the jailer's perspective. I noted these alliances in my journal:

> *Finally, in a burst of frustration, I told these staff members that the students would be surprised at the lecture waiting for them in the classroom. I spoke with firmness and conviction and a show of great frustration. Then, I saw them turn and watch in disbelief at my litany and saw their joy in my decision to give harsh consequences to the students.*

> *I left the unit while the girls changed into class attire and as I walked back to the classroom I again shuddered at the staff's satisfaction expressed in knowing the girls would face harsh repercussions from yesterday's actions. Computer misuse, letter writing without permission, and a student's refusal to give me her written work would all be addressed. I talked with the educational assistant about the need for our united front and our calm and civil presentation to the students.*

> *As we prepared to leave the unit for class, I searched for a face that could lead the line. I scanned the bench and saw that my previous stabilizers*

would not work for this trip. I felt concern and distress as I saw my usual helpers disappear into anger, frustration, fear and sorrow.

Arriving in class was uneventful, unlike yesterday when seat choices sparked verbal blows. I began my lecture, addressing the issues at hand. D was the first to complain, saying that it was time to do school work instead of listening to my directives. Bonnie Parker from "Bonnie and Clyde" is her hero and I knew I could not convince her of the value of lawful behavior. Not today.

The tension mounted and one of the students shot a verbal blow my way, a threat in waiting, not the first but her finest...I was uncomfortable and concerned, considering the best way to remove her from the classroom for a time-out. I continued with instructions for the lesson and a few minutes later I called for staff transport. As soon as staff arrived, she stood, knowing she would be the one returning.

Reflections from the Inside

Now that I have survived the first few years of teaching in an incarcerated setting, I can finally breathe. The barbed wire, the codes, the difference in philosophy with many of the probation staff and the students' angst are familiar and predictable. In a sense, I have redefined my professional goals, expanded them to leave room for miracles in the sense that at any given moment, a student can be inspired, a student can be converted to acknowledging education, and how learning may be the one stable behavior and goal in a tumultuous life.

I have left behind a trail of things that did not work well and have reached far and wide for things that do work, do succeed and offer students a chance to become acquainted with their inner strengths and gifts. Weaving writing projects into curriculum, poetry programs, public readings, meeting inspirational people from all walks of life and supporting students to awaken the gifts within have become an impassioned mission. Now that I am in the library, opportunities to excite and encourage literacy abound. The late Michael Printz, a high school librarian for whom an award is now given in Young Adult Literature, knew that there was, indeed, a book for each student. Our job as library media teachers is to find that book for that student. And so the priority of my daily agenda is to assist students in locating that book. This process transforms students. Some ask for help before they even sit down, knowing that a library is more than a place for books to reside, but rather a place where they are honored as readers, become truly valued as a partner in literature and the written word is valued each time reading occurs.

The setting continues to establish the tone for learners. Respect and kindness lead the way in establishing safety and opportunity for student success. Recently, our students attended a guest presentation in which an elderly person with developmental disabilities and mild mental retardation spoke with the students about a film in which he was the subject. I watched with great respect as the students, all of them, engaged productively, thoughtfully, respectfully and compassionately with this guest. I observed the change in their demeanor as they stood tall and spoke confidently. As they listened to the speaker's message advising them to stay in school and get involved with something good for someone else, some began to realize that they are more than the collection of their crimes and the weeks, months or years of incarceration.

Ultimately, optimal learning occurs in community and in partnership… in that moment of communion between an educator and a learner, in which our students are honored as fully capable of moving beyond their previous scholastic histories. I have realized my best tool for transforming minds and hearts is to be fully awake, fully present with my students. To let the respect and concern I hold for them lay the foundation for the work we will do together. Simple perhaps, but bearing great truth, is that the best remedy for low literacy is reading. In the words of author Luis J. Rodriguez, "Books saved me!"

Former gang member and now award-winning author, Mr. Rodriguez spoke at our local community library last spring. Some of our treatment students attended. I let Mr. Rodriguez know in advance that we would attend. He made a point to visit our section of the audience and shake hands with our students. The autographed copy of his book was held tightly by the chosen student and now has a place of honor in our school library. The learning community of authors, film guests and the one special chosen book all bring our students closer to sparking the love of learning and a quest for accomplishment.

Also required are a teacher's love and devotion—both essential for bringing students to their height of success—plus believing deeply in their capacity and possibility, standing by to provide information, assistance, support, reassurance and respect, and also a relentless commitment to demanding students give their best to the task at hand.

My journey as a correctional educator compels me to see the world through children who have wandered off the path and are waiting for that outstretched hand to pull them back into life's mainstream. It is a giant task, requiring me to see all these students, not just the ones who seize the spotlight through their aggressive behavior or profound educational needs, but also the compliant student, the one who follows structure and protocol and completes his or her work well. The workday is fast-paced and full and I claim my focus again and again to ensure the best outcome. But it is arduous sometimes to address all the concerns of one moment, keeping students both safe and growing.

Nearly four decades have passed since meeting my first at-risk student in a continuation school setting. Patty W—a student—was one of my most profound teachers; small stature, fiery spirit, and a determination to make her life count. Her home life was disastrous and abusive and it was incredibly painful to hear her accounts of abuse, see the scars and learn how her father violently destroyed a favorite family pet. As the years progressed, I visited her at a Youth Authority facility and later she came to the school to show me her infant son. Her delight was dashing and she shone with pride at her accomplishment, now having a husband, a son and a home. A few months later, however, she and her family died in a home fire, her dreams and the hope of a salvaged life reduced to ashes.

Patty has been on my mind and in my heart for almost forty years. She has stood quietly beside me as I strive to teach, honor, respect, inspire, and grow professionally. Her untimely death has fostered a legacy of commitment and dedication, as she lives on in my memory and daily work.

What will be the next step? To ask more questions, listen well, provide cutting-edge curriculum, take more courses, imagine one more creative project, and model lifelong learning in word and deed. To become a quieting voice in chaos, a vital presence in apathy, a diligent reflection of the meaning and definition of teacher. To feel a part of that knowledge flow, immersed in the wisdom and love coursing bravely along the river of life, through its rapids and along its dry banks, holding firm to the natural laws that invite and expect a well-ordered finale.

CHAPTER IV

THE FIRST TWO YEARS OF PRISON WORK:
A PERSONAL NARRATIVE

by Bill Muth

Introduction

My first reading of Wright's (2005) article on culture shock stirred old feelings and memories. He states, "Most prison teachers did not intend to teach in prison" (p. 19). In 1972, when I declared special education as my undergraduate major at the University of Maryland, my future father-in-law, a gifted and decorated New York City policeman, asked if I'd ever thought about teaching at Leavenworth. I politely dismissed the idea. I was interested in child development and considered development pretty much over by adulthood. What difference could a teacher make in the life of an adult prisoner? But I agreed to apply for an internship at the United States Penitentiary in Lewisburg, Pennsylvania for the summer of 1973.

After the Lewisburg internship I turned away from prisons and spent the rest of the 1970s happily engaged in a variety of K-12 special education assignments in the U.S. and in Barbados, West Indies. I had forgotten about an application I had submitted in 1975 for federal teaching jobs when, in November 1980, I received a call from the Federal Correctional Institution (FCI), Parkwood.[1] The decision to leave a model learning center in Rockville, Maryland to work in a prison was the most agonizing career decision of my life. It involved guilt about leaving the children mid-year, doubts about my ability to work with juvenile delinquents, and fear about getting trapped in a job away from home.

Wright notes that new prison teachers "have to work by the seat of their pants" (Wright, 2005, p. 19). True. I expected the youth offenders in my new reading class to do some limit testing. I found it harder to adjust to the prison culture manifested, for example, in the language and behavior of some staff: The case manager who routinely barked to new prisoners during orientation meetings, "You will improve your positive mental attitude!" Or the warden who announced publicly to the staff that prison programs were "B.S." Or the quasi-military discourses that defined our monthly education staff meetings—teachers sitting in student desks, in rows, silent receivers of information while the supervisor of education sat at the head desk, dispensing facts. Or my strange dual roles as teacher and correctional officer. Or the ubiquitous incident report—the teacher's ultimate disciplinary tool—known in prison parlance as "a shot." The attention-getting power of an incident report was often weakened by teachers that over-used it, or by lieutenants

---

[1] This is a pseudonym, as are the names of staff and students associated with FCI Parkwood.

that considered classroom incidents trivial and routinely expunged shots originating from the education staff. Seat of the pants indeed.

Wright correctly asserts that "...prison teaching cultures should be thought of as hybrid...a blend of home and host world behaviors, experiences and identities..." (p. 23). My colleagues and I attempted to create school discourses within our classroom spaces—though each of us brought our own ideas about what that discourse should be. Leroy stoked his pipe and tried to engage students in Socratic-style debates; Mack used individualized instruction and quietly encouraged his students through praise and coaching. I tried to recreate an "open school" design in my reading class, with places for self-guided study, leisure reading, and small group instruction. Beyond the classroom, prison spaces, as Wright aptly describes, were a constant reminder that I was in a strange land: The smells of floor wax and pipe tobacco, the weight and jingling of the Folger-Adams key ring at my side, the ongoing crackle of staff radio communications, the preemptive, nerve-racking PA system and, of course, the slam of the gate.

I agree with Wright that these early prison experiences constituted culture shock—in a most literal way. In this chapter I will try to make sense of some of my early Federal Bureau of Prisons (FBOP) experiences within this framework. I draw heavily on personal journals I kept during those formative years. The journal narratives can be viewed as reflections on my experiences of culture shock, as various themes about "fitting in" cycle through the pages. Recorded on these often heated pages is the rollercoaster ride of my struggle to assimilate, accommodate, acculturate—or, put another way, to keep my head above water and determine my next move.

Summer 1973

My Civil Service career with the FBOP began in 1980. However, in 1973, as a newly declared education major at the University of Maryland, I landed a summer job in the Education Department at the United States Penitentiary at Lewisburg, Pennsylvania. In the following journal entry, written sometime in the early days of the internship, I recorded the exploratory nature of this experience, and my hope that it might inform future decisions about school and teaching:

> I am at a threshold of a decision as to what major(s) to pursue at the University of Maryland. This job will hopefully provide me with some feeling for my capacity to teach men on an elementary level...The penal system is a vague institution about which I've heard so much and know so little. I've come to Lewisburg asking questions: What is life inside prison like? Who are these men classified as criminals? How do they view themselves? Do they feel a need to change? If so, can the prison contribute to the change process?

It is safe to say I was overwhelmed by the internship that summer. I was unprepared for what I perceived as the despair, hardened apathy or relentless manipulations of the prisoners, or my vulnerability as a young, white male in a mostly black prison. Near that summer's end I drafted the following poem as my night bus from D.C. approached Lewisburg early one Monday morning, signaling my return to work:

> *The flight through Purgatory*
> *Arrived on time at Limbo Terminal*
> *What to make of Small Town sun*
> *Early morning shadowed sidewalk*
> *Market Street storefront stillness?*
> *And meet Ira at 7 o'clock for a ride*
> *To society's greatest work of limbo:*
> *The penitentiary.*

My life and my career in correctional education were on hold, much as I felt the prisoners' lives were. After 1973, with the exception of submitting an employment application to the Federal Register for teaching positions in the federal government, my studies and work centered on elementary and early childhood education. I never looked back. Until...

Fall 1980

One day in the fall of 1980, happily engaged in learning and teaching a class of pre-adolescent boys and girls with "severe and multiple handicaps," I got a call from FCI Parkwood. They offered me a job teaching reading to youth offenders, primarily from Washington, D.C. If I was interested, they would schedule an interview and, if accepted, I was expected to report to work two weeks afterward.

In the introduction, I noted the guilt, doubt, and fear that infused the decision to "abandon" my students and strike out so abruptly on this new path. My decision was based primarily on economics and ambition—the federal salary was higher and the career path wide open. In addition, the prison classroom represented a new adventure: I was seven years older than when I worked at Lewisburg. I had successfully managed and taught severely emotionally handicapped children. The students at FCI Parkwood would be younger than the "jaded lifers" at Lewisburg and more malleable. And, I hoped, the FBOP would give me more freedom to define programs and explore pedagogy.

December 10, 1980

I reported to work. My earliest journal entry reflects some unsurprising trepidation. New smells, sounds, discourses, rules, roles and values flooded in from all sides. I learned quickly that many students did not choose to enroll in the mandatory literacy program and had no personal interest in the traditional

27

curriculum leading to a GED. The entry below reflects my earliest attempts to negotiate a relationship with the students, especially the reluctant ones:

> *It felt good going through the controlled readers today—it felt like I was beginning to get a handle on things. My neophyte hopes rose:*
>
> 1. *Winning over students via audio-visual presentations or journals;*
>
> 2. *The [ability to] "laugh-off" [student banter] and sustain interest and order; and,*
>
> 3. *Patience that springs from the realization of the size of the task.*
>
> *But sobering, sometimes chilling counter-thoughts would also enter my head:*
>
> • *If I am too invested they will burn me.*
>
> • *What if I can't hide my fear?*
>
> • *An enormous amount of work and momentum-building lies ahead.*

Fears about appearing to be intimidated or manipulated by reluctant students seemed to be of primary importance. In the same entry I pondered the confusing relationship I had with my inmate tutor, Mr. Rhodes:

> *Me the pushover. Rhodes [my tutor] asked me to sign [his] 4-star evaluation. I should have said "No, I'll write my own." ...I feel manipulated by Rhodes...He is not a student, but my aide. Thus, an awkward role—to ask for his help and yet keep him at bay. How to [manage] him?*
>
> 1. *He listens selectively and can turn statements inside out, to make himself look good;*
>
> 2. *He doesn't stroke [provide positive feedback] the students enough;*
>
> 3. *He may project an air of arrogance to the students;*
>
> 4. *He wants to impress the guys, not help them;*
>
> 5. *He gets off track with his advice;*
>
> 6. *He oversteps boundaries; and,*

7. *He isn't patient enough to let the students answer for themselves.*

Toward the end of that journal entry I worked out a tentative solution: Use Mr. Rhodes to do outside the classroom prep work and rehearse some "scripts" to confront his manipulation. The entry ended on a successful note about an instructional and motivational breakthrough–the use of a tape recorder to have one learner interview another about his goals in life:

> *Developed a strategy to use Rhodes to do outside of the classroom prep work. Rehearsed LSI's [Life Space Interviews—a counseling method developed by Redl and Wineman (1952)] to confront his behavior. …Impressions of Williams interviewing Rollins. Two bubbling child-men, given a chance in the limelight. Of their impulsive energies: Wow, they're really living for right now, for that tape recorder, and the seductive glop of their born-again pontifications!*

February 3, 1981

Unlike most of my colleagues at the Sandburg Learning Center (the school I had recently left), some of the teachers at FCI Parkwood had very jaded views about prisoners and their chances of transforming into law-abiding citizens. These views pierced the armor of my idealism and created doubts about my own belief system:

> *Although I am a bit run down physically, I hear [staff teacher] Smith's unabashed admission that working in the joint is awful and I can't help but succumb. Surely his shallowness is an admission of the low price tag [he places] on his own head. But…where am I in all this? Am I inspired? Can I continue to invest extra energy into this work? Or is it true, "they're not worth a shit—the whole bunch of them" (another Smith-ism)?*
>
> *[Regarding mediocrity]: It has got to be all or nothing! Either I [take this job seriously] or I leave [the FBOP]. I will not waste my talents on the ugly rock of prison, on the smallness of kiss-ass bureaucracy, on the meanness of secondary gains (power and sadism), on the relentless impotency of failure to effect change.*

February 2, 1981

I lectured myself idealistically about how to develop the right relationship with youth offenders and prison staff. Unstated, but implied in this passage is the cause for this lecture—the coercion and mistrust endemic to the prison's culture:

> *The controls needed in the classroom must be forceful yet non-physical— based on eye-contact, relationship, and a sense of respect, communicating*

an unambiguous belief that we can change. Give up the need to be one up, to be threatening in order to not be threatened.

[Regarding my peers' view of me:] I've worked as much as anyone [for the cause of change]. I have the right to look any social [cynic] in the eye and ask him for "his" credentials.

I accept the pain and weight of my work because it is the cost of being true to myself and my beliefs.

February 11, 1981

More of the students were engaging in learning activities. One student, Mr. Dorsette, was a highly impulsive eighteen-year-old. Despite his minimal print skills, he projected an annoying and pathetic sense of intellectual prowess. Of course he needed no assistance from an ABE teacher. He could never understand why he was placed in my class with these losers in the first place! Mostly to keep him from interrupting others in the room, I let him record his grandiose ideas into a tape recorder. After a while, to the disbelief of other staff, I began transcribing these homilies into print. The transcripts formed the first text Dorsette ever cared about. He used the texts to build sight words and to learn phonics and spelling rules. Eventually his stories became more "real" and his strutting gait transformed into an open, enthusiastic, though still impulsive one:

My work [Language Experience Approach strategy] with Dorsette is absurd. Yet I am fond of him. His ideas are raw and honest, and he is responding to the methods.

Dorsette, Rollins, Vines, Markham, Golden, Baynes, Lindsey, Carlton — I've reached so many of them! And they say, "It's hopeless — these kids don't deserve what kids from stable families deserve."

Still, in spite of (or because of) these small victories, my nostalgia for the Sandburg Learning Center was gripping and raw:

I will never forget that bittersweet day, December 12, 1980, saying goodbye to my friends and colleagues at Carl Sandburg School. How I miss those days at the Smith Center [outdoor education programs]…the kids, Sandy's breakthrough in her journal writing…

February 12, 1981

On this day a student (or students) stole a bag of mine with some possessions in it. I did not understand the motivation for the crime, and left no record in the journal about how (or if) I handled it. I doubt that I confronted any students, given the tone of resignation. It is interesting now, looking back across the years, how my wounded sense of competence was projected onto the "profoundly damaged" students:

> [Today] one of the students stole my blue pen that [my wife] gave me, an atlas given to me by my mother, a library book I will have to pay for, and Williams' class work. So why were these things—useless to the thief—stolen? To get me back for making them come in from the smoking area and sit down? Or just out of curiosity or greed?
>
> How vulnerable one is, who places himself in the path of criminals—who flatters himself with delusions of "making a difference" in their lives. The depth of the damage is profound.

February 15, 1981

Here, for the first time, I overtly questioned my current and future career with the FBOP. My sense of isolation lacks the fascination of a tourist, and sounds more like a stranger beginning to feel trapped in a very strange land:

> What am I getting out of this work? At some point I must sit down and think about my professional future. The Ivory Tower seems to be floating away, far above us poor peasants toiling in thickets outside the city gates. If I did not have family commitments, would I walk away from this job tomorrow?

February 16, 1981

This rant extended the downward spiral of negative feelings (isolation, self-doubt, vulnerability and cynicism) of the past week:

> I get repulsed by Markham, loathe Rollins, am frustrated with Dorsette—and this depletes me. Maybe [as staff teacher] Smith said, "They aren't worth a shit—the whole bunch of them!" Why should I throw my life away on unappreciative—and undeserving—dull children. Let me quit today and take to the gardens.

March 2, 1981

Two weeks later, a feeling of potency had returned:

> Kent [a student] says I am "soft" towards them. No, just the opposite—when I am not intimidated by them, have no fear of them, I feel no need to have excessive power over them. I see them more as threatened than threatening, needy more than greedy. So, let the classroom be democratic. Let their voices carry weight.

I will miss Carlton—he has really blossomed in the class. The week the hostages [from the U.S. Embassy in Iran] were released he was saying, "Boy, if my sons are about to be drafted I'm gonna tell them to get all shot up with heroin." I hated him then; found him to be lazy, evasive, and distracting. Now he's the leader of a great surge of self-help [that has motivated other students, such as] Williams, Rollins, Goines, Dorsette, Hathaway; and, now, a third generation: Dillwin.

To defend my stance…to defend this commitment in the eyes of Jennings [a cynical staff member]…Hell, yes! I care about [their] rehabilitation.

March 16, 1981

In this day's entry, the job's challenges seemed more manageable and less threatening to my overall professional identity. Past teaching experiences were not so much a source of stifling nostalgia as an instructional resource to draw upon for ideas to help current students:

Wanting to recreate the Sandburg [Learning Center] strategy of using art to spark Language Experience Approach lessons… But one of the things I have great difficulty with at FCI Parkwood is [getting students to] take risks. How can I encourage them to do anything [reflective] with creative interpretation [through art] without having them accuse me of psychoanalyzing them?

Further, I felt empowered to enforce prison policy and rules, and examined the ethical use of this power:

A moral problem: Should I allow Anderson to cop out of school? He hates being here. Yet he has acknowledged that we might be able to help him. But he resents "having" to be there, having no choice. I think his resentment overshadows his fear [of exposing his limitations in the classroom]. Do we have the right to force education upon [him]? If we let him go, would he choose to come back?

Why he resists:

- *Better life hustling?*

- *Emotional block towards school?*

- *Angry at life?*

- *Angry at coercive prison policies?*

Why I want him to stay:

- *To keep our quotas up so I don't lose my job? (Not really.)*

- *If we allow him to quit, it will encourage others to want to quit. (Possibly.)*

- *If some students aren't pushed, like Carlton, they might never realize their potential to learn. (Yes)*

Are any of the "reluctant students" learning? [An inventory of fifteen students revealed that four were learning, two were questionable, and nine were not]...The lower literacy level students seem most responsive [to my pushing them to stay in school]. The functionally literate ones are least responsive to being pushed. Perhaps this will change when I get a better handle on interesting materials at the upper ranges.

At this point, my vote is to "impose education" on Jose for ninety days, then let him choose to stay or quit.

March 31, 1981

Part of the culture shock experience, of course, was getting to know the students and what I perceived as their surprisingly appealing or repulsive characteristics. In this journal entry I expressed repulsion by the way some students reacted to President Reagan getting shot:

Reagan got shot yesterday; Jim Brady lies in a coma with a bullet in his brain. I witnessed the "lows" of inmate-think: Dorsette, "Join me in a round of applause for the assassin." And Billingsly, "He [Reagan] needed to be brought down a notch." These quips may have been heartfelt, inane, or meant to impress someone. But they made me sick to my bones.

April 2, 1981

I regarded some of my colleagues at FCI Parkwood as being compassionate and talented teachers, others as antagonistic and cruel. When I look back on some of the more cynical staff today I forget that, at the time, I valued their opinions of me. (One—my boss—had the power to promote or fire me.) They were a large part of my world, and I longed for their approval and acceptance into their world:

Luke [my boss], seeing Lindsey [a student] sleeping in class today (he had another seizure in class yesterday; his Thorazine really knocks him out) gave me a disapproving look that made it clear he thought I could not control my class.

...Why do I feel so exposed sometimes? What is it I have to hide from Jennings, Luke and "the good old boys?" ...my "soft" view of convicts?

My aloofness? I fear that nobody cares about me. I wish I could be
stronger and more independent...

And then the self-directed advice:

...What is needed here is a little levity, easy confidence; not defiance or
huffy confrontational show-downs...

April 10, 1981

To this end (i.e., the need for acceptance by peers), an opportunity for a
breakthrough presented itself the following week:

...the camaraderie of Luke's easy tales yesterday afternoon at Blackstone's
Pub; the ease and good fun of Dusty, Leroy and the others around a
pitcher of beer. Talking about gun control and herring dipping. They
want to start a Great Books Society...

Two ways to get closer to the staff: (a) [work on] my attitude;
(b) [establish some shared] activities and projects. A good laugh can
wash away a mountain of grief.

April 15, 1981

Teachers are not the only professionals that experience culture shock
in prison. After a conversation with one of the FBOP doctors, I recorded this
observation:

An FBOP physician questions why he busts his tail to help save a dying
prisoner serving a life sentence. He knows he won't get the support
he needs from the top to use heroic means to save the life of an Aryan
Brotherhood gang leader—so he tells his patient he's trying as best he
can, but he really isn't.

The advantage of prison education over prison medicine: Education
provides an avenue (space) for growth. To see an inward effort, a small
change, an outward skill develop, a relationship evolve...Trust and risk
taking. With medicine you are merely (sometimes literally) patching up
holes; in education you are planting seeds.

April 20, 1981

While more basic needs (i.e., physical and psychological safety),
discussed in prior journal entries were not evident in the one that follows, I was
becoming aware of a higher level need, in terms of Maslow's (1952) hierarchy—
the need to teach creatively:

It's not the loss of [professional] identity I feel right now; it's the awareness of a loss of freedom—to explore, build, compose, create—in the classroom...

April 21, 1981

Although I never thought of the youth offenders in my class as simply victims of the system (many were doing time for murder, rape and other violent crimes), the following excerpt reflects my identification with the system to a degree not seen in earlier journals entries:

We Americans are traditionally for the underdog. Perhaps it is time to resist cheering on the bandits. To look ourselves in the eye, and say we're not for the underdog in this case; we're for the benign strength of the people who struggle for solutions and do not hurt others in the process—the shop owner that hires an ex-con or supports social change, a community leader that starts an after-school program to keep youth off the street. Let's bury Billy the Kid and Bonnie and Clyde. We act out of kind-firmness to protect our society.

July 13, 1981

On July 13, 1981, I got a rude reminder that, in the FBOP, teachers are correctional officers first. I had already done my share of fog patrols (walking the outside fence perimeter armed with a shotgun during periods of heavy fog when escape risks are highest), tower duty (manning the gun tower, usually during the slower "morning watch" shift from midnight to seven A.M.), and correctional officer relief (in housing units or the cell house). But on this day I became a member of a riot squad. The prisoners had enforced an institution-wide hunger strike by stabbing one inmate who had attempted to go to the chow hall for breakfast. All staff, except for a few unlucky officers stuck in housing unit, reported to the visiting room and were assigned to the riot squads. The following notes were scribbled down throughout the day, as events unfolded:

As I dropped some school materials off at the camp this morning, [Officer] Donnelly told me about the food and work strike inside the compound. Ten minutes later I found myself with gas mask, jump suit, baton and helmet, taking notes on how to break into line, wedge, and echelon formations. I was—and am—part of the goon squad! Squad B: Clean up and restraining. With Elton and Leroy [fellow teachers], and others. Mr. Wilkinson, our squad leader, seemed irritated and nervous, like the rest of us. But the Captain briefed us thoroughly every hour: So far no outbreaks; only six inmates ate breakfast; dorm officers are cleaning up potential weapons (pool cues, broom handles, etc.). Negotiations are still going on—dorm reps (inmates) from each of the seven dorms are meeting with Dr. Thornton [psychologist], Luke [my boss] and other staff. They're (inmates) disorganized, mostly complaining about the food service. About noon Mack and I walked down to the cafeteria to get sandwiches for the dorm officers (locked into the dorms with the inmates). Mr. Bishop [correctional officer] was pissed off because the Administration was too easy going, letting the inmates watch TV and use phones. "No work," says Bishop, "no play." Dorm officers were tense and sweaty, but one in Carolina Unit at least showed some signs of humor when we arrived with the [plain] sandwiches, "What's this, fried chicken?"

The afternoon ticked by in suspense. There were continuous lines to use the bathrooms. I got some scissors from the warden's office and sheared off as much of my beard as possible so the gas mask could get a good seal. Some guys read books. Most sat around and made small talk. Then the deuces [alarm] went off—a stabbing in Virginia Hall! B Squad (mine) was sent down in plain clothes, A Squad was suiting up and on standby. We found out that Rhodes' [my tutor's] roommate was stabbed as a punishment for breaking the strike and going to breakfast this morning. Shakedowns. Strip searches. Going through filthy underwear, staring up ass-holes for contraband, tearing apart mattresses (one inmate is writing a BP-9 on us for leaving his room a mess). He should. It was. Contraband: knives from dining hall, two shanks probably made in the machine shop, a box of plastic bags, a sack of gungy [fermenting fruit juice], a bag of marijuana, a bag of white powder.

The rest of the afternoon passed without incident. Opened up education: No students. But inmates did go eat. Scared silly, quivering Lindsey [one of my ABE students], was one of the first to set foot in the dining hall. Soon many inmates—150 to 200—went through chow to get to commissary. At 9:00 P.M. we prepared for a recall hassle, but every inmate went back to his dorm peacefully. The question now is: What will tomorrow bring, with 500 inmates still striking and the others stocked up with food?

August 11, 1981

Anita Wilson (2003) found a third space in juvenile prisons in Great Britain, where the personal voices of incarcerated youth penetrated the highly regulated and impersonal first spaces of prison routines and regulations. Their graffiti, poetry, posters, letters and music reflected a resilience of spirit. In class on August 11, 1981, a dance film sparked a spontaneous, highly risky form of third space expression by one student. Or was it? It seems more likely that the student was playing a game about the absurdity of self-expression in dangerous prison spaces. Either way, the episode provided a rare opportunity for laughter and levity:

"Rhythmetron," a film about the Harlem Dance Theatre, brought the usual cat-calls and crude remarks. "Boy she'd get hold of your dick and wouldn't let go till she was good and ready"—Cosner's comments

about one female dancer. But there was one magical moment when we thought Watkins really lost his mind. He jumped up in front of the projector, raised his arms out to either side, and slowly bent his knees, repeating an up and down ballet-like motion, and then executed two pirouettes, all the while in a trance-like state. No one (student or staff) knew what to make of this, as we glanced at each other in dismay. Was he hallucinating? Was he really doing a spontaneous dance here where self-disclosure is considered weakness, and weakness an invitation to extinction? Fortunately, as he finished his last rotation, he broke through the trance with a mischievous grin and sat down chuckling: The joke was on us. Nervous laughter gave way to a hearty "well-done" uproar throughout the room! A triumph of the human spirit...

August 14, 1981

Usually students were on their best behavior in the classroom. Not necessarily because they wanted to learn, but because they were under close scrutiny by staff. When fights did break out in school, they sometimes provided views of a student world I knew nothing about. In the event recorded below, I found both pathos and virtue in the two students involved in the fight. One of the students, Mr. Young, was developmentally delayed and frequently seemed to set himself up to be victimized by others. Prison is dangerous enough for students with highly developed social skills; for those with mental illness or other limitations, prison can be as deadly as it is confusing:

Last night Young and Ellis got into a fight in the bathroom of our school. Leroy [a teacher] counseled Ellis out of slugging Young. Poor Young was so dazed and upset when he came back into class...His hand was cut, rubbing his ear and neck and wearing a look of "I'm-lost-again" bewilderment.

I believe that even though Ellis was ticked because Young had ripped him off (locker-knocking), the fight tonight came as a surprise to both of them. They exchanged a few unprovocative words in my class before the switch. Then I think sheer, stupid bravado in the face of peers forced them to call each other's bluff. I'd expect that of Young, but [not of] Ellis: Such good controls in the classroom and yet he got sucked into a duel with someone as vulnerable and non-threatening as Young. He must be much weaker socially than I thought.

On the other hand, from somewhere in Young's dazed face, a higher virtue—a courageous stance, a commitment to some deadly, unquestioned code, stared back at me.

August 16, 1981

Unlike teaching at Sandburg Learning Center, where I felt confident about expressing negative feelings such as anger and disappointment in controlled ways, I had not found a way to show these unavoidable emotions to the youth in my prison classroom. I worried that these suppressed feelings would surface outside the class in, for example, my interactions with my five-year-old son:

> *I am concerned about the professional arm-lock on my feelings of anger in the classroom. Whereas with kids I can find ways to express these intense feelings caused by frustration, or a selfish or cruel act, there seems to be no way to vent my frustrations constructively here at FCI Parkwood. I swallow my anger. Where does it go? When does it surface? My moments of exasperation with [my son] this weekend—were they linked to the exasperations of the classroom?*

August 19, 1981

A few days later, confidence in my ability to confront student behavior seemed to have improved:

> *I have confidence that I can be emotionally direct and honest with the students, to reflect my anger at lazy, childish or phony behavior. I sometimes avoid confronting their [anti-social] behaviors [toward each other] for fear the student will retaliate verbally or physically. But this is rationalization. I must, and can, confront them.*

August 29, 1981

The FBOP maintains a staff development center in Aurora, Colorado. In 1981, I attended an in-service program for new teachers and met for the first time, regional and central office education administrators and colleagues from around the country. The following excerpt reveals how isolated I must have felt at FCI Parkwood and how important it was for me to be accepted by colleagues that shared similar values:

> *Denver was a success. I connected with K. Kallish, S. Lonnigan, and D. Clark, [Administrators] and with turned-on teachers like Jossey [and a list of others]. My presentation was effective; Kallish told Clark the best thing he ever did was hire me! She [Kallish] talks to students the same way she talks to wardens and everyone else. She told me, "Who am I to tell a student 'that's as much as you can learn,' and give up, just because of some low IQ score?"*

October 30, 1981

My current stance toward prisoners and correctional education was anything but well formed when I started out at FCI Parkwood. Again I am reminded how much the belief systems of peers—especially those I regarded as sympathetic to a transformational view of correctional education—influenced my own views of prisoners and their capacity to change:

Why do I get so down and repulsed by my work? T. Pagel's (psychologist, most gifted and positive of all colleagues here at FCI Parkwood) only statement concerning Thompkins [a student] was, "Be wary of his type of personality; he'll look for chinks in your armor and try to tear you down." Yes, but what steps can we take to try to help him change? Is Pagel, a five-year vet, trying to tell me something?

Long hours back at Sandburg Learning Center were draining, but nevertheless seemed framed in light; long hours here seem to leave me feeing bitter and dark.

November 11, 1981

The journals provided a space to guide and construct my emerging—if rather middle-class—beliefs and hopes about correctional education. But they also recorded some of my existing views about students as "cripples," and prison classrooms shaped by power struggles, mistrust, and coercive policy:

What I seek in the classroom is to help my students reach a [love for learning]. Direct moralizing is repugnant to me—demanding them to conform to my values. What I want for them is to experience concentration, intense work for the joy of it, their inner voice. This can be achieved through drama, reading, art, and relaxation. I would like these emotional cripples (for some truly are!) to be able to experience shades of feelings. The ultimate goal: To trust—inside and out.

November 20, 1981

I think this next entry marks a significant shift in thinking. For the first time since joining the FBOP, I critically reflected on alternative career paths within the Bureau, and seemed to seriously consider the possibility of staying on:

What to do about my career in the FBOP? What kinds of jobs would be right for advancement? Returning to school to major in an Ed-Psych-Sociology area is critical. Is the path to warden [the typical Bureau trajectory] a possible avenue for me? Could I manage the use-of-force side of things (riots, routine security functions, correctional staff)? I know my abilities and limits: The answer is no. So, if the Bureau doesn't kick me out for avoiding the warden track, there are other [tracks], such as supervisor of education.

November 23, 1981

Here I seriously consider the possibility of remaining an FBOP classroom teacher, and how that experience might support my need for professional growth:

Although the blackness of violence and dehumanization sometimes looms over my mind like a cloud, I dare consider the Adult Basic Education path…a noble calling. There is much work to be done. It [the ABE path] cries out for science and art to embrace it, study it, notate it, reshape it, and refine it.

December 10, 1981

A sub-theme running through the early journal recordings was my ability (or lack of) to maintain integrity as a teacher-coach while, at the same time, establish control and earn the respect of students in a system that required respect to be earned by asserting authority and strength over others, not with them. In this entry I felt triumphant about asserting this power over others, while still wanting to parlay this to a more "therapeutic" kind of potency:

…Asserted myself today. Made [student] Winters wait until I checked out his statement (that DAP inmates can go without a pass). His assertion was right. But now I know I can make it as a hack if I ever want that job! (I wonder about the potential of using the dorm counselors as "real" counselors—a therapeutic milieu approach to corrections. Sorry, Fritz Redl, not in this fiscal year…)

December 25, 1981

The journals were a refuge, a place to find resolve. The following Christmas "mantra" typified an ongoing, conscious effort to make sense of my early correctional education experiences:

The struggle of my job: Let me use it to burn a brighter character—warmer, harder, bolder, truer. Through the great backdrop of hopelessness let me transform outrage into energy—professional, intellectual, moral.

December 29, 1981

Despite my progress finding footing over this first year, the struggle to create a stable, consistent learning environment was in perpetual conflict with the prime security mission of the prison. In the FBOP, teachers are trained to be correctional officers (CO's); and, when the need arose (as it all too frequently did), teaching functions were preempted by custodial ones: Manning gun towers, substituting for unit officers, walking the perimeter fence. Most disturbing to me personally was not the actual custodial work, but the regular interruptions to instruction and learning caused by pulling teachers out of the classroom. In an environment where positive momentum depended on the constant coaxing of mercurial classroom dynamics, these almost-constant interruptions were destructive and frustrating.

Here I chide myself for volunteering to cover a custodial post. The entry provides a small window into one kind of double-bind faced by FBOP teachers (and, I suspect, correctional educators in other systems) to this day: The need to fit in and support the larger prison community (upon whose support your life might someday depend), versus the need to protect the integrity of the classroom.

> *I am angry with myself for volunteering to do another stint as dorm officer. Why did I? For acceptance and praise? Of course! But I thought I was opposed to this work, in principle, on the grounds of weakening education's stature by allowing ourselves to be pulled out of the classroom even more. But we all (custody and program staff) have to live together, be there for each other.*

Another entry that day provided fragments of insights about individual students, group dynamics, and larger prison-system conflicts—the everyday stuff of teaching in prison. In these reflections, even the ones about my own interior states, I seem more detached and less overwhelmed than in earlier entries that addressed some of the same puzzling experiences:

> *The puzzlement of older students: Note Golden, "No man wants to learn after the age of 35."*

> *Tutor burn out: L [my tutor] B-S-ing with other students; Dana [another tutor] off reading on his own; Acton [a third tutor] harshly criticizing a student...*

> *The large group is bored with readings...*

> *Interruptions! Holidays; second group coming into class after having first period off (Mack [first period teacher] is sick)...*

> *Saturation with student requests. I am overwhelmed with small, legitimate concerns (help with letter home, frustration with commissary staff delaying a purchase order, fear of visit...). I feel overworked and frustrated, but want to distance myself from this inadequacy by characterizing the student requests as "con jobs" or manipulations, to avoid guilt.*

December 31, 1981

Here again, I expressed feelings of being overwhelmed, but there was energy left over to note the injustices inherent in some prisoner-staff discourses:

> *How can I possibly solve these riddles day after day? The sad fact is that no one wants to be bothered listening to the problems of inmates. Commissary put me on hold trying to solve a cash transfer problem for a cooperative, and patient [inmate] Saul, who has been trying for three*

weeks to get his order placed. Receiving and Discharge sighs irritably when I ask them to call Allenwood [Federal Prison Camp, Allenwood, Pennsylvania] to check on M's property.

January 9, 1982

I return again to the theme of a potential Bureau career. My thinking about this seemed to grow less emotional and more rational as time progressed. A small marker, but one of great personal importance, is tucked into the end of the passage below ("a la Thom Gehring"). Thom, cherished friend and mentor, correctional education leader and historian, entered my world serendipitously in 1981. His friendship provided immeasurable support, with new words (good-old-boy networks, criminal plumber, new role models),Thomas Mott Osborne, Austin MacCormick, new ideas (democratic methods, correctional education professional identity), new networks (Correctional Education Association, Rehabilitative School Authority), and, above all, a sympathetic ear and a steady, reassuring presence. Where my teaching path would have taken me had I not met Thom is impossible to say. But he, and shortly thereafter his friend, fellow correctional educator and future wife—Carolyn Eggleston—had a profound influence on my life and vocation.

These new friendships and intellectual tools helped me cope, but could not buffer me from the day-to-day drama of FCI Parkwood. Leaving the Bureau was a viable option. Here are some of my career thoughts a year and a month into the prison sojourn:

Why I should not leave:

- *Federal pay (higher than most school systems);*

- *Abandoning students again: Thoms, Vines, Golden, etc.;*

- *Stepping backwards (admitting I made a mistake by coming to work at FCI Parkwood); and,*

- *Letting down family members.*

And why I should stay:

- *Develop a social justice stance;*

- *Create a reading lab;*

- *Create a safe place for students to explore/develop identity; and,*

- *Pursue professional growth in correctional education (a la Thom Gehring).*

January 11, 1982

The physical and psychological isolation of prisons, their disconnection from the outside world, was a prevailing theme in the journal from the start. But in this journal record, concerns have shifted from my isolation to that of my students:

> *Knowing there are trees outside my window and that they are connected to the sky and I am connected to them is important. So it is with my work. If my students can touch the outdoors—snowflakes, vegetation, woods—if they can see they are connected through the fuse of their parents to history, if they can see how this indoor classroom is connected to the outdoor world; then they will love learning.... Maybe we can create a community service program...*

January 12, 1982

Again the themes seem to be broadening to include my struggle, my students' plight and, now, prison policy:

> *I see men crammed through ABE, GED. So what? They never learn self-pride, self-responsibility or a sense that they can be masters of their own fate. That is the only education that really matters. What have we really taught [students] Baynes? Seymor? Matthers? It must start with diagnostics: If we do not know their [personal interests and individual needs], how can we help them master life or reflect on their own understandings?*

January 20, 1982

The shift toward reflections on FBOP policy and curriculum—and even the larger correctional education community—continues. Thom Gehring introduced me to the works of correctional education leaders. I used Ryan's (1975) Adult Basic Education model to develop a set of social-communication skills that would support social learning experiences in an FBOP program:

> *Inspired by T.A. Ryan's model of Adult Basic Education, I've sketched out the following skills, knowledge, and attitudes that might be relevant for the medium-security Federal Correctional Institution ABE classroom:*
>
> *[Cognitive] Social Skills*
>
> *1. Sharing: Ability to share instructor's time, materials; take turns in discussions.*
>
> *2. Confidence: Ability to express one's views, to argue effectively.*

3. *Risk taking: Ability to participate in reflective literacy-based activities, to volunteer answers.*

4. *Respect: Listening to and learning from others, using a quiet tone of voice in the classroom, not smoking or sleeping in class.*

5. *Impulse control: Perseveres when frustrated; vents frustration in ways that are not harmful to others.*

6. *Reality testing: Checks out others' messages (content and intention) before becoming defensive; responds with emotional intensity that is proportionate to the situation.*

7. *Ownership: Accepts responsibility for his contribution to a problem, takes initiative for growth and learning, establishes personally meaningful goals.*

8. *Problem solving: Troubleshoots a problem to determine its underlying causes.*

9. *Self esteem: Makes realistic goals, takes pride in work, accepts constructive criticism, makes honest self-appraisals.*

10. *Cooperation: Works as part of a team, accepts direction from others, leads discussion or project, is tolerant of others' views, is supportive of others' efforts, competes and handles both winning and losing.*

January 23, 1982

If transformative learning begins with an acceptance of the adult learner as he or she is (Kegan, 1994), then the following vignette, in which some students reveal their beliefs about street life, marks a potential starting point in transformative dialogue. It also signals the willingness of a group of reluctant learners to open up in class, and a growing confidence in my ability to support more meaningful, if fleeting, learning experiences in prison:

> *After reading "The Hold Up," a story about a kid who attempts to enact his first stick-up only to be talked out of it, and [ultimately] employed by his would-be victim (a gas station owner), I asked the group what happened to the kid? Harrison said, "He was conned instead of doing the con. The man took away his street pride. He lost his respect." Pritchert added (somewhat tongue-in-cheek, as if he were just responding with what I wanted to hear), "Yeah, but he gained some work pride." So I asked the group if there was such a thing as work pride? Harrison replied, "No. Everybody says, 'There goes the chump who works all day and just has barely enough money to pay the rent and eat baloney sandwiches. They've lost their street pride.'"*

February 4, 1982

Open dialogues with other students were noted in this day's journal entries. One such dialogue started just as the prisoner was about to leave prison:

> Paulson (forty-five year old, white inmate with drinking problem), after reading about how the clitoris and penis develop in utero, said, "So it really is up there, huh? Right above the vagina?" Forty-five years old and unsure whether the clitoris is a myth or real. Sex education in prison is desperately needed...

> Paulson is scared to death about going home. He came into the program so "fly" [with a cool and smooth demeanor] he gave me his "fast rap" — man is words, words are thoughts, etc. [high-sounding gibberish]. He was impressed with his own profundity. Although many people were turned off to his jive-ness, he could describe the cold, hard game better than anyone else: How ninety-five percent of women are "ho's;" how to spot a con; how the little "turds" start taking over the turf and must be watched; how to pick up chicks; how, once when he was taking LSD he saw little splinters of light burst forth from the sidewalk into millions of ideas...Paulson excels at seeing through shams, but is clueless about seeing through to genuine friendship or a caring family member. Today Paulson is nervous about his "life-sentence to the street" [his words]. He seems humbled, lost. After five and a half years down and knowing he's going right back to the hustle, he seems to be crying out for guidance.

February 6, 1982

With a clearer idea about the need for cognitive-social foundations for correctional education, I expressed frustration at the lack of support for this kind of learning at FCI Parkwood:

> Is there no hypocrisy in an organization that sees itself as correctional, that supports rehabilitation and re-integration, that spends millions of dollars on personnel and equipment...but invests nothing in quality control, and knows nothing about the quality of what is really happening in its classrooms? ...If we're not using literacy to develop introspection and socialization skills then we are not teaching. Period.

February 13, 1982

Here is another mantra for self-preservation—I wonder what happened that day to cause this admonition:

> I must become more like a detached observer at work. This even-mindedness (if possible) might allow me to actually get closer.

March 1, 1982

The following anecdote records my attempt to organize teachers at FCI Parkwood. Although the request was denied, the account reveals both the degree to which control at FCI Parkwood remained in the hands of one person—the supervisor—and also a growing awareness of my ability to assert myself:

> *Submitted a letter to Luke [my boss] today, in light of the [current mission change at FCI Parkwood], on behalf of all the teachers. The letter called for the development of a program-development committee consisting of all the teachers—that would meet once a week to discuss program development, recruitment, discipline, school rules, challenges, ideas and best practices, latest findings from professional journals, etc. We would be willing to stay forty-five minutes late that day, if the FBOP would provide us forty-five minutes of planning time (during the work day).*

April 15, 1982

This is another "day in the life" anecdote that presents little pieces of a daily mosaic. The first paragraph addressed my exasperation with constantly working against the grain to create psychologically safe learning spaces for learners at lower literacy levels. The second provides an example of how class integrity was frequently interrupted. (At least in this case, even if no learning was going on, the situation was manageable.) In the third paragraph, more student breakthroughs are mentioned.

> *Today [student] KA "rung my bells" by laughing when I told Lance he had more work to do. Anderson, Jones, and Harrison are all developing poor attitudes. (Or should I say that the flood gates to the FCI Parkwood ocean of rage are breaking down?) The oasis I try to create using art, music, journals, etc. to try to shelter Lindsey, Williams, Paulson, Baynes, Jenkins is so crazy—bringing tigers into an oasis and trying to protect them! Domesticate them! Tap some hidden source of self worth....*
>
> *In the afternoon, Luke [my boss] forgot to tell us that [staff teacher] Coats would be out, and that I would be combining his students with mine. Despite the overcrowded conditions, things went well. There is an equilibrium that is maintained in the class...so that sometimes it's easier to manage twenty than six. There seem to be less games, more peer pressure to be civil to each other.*
>
> *The last class is my favorite. Capponella—crazy, but plugged in to his assignments. Baker, who was very hostile and mistrusting when he first came into the program, now uses phrases like "decent!" and "no sweat!" It is obvious he is satisfied with his progress in Hip Reader. Jones is plugged in also....*

May 28, 1982

Here, eighteen months into the job, I seem to be reacting to a slight by my supervisor and pondering the qualities of an effective one. I think this reveals another step toward my assimilation into the FBOP, and an indirect experimenting with putting on new coats from the career wardrobe:

> *Luke [my boss] became furious with me today when I suggested separating Harrison from Markham because of the dynamics between them. "Jennings [a veteran staff member] will take care of the discipline problems up here," he barked. "I guarantee it."*

> *It must take a very courageous person to be supervisor of education — someone who has to live down the mistrust and ridicule of the rest of the institution staff. A person who doesn't get sucked into proving one's manhood by buying into a constant state of siege mentality. Who acknowledges the need to tolerate some inmate behavior. Who understands that absolute control is not the ultimate goal. Who sees caring and helping as strengths, not weaknesses...*

November 1, 1982

The FBOP provided two days of Refresher Training annually for all staff. Topics typically included safety, self-defense, firearms and other custodial issues. The institution's staff training center was located outside the fence, but on the federal reservation, along a sleepy bend of a river. Sitting by myself on the bank during a break, wishing that the training were related to teaching, I was conscious of my self-imposed aloofness from the other staff—primarily correctional officers. Halfway across the river, some poles stood four feet out of the river, foundations of an old dock. Clumps of moss and other vegetation grew out of their sides, apparently without need for soil. I recorded this scene in verse below. Almost two years into my assignment at FCI Parkwood, the themes of isolation and resilience still haunted me:

> *Sitting on this skinny old boat platform*
> *Gazing across this... tributary*
> *I behold strange daisy-like plants*
> *Growing from the jetty.*
> *Their soil?*
> *The algae-crusted bark of*
> *Wooden posts.*
> *From these muddy posts*
> *Their roots wave languidly*
> *Down to the river –*
> *A foot or two below.*
> *No question as to their survival.*
> *But their frame:*

Stark desolate naked.
Yet the lapping river
Doubles back for
Another and another embrace.
An inchworm observes from above.
Ants conduct business,
Never considering the delicate balance.
The perennial metaphor stubbornly resists.
Life fills space.

November 13, 1982

On this day, after numerous cycles of success, failure, resolve and renewed effort, latent feelings of vulnerability and self-doubt were as robust as when I started in the FBOP:

> *At FCI Parkwood my assertiveness rises and falls with my energy level. But one of the great ego-boosts of working with children is missing: The emotional power. There are times when fear and exhaustion take the edge out of me. This happens with students as well as with Luke [my boss], although in different ways. But in both cases it is [the feeling that] I have not stood up to others that cuts deepest and tears down my will. Surely there have been many triumphs of assertiveness, but when my perceived weakness sets in, they [the triumphs] are quickly forgotten.*

November 30, 1982

On the other hand, breakthroughs, in terms of open dialogues with students, continued to provide emotional power, contrary to the lamentations of the previous journal entry:

> *When Fillipe said, "If you fell over with a heart attack, I wouldn't touch you," I asked him why. First he said because, "You are a Fed and Feds degrade us, call us 'convicts,' 'lower than mud,' 'pieces of shit.'" Then he paused and said, "If I put a hand on you, you never know what those Feds would try to pin on me."*

> *During the reading of Jack Henry (a black World War II soldier who had to take orders from a racist sergeant and ended up saving his life), Fillipe said, at the beginning of the story, "I wouldn't save that racist bastard—he'd get up and kill me anyway. But by the end of the story and ensuing discussion, he was able to empathize with Jack's efforts to "reach out" to the sergeant. The cathartic discussion about Gandhi and altruism seemed to touch him and marvelously, though briefly, transformed him. During the discussion he also said, "Fast money is death money; slow money is life money." I really cherish these privileged glimpses into these men, illuminated by the power of literature.*

Conclusion

I make no attempt to arrange these recollections into a linear story. The reader can see evidence of assimilation, isolation, despair, hope, doubt and epiphanies throughout the two-year chronology. Perhaps these experiences constitute not so much a rollercoaster ride (the metaphor used earlier to characterize them) as a spiral, with cycles of acculturation and culture shock moving in a certain direction. (I believe there is some evidence of that here.) But I will leave that to the reader to sort out. My purpose here was not to interpret, but rather report, as faithfully as I could, on the things that most demanded my mental energies during those first years "going to work in a prison."

Looking back, it seems strange and unlikely that I would end up working in the FBOP for twenty-five years. Or that I would find ways to grow professionally, sometimes in spite of the work, more often through the work and the many great FBOP educators that inspired me to keep fighting. I am thankful I survived those first years.

I attribute my FBOP survival to three things. First, I was exposed to strong teachers and teaching models before entering the FBOP, so I knew what could be done in classrooms, even with the most challenging of students, when the proper supports were in place. Second, new friends—Thom Gehring and Carolyn Eggleston—mentored me in those vulnerable early days and introduced me to our professional community, the Correctional Education Association. And third, the journal writing itself provided a safe place to rage, rant, reflect, discover, test, recreate and sort out confusing and messy events.

It is hoped that readers, especially those teachers new to prison work, will recognize some of the experiences presented here and find insight or catharsis in doing so. I am grateful to Randall Wright for allowing me to contribute to this important volume on culture shock.

Postscript: July 17, 1983

I read ahead in the journals to try to find a point when it seemed like I turned a definitive corner in professional identity away from K-12 and toward prison-based teaching. Hints of this change were evident in an entry written two-thirds through my third year at FCI Parkwood:

> *I've discovered tonight (I think) that I have accepted the limits of teaching prisoners. At least I am presently liberated from the crippling nostalgia [for my past teaching experiences with children], and have energy for today. I plan to continue to pursue the knowledge, artistic expression and philosophy of correctional education.*

CHAPTER V

HOW I LEARNED TO TEACH IN A WOMEN'S PRISON: A TALE OF GROWTH, UNDERSTANDING AND HUMOR

By Jane Penwell

Introduction

In January 1989, I walked into a new women's prison and heard the doors clang closed behind me for the very first time. I was new to this small, closed world of women locked up together and had no idea how much I would need to learn to operate effectively as a teacher and a human being.

I had been hired by a small college to work full time in the prison as a prerelease coordinator. Ostensibly, the prison was a prerelease center. Yet rarely were inmates given the opportunity to learn to work or function in society prior to their actual release from custody. So we, the staff, and they, the prisoners, were cramped in a minute space that had been originally designed as a work/study center for people who were working or studying in the community and only in the facility on nights and weekends.

Luckily for us, the entire staff was new: We all were transferred from other facilities or recently hired, so nobody actually knew how the education department should function. We were able to re-invent ourselves repeatedly as we learned and were changed by what we learned. We all were female, except for a former minister who had left his church and was going through a difficult divorce—something many of us, both teachers and students, could understand.

As a group, we had a wide variety of teaching experience—one was an academic who had taught at the college level; another had taught in an orphanage. I had worked as a trainer in a state agency after leaving a position as a high school instructor. Our director also had taught at the college level and was an employee of the college that had hired us. Since this college was very involved with correctional education, our director had also taught at a men's prison, and so had some experience with how prisons operate.

In time we added a computer lab and another female instructor, who taught at the local community college.

Some of us were black, some white, some straight, some gay, some married, some divorced, some mothers, some not, but all of us were committed to the success of our program.

In the beginning, we huddled together, finding comfort in numbers in this alien environment and clinging to our old routines—setting up our offices, arranging our furniture, booting up our computers and waiting—waiting for them to arrive, and then one day, they came. But by the time hundreds of them came, we had learned the prison routine—we knew about chits and counts and chow, lock ups and lock downs, belly chains and cuffs. We had created our program and assigned ourselves duties, we had worked with the few women who were in the facility as cooks and clerks, we had taught mock classes and ordered more books—we were ready, or so we thought.

When we discovered our students were coming before we were ready with our pre-release programming, I decided to begin by teaching basic English classes. I was an English major, had briefly taught English at a juvenile boy's facility, and had taught high school English. So, I prepared for my classes by imagining my new students would be the equivalents of the bad boys and girls that attended my high school classes. In other words, I thought the adult incarcerated female student would be an older version of the boys and girls I had taught previously and so those were the women I prepared myself to teach. Unfortunately, those women never arrived.

Instead, the women who filled the seats in my classes were introverted, unresponsive, angry, bitter and resistant to group activities (which I had thought would work quite well). These were not the wisecracking jokers from my high school classes or the bad boys who squirmed in their seats and loved it when I read to them. These were adult women whose lives had been ruined, whose children were with strangers, whose men had betrayed them and whose parents blamed them. These students, when asked to write an essay, wrote about rape and beatings and drug deals gone wrong in which people were killed or seriously wounded. They wrote about drive-by shootings and gangs—a world that I had read about in the newspaper or seen on TV but hadn't really understood existed. They accused me of using their stories to get attention at parties, of not caring about their traumas, of walking out at night and forgetting them and, worst of all, of trying to get them to learn something that just didn't matter in their lives. They were looking for help finding housing and transportation and getting their children back, not in learning that subjects and verbs should agree. They needed information about services available in their home communities, not essays written by well-known authors, no matter how well meaning. They wanted to leave the institution and be safe and have a safe place for their children, then, maybe, find a job flipping burgers would be fine—their aptitudes for jobs were irrelevant in the world they would re-enter. Underneath all of the anger and tough talk and resistance was paralyzing fear—fear of AIDS, fear of a man who had sworn to get them, fear of a habit that was too strong to fight for long and fear of losing everything again.

So, how do you teach English to the real incarcerated female student? How do you persuade her that subject-verb agreement really does matter and that understanding a short story will help in the long run? How do you get the real student to forget about that violent, unforgiving world of drugs and money and men long enough to think about how to write correctly, choose a topic and create a great topic sentence and then end with a dynamic conclusion? How do you motivate her to want to correct errors and go beyond street speak to a proper English that, in her opinion, she would never use?

The psycho-babble of our day is self-esteem—why people don't have it, how they can get it and how it would improve their lives. There are many theories and methodologies for creating and nurturing self-esteem in those who don't have it, but none of the literature has dealt with women who have lived lives of degradation and hopelessness, robbed of any self-esteem they may have retained after an abusive, neglected childhood. Of course, I thought, if they could just realize how people would take them seriously if they spoke correctly, how employers would react positively and landlords would be impressed with well-written letters and subjects and verbs that agreed, their problem would be solved. So, I tried to persuade them that learning correct English would make a difference in their lives. I spoke eloquently about how people in the straight world react to street talk versus proper English and how a well-written letter could open doors. What happened? A hand was raised—great, I thought, somebody gets it—and the owner asked in a bored and disinterested voice if I really talked like this at home.

I was speechless. I couldn't understand the question. Did she think I had created an educated persona strictly for teaching and then went home and became Jane from the block? Absurd, I thought, so I said, "Yes, and my mother talks like this, my son talks like this and so does everyone else in our family." I could see looks of doubt and suspicion, so I asked what they thought about a whole family that talked like me. Well, one person said, "I bet you had trouble in school." Another said that she thought people who talked like me were just on TV and not for real—I had already thought the same about her and her fellow students.

After several similar sessions, I finally understood that my students lived in a world comprised of people that did not talk like me, did not think like me, did not look or act like me and they really had little use for someone telling them their whole world—which was just as incredible to me as mine was to them—was wrong. In fact, one student asked me if I understood that it would be just as difficult for her to attend a job interview with a resume and make a presentation as it would be for me to stand on a street corner and sell drugs. Well, no, I didn't understand this because I viewed their lives as examples of what happened when people got addicted and lapsed into addict behavior. I did not realize most of my students lived their chaotic lives and committed crimes as routinely as I looked for a part-time job—this life was normal for them.

This revelation had a great impact on my lesson planning and my presentation. I went back to square one and tried to understand how to present an English lesson to students that really didn't think my world and its emphasis on correct grammar existed and, if it did, could not see the relevance to their lives. What would work, how could I create lessons that would penetrate their belief that nothing I said was useful or important to them? I tried several approaches: finding books with stories about gangs and urban life; preparing my own worksheets with questions oriented to their interests; journaling for ten minutes each day with carte blanche to write about anything; and, developing many more lessons to find something, anything that would work.

Each solution I tried worked to an extent. Most students did enjoy stories that spoke to their lifestyle, but many could not read well enough to really understand the stories. So, this began our read-aloud classes. I would begin by reading a page and then everyone else would read a paragraph and then I would read a page. Next, I would question them about what we had read, ask for their opinions and voice my own. Many times a student would say she didn't have an opinion, she was just listening, so I would skip her and go on to someone else or take the opportunity to voice what I thought. Usually, my opinions elicited groans and hoots because I was seen as such a Pollyanna, so green, so square, and sooo white—and pretty soon they could predict what I would say and would say it with me. I found that only a few students would actually respond to my questions by stating their own opinions, so I began to wonder why always the same women would respond.

By this time I had a clerk that I could trust, so I asked her why certain women would always respond and the majority would not. "Well," she said, "those ones that answer don't care what anybody thinks about them and the ones who don't talk are afraid that if they do, somebody will call them out in the pod." (Hmm—so anything that was said in class could harm a person in the living quarters, maybe even cause her big trouble if it was repeated.) "Why did the other women speak out?" I asked, curious about the students who did talk. My clerk rolled her eyes (an eloquent form of communication that I had never seen used so effectively prior to entering the institution) and proceeded to tell me that one was a big-time, wealthy drug dealer who didn't need anything from anybody in the joint, another was a bull dagger (lesbian) who could beat anyone to a pulp, another had a boyfriend on the outside who would take care of anybody's family if they bothered her and so on.

So, I discovered that the institution did not exist in a vacuum, but rather was an extension of the street, with all of the same games, status and payback activities that characterized the every-day dealings of most of the students on the outside. I also learned that most people knew the life stories of everyone from their city, who their mothers, fathers, boyfriends and children were, where they lived, how they got their money and what they had done to get locked up. I learned about boosters and mules and ho's and strawberries and street names—a whole new vocabulary that replaced the given names and vocations I used to describe people. And, I learned that there were nuances unsuspected by me prior to learning this new terminology. If my clerk dismissed somebody by saying she was just a ho, this was different from her attitude toward somebody who "hoed" for a certain well-known pimp. I began to see an entire culture had been created around drugs, prostitution and other criminal pursuits and that the people who were part of this culture saw the majority of the activities as normal, at least for them.

As I learned more about the lives of my students, I began to see increasing opportunities to insert a learning dimension into our class discussions. For example, I might bring up a student in another class who had told me she was incarcerated for letting a drug dealer distribute drugs from her kitchen, using the back door as a hatch to pass drugs out and money in. Then I would say she had done this in order to buy Christmas presents for her children. Everybody would nod, understanding this reasoning, since they had probably done it themselves. I would state that I would prefer my children got nothing for Christmas rather than something bought with drug money, and a furious discussion would erupt with everyone shouting and arguing about how stupid I was. When things calmed down, I would talk about my reasons for not wanting to give children things bought with drug money—somebody has to suffer and maybe die for me to get the money, it's illegal, what good would presents do my children if I were in jail, the drug dealer makes the money and I take the risks, I could lose my apartment for nothing, etc. Of course, I had to admit that I was white, middle class and had never had to steal or deal drugs to buy Christmas presents, so naturally I was merely speculating about how I would feel if I were in this predicament. Amazingly, some students would come to my defense and assert that I was right and that kids should understand that everybody's family cannot afford Jordans or Starter jackets or whatever is popular at the time, so they should just be proud of what they get. Less frequently, someone would muse about the rights and wrongs of teaching kids that these things are so important that their mothers would risk prison to get them and maybe this is what makes the kids kill each other for them.

After one of these heated discussions, I would ask everyone to get out their journals and write for five minutes about the topic we had just discussed. When I reviewed the entries, I would occasionally find that students who had not responded in class, who had looked out the window or appeared to read a book, had written passionately about the topic, and so I learned that oral communication was not even half the battle in my new environment. I also learned not to push students that did not respond, but rather to ignore their unresponsive behavior and continue with the class. This way, I avoided confrontations I could not win and students who just needed to have a time-out from classroom discussions could get that time. However, if a confrontation did erupt and I had to respond to a student's negative behavior, I also learned to discuss the situation in private, not in front of the class. Frequently, I would get an entirely different reaction in my office than in the classroom and find that the student had been upset by something totally removed from the classroom. Sometimes, I could resolve the issue by talking with the student; other times I would have to act—do a write up, call the officer in charge of the dorm, talk to another teacher or pass the situation on to one of the prison counselors.

In the midst of all this, I still tried to develop exercises for subject-verb agreement with a message—a subtle message, I thought, but often after class students would tell me they recognized what I was doing and weren't fooled for a minute. But they kept working to discover what corny saying or silly observation I would use to conclude the exercise. When we reviewed these sentences in class, everybody would chuckle and smirk while I pretended not to know they were wise to my little tricks and, amazingly enough, I got some positive reactions to my lessons. So, I grew bolder and made the mistake of actually introducing a reading assignment that called for a moral judgment.

One of the stories I used was O'Henry's tale of the poor man who sold his watch to buy hair combs for his wife, who had sold her hair to buy him a watch chain for Christmas. I thought they would enjoy this tale of love, devotion and sacrifice and that we could discuss the whys and wherefores without problems since it had all happened so long ago. Instead, everyone agreed the guy was stupid, the woman was crazy and that sweet little story was scorned as if it was about people who were either demented. The students had no empathy or understanding or interest in the fictional couple and felt that anybody, even me, could think of a better way to solve the problem of how to get Christmas gifts if you have no money. They all agreed that I would do something corny like make a gift using a dishtowel or my underwear, but they would just boost (steal) something useful for the guy. So, I learned that above all, the stories and lessons must be pragmatic. The students would rather read directions for programming a VCR than stories about Christmas written by long-dead white men, and they made this very clear.

So, most of my original lesson plans ended up in a file and I scrambled each day to find a plan that would work for the students and for me. I learned that teaching in a prison is a process very different from teaching in any other environment. In a prison, anything can happen at any time: There can be a fight in the yard that causes everyone to be locked down. Five of the best students can be accused of something and go to the hole to wait for a hearing. One of the students can get bad news from home and totally disrupt the class and so on. Also, because one day is just like another, except for the days when something huge happens, everyone suffers from almost terminal boredom—"same old, same old" is the mantra. So most days are the same except for the days when everything is in turmoil—there is rarely a chance to just make a change for your own mental health—like I might go to Bob Evans if I were bored with my own cooking, the students craved something different.

As I began to understand this, I tried to satisfy the students' hunger for something new and different. I would bring a newspaper article to class and read it for class discussion or find a video to play or take the class outside to the yard to look for something—anything was better than "same old, same old," I thought. But not so—I found that what we did had to relate to our lessons. Nobody is more alert to rights\wrongs or fair\unfairness than an incarcerated student. If I proposed doing something that did not relate in any way to our topic or lessons,

I would find dissention in the ranks—someone would say, "But miss, ain't we supposed to be studying English?" And everyone else would agree, so I would be faced with some very suspicious and doubtful looks, even if I tried to make a joke by saying, "Ain't, ain't a word." About this time, somebody said to me for the first but far from the last time, "You can't con a con," and I had to agree. My attempts to bring some change to the class were acceptable only if they had an immediately apparent point that related to class activities; otherwise, they were a waste of time and nothing I could do or say could disguise that fact.

Then, one day a student came to me to complain that other students were cheating. She was very upset that these students were getting good grades while she was failing. I had not realized the extent of the cheating and promised her I would get to the bottom of it and adjust the grades accordingly. "Good," she said, "cause when I get an 'F' I want to earn it."

So I learned that my students cheated routinely, for no good reason except they loved to beat the system, no matter what the system might be. I worried and talked to my colleagues about this matter—what to do when the grades actually meant nothing—and found it was happening in all of the classes. Finally, we decided that we would all announce a new policy—anyone caught cheating would go to the director's office for a talk and then would be banned from classes for a week.

This turned me into Nancy Drew. I was determined to catch the worst offenders and make examples of them. How silly, I now realize, as they were already in prison, but nevertheless I watched and waited and finally caught somebody copying from a crib sheet she had tucked into her sleeve. I pounced on her, took her out of the class and into the office, gave her a good talking to about cheating and left her looking mutinous, sitting with the secretary, waiting for the director. I returned to class and proceeded with the lesson plan, collected the papers at the session's end and went to my office, feeling pretty good about teaching a valuable lesson.

As soon as I sat down, my clerk told me that the entire class had erupted into a fight when I left the room. "What about?" I asked.

"Well," she said, "they was all trying to get a hold of that paper you took off the girl."

"What?" I screamed. "You mean I left it there?"

"Yup," she said, "but I got them to quit fighting."

"How?" I asked.

"I told them," she said, "that their girl didn't know shit and all the answers was probably wrong."

So I learned the futility of trying to enforce meaningless rules—just as our captain, who was an "out" lesbian who lived with a woman, came to work each day to punish women engaging in the same behavior, I was repeating the middle-class schoolmarm behavior that I hated in high school. I felt the only way to make any difference in the lives of my students was to actually address their real problems—to try to help them do something constructive about these problems and not worry about the rules and regulations of the institution. All my colleagues had come, by different paths, to this same conclusion. We knew we were needed in the institution, not as quasi-school teachers but rather as people who knew how to help. Also, at this time, our institution was headed by a female warden who was very interested in anything we could do to improve the women's chances of getting and staying out, so we were allowed to do what we could.

We interviewed people who were ready to go home and found that when they left the institution, they would be given a ride to the bus station, some money and some old, outdated clothes. That was it—no referrals, no plans, no help, unless they had family or friends who would come to their aid or an institution counselor who had the time and energy to make some phone calls for them. So we began to make contacts in the various cities in our state and found agencies willing to accept referrals from us, places where people could go to get clothes, shoes, furniture, etc. The students eagerly devoured all of this information and we felt good about what we were able to accomplish. However, we soon learned the best of plans was not good enough. Within six months, many of our students began to return, sheepishly saying that they had messed up "on the outs."

Our little prison family, all teachers with degrees who had lived lives of delayed gratification, proved to be poor planners for women who had lived by their wits, sold drugs as a job, boosted if necessary or not and were unready to embrace another way of life. We made plans for them that would have worked for us, so naturally, those plans failed. Back to the drawing board we went, to try to determine how to do this thing effectively that we all desperately wanted to do: Help. We began to dream of a drop-in center where people could go when they were out of options and ready to do something that could lead back to prison. We thought about having "old girls" who were successful come back to tell how they made it.

By asking the women who had returned, "What would have made a difference in your life at the time you were arrested?" I found that at least half had returned to drugs and nothing would have changed that. The other half had tried for about six months to do the right thing, but a variety of situations had sidetracked them. For some it was a return to their old neighborhood and associates, while for others it was a death in the family or a financial disaster— almost any situation could trigger old behavior that was comfortable and frequently effective. So we learned that to stay out a student must want to stay out, but she also needed information and tools, which we provided by putting on job fairs inside the institution to augment our pre-release classes.

Our program operated in the same institution for about nine years, and looking back, I realize all of us became increasingly effective as we became more familiar and accepting of our students' lives and lifestyles. As we learned the language and mores and stopped imposing our own, as we relaxed and began to forget about the lesson plans and think about each individual, as we became a family of people inside the institution who were there to help, we became progressively more effective. Time and daily contact with students, whose lives were so different from ours, revealed we also had many things in common—we were mothers, we told jokes and laughed, we had parents and siblings and we all wanted what was best for our families.

What is my final advice to anyone who is beginning a career teaching in a prison? Endure and learn—learn to understand and accept your students and let them teach you about this new world you have entered. Then show them you have knowledge that could be helpful to them and offer it to those who are interested. Make your classes fun, laugh a lot and constantly bring in stimulating materials from the outside, including speakers and videos, if possible. But be sure everything has a purpose and a meaning to the students; they are not children to be entertained but adults who will pick and choose among the various pieces of information you make available. And last but not least, help when and however you can, because providing that help is what you will remember proudly long after you have departed.

CHAPTER VI

IN THE NAME OF LIQUIDITY AND FLOW

by Madeline Kiser

Throughout the world today parallels exist and they are notable: Rivers run dry and die, because dams and other human-made constructions stop their natural flow, and societies with their own form of flow—that of affection, old to young, children to parents, sibling to sibling—are blocked in part by the feverish building of prisons. This is especially true in the U.S., which has the world's highest incarceration rate, according to an August 18, 2003 article in *The Christian Science Monitor*. About 5.6 million Americans—that's one in 37 adults—are now in or have served time in prison. According to the Bureau of Justice, there are approximately 800,000 law officers in the United States. Many of these work for state and federal prison systems.

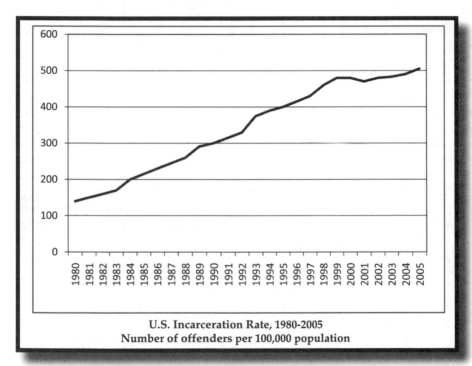

U.S. Incarceration Rate, 1980-2005
Number of offenders per 100,000 population

This graph documents the dramatic increase in the U.S. prison population of the last 30 years.

In the past thirty years, since the war on drugs and mandatory sentencing took root, we've managed to create both a prison mentality and a prison industry, with entire communities economically dependent on the prison. It's becoming hard to imagine what our country would look like without its abundant prisons, especially rural agricultural communities, which have come to depend on them as a source of income in the wake of losing their traditional economic base of family farms. They would no doubt suffer without them. But in numerous, notable ways, prisons are like dams: No river can survive over time whose innate pattern of flows, a kind of signature or personality, is interfered with and altered.

In February, 2002, I assumed the position of bilingual writer-in-residency at the Tucson Federal Prison. Sponsored jointly by the Federal Bureau of Prisons and the National Endowment for the Arts, this position was part of what was called the Artist-in-Residency Program (AIR.) I was hired as a bilingual Spanish/English poet. I taught in both languages. This position bridged for me a background in journalism, poetry (I hold a M.F.A in poetry) and social justice programs for the disenfranchised and marginalized (youth on parole, young mothers, and single, teen fathers). With a master's degree in Latin American Studies, I was passionate about modernization and globalization and their impact on the peoples of Latin America and on Spanish people in general.

Despite my enthusiasm, the program was cut in 2004 when funds for it were discontinued. After my contract expired, I continued teaching as a volunteer, at first once then twice a month until April 2004 when, for the second and last time, my badge and teaching privileges were revoked and I was asked to leave.

At the Tucson prison, about 200 inmates took a variety of writing classes. I taught five, three-hour classes each week. These included a writers' workshop, a course on Latin American and Spanish poetry, a prerelease writing class, a children's story writing class for women, and weekly "tutorials," where I'd work one-on-one with inmates, reading their manuscripts, scolding them— one conversation comes to mind about "being intellectually lazy"—talking with and listening to them about their lives, sharing poems and stories and novels and CDs. We'd argue and debate: What does it mean to lead a good life? Does altruism exist? How to live with anger, and rage? Are current immigration policies in the U.S. fair? (Many of my students were Mexican nationals.) What are the roots of migration? Also, centrally: Can the sorrow we endure transform into gifts for others?

Over time, as inmates spoke, it became apparent they had stores of knowledge, pools of hard life experience that could be useful to others— especially to increasing numbers of youth outside prison walls yet shaped by the life before them; youth, dropping out of school and finding temporary release and meaning in that predictable trilogy of violence, sex and drugs.

At the start of my residency I was given a wheeled suitcase to bring in library books and other materials for days when tutorials were held. Ultimately it was probably the generosity of this lending, or my interpretation of it, which gave me an entrance into trouble. In another sign of largesse and the willingness to cooperate and be creative, staff agreed to let many different volunteers—more than twenty—enter the prison and speak and join classes, and they generously processed the multiple forms for all these people.

Poet, novelist and filmmaker Jimmy Santiago Baca came to read from his work and speak to a large group of inmates (over a hundred gathered), about how writing transformed his life. Along with *Sierra Magazine* editor Marilyn Berlin Snell, members of the writers' workshop interviewed, in the prison visiting room, author Ken Lamberton, whose *Wilderness and Razor Wire*, a memoir about how writing gave him strength and helped him change during the twelve years he spent in an Arizona State Prison, won the prestigious Burrough's Award for environmental writing. Afterward Ms. Snell (2002) wrote an article about Mr. Lamberton with help from the inmates. She was kind and patient when reviewing their pointed, acerbic comments as she prepared her article for publication.

A Tucson pastor joined us. A dancer and midwife from Colombia whose father was kidnapped and murdered performed, for inmates and staff, a dance-narrative she choreographed to honor him; it was originally presented in Medellín. A young woman who taught African dance to youth in the community gave a lecture about the role of movement in bringing joy.

Staff also gave permission for, and coordinated, what came to be known as our bi-annual Poetry Jams. A month prior, colorful posters advertising the jams would appear throughout the compound. With fanfare, they were held in the chapel. At the Spring 2004 Poetry Jam, our last, the literary director of the University of Arizona Poetry Center—which is internationally known and respected—joined inmates in reading from her work. At the microphone, one inmate said, "To my white brothers, my Mexican brothers, my brother-brothers, I want to say: The poetry we are sharing tonight is a way of bringing us all together." At the end of the reading and as guests were leaving, another student remarked, "It almost feels as if we weren't in prison," and then, joking, to one guest in particular said, "Hey, can I walk you out to your car?"

We have entered dangerous, unpredictable times in the world-at-large that are making it hard, at both state and federal levels, to continue spending to incarcerate large numbers of people. We're spending money that enables us to be present in many different places outside the U.S. Moreover, thirty years of what is being called "mass incarceration," has had an adverse effect: In some communities, youth see and describe going to prison as a rite of passage, or "gladiator school," a term brought to attention in former Crips gang member Sanyika Shakur's autobiography, *Monster: The Autobiography of an L.A. Gang Member*. Given that we have less money to spend on prisons and that they may be losing some of the power they once had to deter crime, there is more fluidity, in myriad ways, over and through walls than we are willing to admit. The question, "How do we best prepare inmates to re-enter society?" is becoming prevalent.

Paul Gendreau (2000), a well-known Canadian criminologist, represents this trend. Based on extensive meta-analysis of incarceration and recidivism rates, his conclusions reflect a growing sentiment with regard to the effectiveness of incarceration:

1. For most offenders, prisons do not reduce recidivism. To argue for expanding the use of imprisonment in order to deter criminal behavior is without empirical support. The use of imprisonment may be reserved for purposes of retribution and the selective incapacitation of society's highest risk offenders.

2. The cost implications of imprisonment need to be weighed against more cost-efficient ways of decreasing offender recidivism and the responsible use of public funds. For example, even small increases in the use of incarceration can drain resources from other important public areas such as health and education.

3. Evidence from other sources suggests more effective alternatives to reducing recidivism than imprisonment. Offender treatment programs have been more effective in reducing criminal behavior than increasing the punishment for criminal acts.

I mention that in our tutorials we talked about altruism. In the Tucson prison where I taught, inmates received classes on résumé writing, life skills, job interviewing, parenting, waste water management, GED preparation, history and other academic subjects. It is striking, though, how few of them can envision a life for themselves that doesn't center on money, power and prestige. Teaching, one wonders what to do to help students enter into a kind of imagining that has a different focus. The answer seems to lie in the power of narrative. Narrative is everything; narrative and stories. Laurel Richardson (in Wright, 1998, p. 51) underscores the importance of narratives or stories, in the formation of cultural and personal identity:

> Cultural stories provide exemplars of lives, heroes, villains, and fools as they are embedded in larger cultural and social frameworks, as well as stories about home, community, society, and humankind. Morality and cautionary tales instruct the young and control the adult. Stories of one's "people"—as chosen or enslaved, conquerors or victims—as well as stories about one's nation, social class, gender, race, or occupation affect morale, aspirations, and personal life chances. These are not simply stories, but are narratives, which have real consequences for the fates of individuals, communities and nations.

All of the visitors who spoke to us had two characteristics in common: they had suffered a loss, a disease, some personal disaster or misfortune, and subsequently live loss by working to lessen others' suffering; and they are capable of narrating this loss in a way that's engaging. Hearing these narratives, participating in them for a while, inmates were made to feel part of a community *before* leaving prison, and not just part of any community: Part of a group of people who don't live predominantly for money. Surprising numbers of my students hadn't been exposed to these kinds of people. It's not that altruism doesn't exist for them; rather, it isn't dominant among the ethics and reality they've inhabited. "You work for HOW much?" they liked to ask, when I'd share my hourly rate. "Man, you're nuts," they would say and think. Then, I'd see them, changed from tan prison clothing to tennis shoes and jeans, and walking through prison doors to the taxi waiting to take them back to where they came from.

Prior to teaching at the prison, I taught poetry in another program called AIR (Art in Reality). It serves youth, ages fourteen to twenty-one in the Tucson community who've dropped out of traditional schools. Many students in this program have fathers, boyfriends, sisters, mothers, uncles and neighbors in prison; many have been locked up themselves, in juvenile detention. Watching students from prison get ready to leave and return to their communities, it was these youth, the daughters and sons and girlfriends, who would come to mind: The liquidity of their lives that transcends walls. These same family members and friends, visible on prison visiting nights with their clear purses—change in them for snacks from machines in the visiting room—and toddlers, helped by correctional officers to make their way through metal detectors, motivate inmates to the extent that some of them can turn from crime. From the stories they shared with me, it's clear that they want to be of use. They want their stories and their experience and their narratives to address someone else's suffering.

I became deeply curious, as writers in their mischief can when questioning, about what would happen were inmates made to feel a part of a community while still in prison? With all this in mind, I let inmates take magazines back to their cells when I saw them engrossed in them in class. On the occasion of my first Christmas teaching in prison, I gave out cards to everyone I knew, both staff and students, and I left hanging in the women's unit, on the morning of December 24, a Christmas stocking used for decoration during a poetry reading we'd had. Last, in the name of liquidity and flow, I shared poems and stories, without names on them, always anonymous, first between different groups of students inside the prison, including male and female inmates, and then between students on the inside and out.

I was twice dismissed from teaching (after my first firing I was given a second chance), because of all of the above. I was suspended, first, because of holiday decorations I left hanging in the women's unit after a Christmas poetry reading. I thought I had permission to leave them up, but didn't. Correspondingly, I gave all of my fifty or so students, as well as staff, Christmas cards—more contraband. Later, I was allowed back in to teach once a month.

I was dismissed again, permanently, after seven months. I'd allowed my students to take books and magazines they were reading (poetry, history and current events) back to their cells and these were found—more contraband. Also, I'd been sharing my students' writing, anonymously, with youth on the outside in detention and sharing students' writing anonymously with inmates. I thought I had permission to do this, but didn't.

I was asked, first, to give back the suitcase—symbol, to a poet's mind, of mobility—and later to leave the prison.

Luckily for me and more important for students in the prison, one of the visitors who came to our program started a program of her own: Retirees Available to Inmates to Supplement Education, or RAISE. Under its auspices volunteers in a prominent local retirement community teach a number of courses at the prison including creative writing. They also provide other needed services such as driving to estate sales and finding books to donate to the prison's small library. At a public event held not long ago at the prison, RAISE's founder, Jan Riding, was formally thanked by staff for giving so much to the prison, to which from her seat in the audience she responded rather tartly, "We're not givers, we're takers!"

To state it tritely, inmates need to be needed. All people do—perhaps those who've suffered more than others, because how else is pain to be transformed? And the communities they come from and return to have a real need for them—for their stories. The acronyms like AIR and RAISE that describe programs for those left out of society's mainstream aren't stumbled into, they are keenly felt. Perhaps there remains to be discovered a water-related lettering that likewise calls forth free and upward movement, of liquidity and flow.

CHAPTER VII

CROSSING BORDERS:
THE PROBLEM OF PROFESSIONAL BOUNDARIES

by Paul Ropp

Introduction

When I started teaching in a medium-security prison, the extent of my training consisted of being handed a set of classroom keys and being told, "Now don't take any crap off of anyone." It was definitely a learn-as-you-go experience from that point onward. Fortunately, none of the mistakes I made while working as a front-line correctional educator were of the career-ending variety. I want to share with you my personal experiences of prison teaching, and some of my observations and conclusions based on that experience.

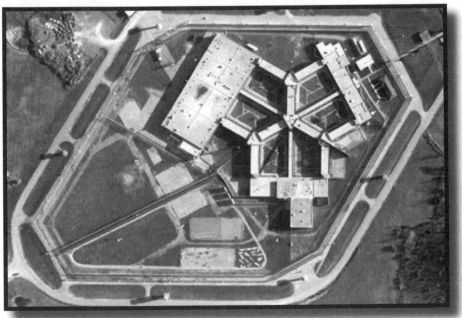

Millhaven Institution in Bath, one of Ontario's 13 confinement facilities.

Having survived (and actually thrived) during seven years of teaching in various prisons in Eastern Canada, I was later promoted to a managerial position (Director of Program Services) responsible for overseeing the work of a group of correctional educators. My duties included the hiring, managing and training of correctional staff in the Ontario Region of the Correctional Service of Canada. As a manager for the correctional education contract, I had the authority to hire and fire staff according to the principles in the personnel manual developed by my employer, the contracting company. I have dealt with a variety of situations involving correctional educators who stepped outside of their professional boundaries. I have personally encountered correctional educators bringing in contraband, giving money to inmates, having intimate personal relationships with inmates, gaining financial benefit from deals with inmates and stealing government property.

The least pleasant aspect of my management job has been to tell correctional educators they can no longer work in the prisons because they, for whatever reasons, have committed serious professional infractions. In some cases, the individual being let go desperately needed the job, but to place the person back in the prison would have created safety or security issues.

On the other hand, one of the most rewarding aspects of my job has been salvaging situations involving correctional educators at risk of losing their jobs due to professional infractions. In those cases, I was able to work with both the employee and the prison authorities to arrive at the conclusion that mistakes had been made but the end result was a better-informed and professionally stronger correctional educator.

Border Crossings

The violation of professional boundaries by correctional educators has had a direct impact on my professional life, so the reasons some correctional educators step outside of their professional boundaries is a topic that holds much interest for me. My advice to prospective correctional educators is: Constantly monitor your professional behavior in relation to applicable ethical/ professional guidelines and don't take any crap off of anyone.

Shortly after making the transition from front-line correctional educator to manager of correctional educators, I worked with a teacher who I will call "John" (not his real name). John worked as a correctional educator in a medium security prison. He was already an experienced teacher with years of working in community schools prior to teaching inmates. As a correctional educator, John was very popular with his students, maintained a busy classroom and seemed able to work productively with certain inmates with whom other teachers struggled. For most of John's first year working in the prison, he seemed to do a solid job as a dedicated teacher.

Then, during a routine prison-cell search, it was discovered that one of John's students had some straight pins, which were unavailable through legitimate prison purchasing channels, in his cell. Straight pins can be used in making tattoo devices. Straight pins coated with blood containing the Hepatitis C virus could also be used to inflict small skin punctures to deliberately transmit the virus to another person. Questioning of the inmate and an ensuing investigation revealed that John had brought in a number of contraband items for that particular inmate. The list of identified items also included shoe polish and perfume. Shoe polish is one of the more popular inhalants (along with paint thinner and gasoline) used on the street. Based on further information from inmate sources, the investigators eventually surmised that John, in addition to bringing in pins, shoe polish and perfume, had probably brought in a number of other unidentified contraband items that ended up in the hands of a number of unidentified inmates. Exactly what those items were and who ended up having them was never discovered.

John lost his job at the prison following the investigation but steadfastly refused to acknowledge he had done anything wrong. He was simply trying to "help out some of his guys" who could not buy certain essentials through regular prison purchasing processes. John could see no risk in providing inmates with the items and, from his perspective, the prison was being unduly harsh in not providing the inmates with those essentials.

When a correctional educator makes a serious error, as John did, the reaction from those aware of the story details is often, "What on earth was that person thinking?" In John's case, as well as other situations involving correctional educators who erred, we will never know exactly. We can, however, examine some of the factors that may have contributed to professional infractions. The intent of this chapter is to examine some of the factors that, acting either individually or in combination, seem to lead some correctional educators to overstep their professional boundaries.

Most teachers are guided by some jurisdictional or organizational code of ethics or by a code of conduct that defines, in general, the acceptable boundaries of professional behavior. Because all teachers occupy positions of authority, trust and influence, relationships between teachers and students must measure up to the closest scrutiny:

> Ethical codes contain two types of statements: broadly worded positive exhortations representing general principles and more specific rules that forbid certain types of behaviour. (Bezeau, 2002, p. 4)

One example of guidelines for professional conduct comes from British Columbia's College of Teachers. Within the British Columbia guidelines are statements such as: "Professional educators establish and maintain the boundaries of a professional relationship;" "professional educators act with the understanding that they are role models for students"; and, "professional educators are accountable to students, parents, employers, the profession and the public" (British Columbia College of Teachers, 2004, pp. 15, 17).

In addition to the standards governing every teacher's professional behavior broadly outlined by a professional code of conduct, teachers working in a prison environment are also regulated by a second code of conduct that applies to employees working in prisons. This second code of conduct is described in the Correctional Service Canada's Code of Discipline

(Correctional Service Canada, 1994). This code states that it is an infraction if an employee "improperly uses his or her title or authority to personal gain or advantage," "enters into any kind of personal or business relationship not approved by his or her authorized superior with an offender or ex-offender, or the offender's or ex-offender's friends or relatives," or "gives to, or receives from any offender or ex-offender, or the offender's or ex-offender's friends or relatives, either directly or indirectly, any contraband" (p. 5). By virtue of teaching within a prison, the correctional educator, therefore, is subject to two professional codes of conduct; one code defining professional conduct as a teacher and a second code defining professional conduct as a worker within a prison environment.

Outside the prison environment (within community schools), the transgression of a teacher's duty to engage only in behaviors that meet the accepted standards is addressed through disciplinary hearings conducted by professional associations. If it is established that a teacher has violated the applicable code of conduct, the result is often sanctions against the teacher accompanied by open expression of anger from members of the teaching profession and from the general public at the violation of public trust. Among the coworkers of the implicated teacher, behavioral norms with respect to the teaching profession are reinforced and the consequences of violating those norms are publicized.

Periodically, similar violations of professional standards occur involving correctional educators. However, in contrast to professional disciplinary processes outside the prison environment, where the nature and consequences of proven infractions tend to be well publicized, professional disciplinary processes within prisons tend to be fairly secretive. If a prison staff member has violated professional standards, the result is often a low-profile corrective action or a quiet dismissal. There is a general absence of information made available to coworkers. In this fairly secretive environment, therefore, it is more difficult for correctional educators to learn from the mistakes made by other staff members.

What motivates that small percentage of correctional educators to overstep their professional boundaries? Although each individual incident is unique, there appear to be five factors at work which often overlap and work in conjunction with each other:

1. Lack of training

2. The influence of groupthink

3. Isolation (The Mad Trapper Syndrome)

4. The Maverick Mindset

5. Personal vulnerabilities

This chapter will examine each of these five factors in turn.

Lack of Training

The need for both introductory and ongoing training of correctional educators is often re-emphasized after some incident has occurred that could have been prevented through more comprehensive training. In some cases, a new teacher is simply not aware of specific professional expectations being placed on him or her by colleagues or managers. Training for correctional educators should cover both the broad expectations outlined in the applicable codes of ethics and codes of conduct and the very specific, practical "do's and don'ts" of working in a prison classroom. They should derive from their training a strong sense of their professional duties both as a teacher and as a staff member in a prison.

Veteran correctional educators can become so comfortable with working in a prison environment that they lose their "edge" in terms of following some of the fundamental guidelines that they learned when they first started teaching in prisons. Because of the secretive nature of prisons, incidents involving staff committing professional infractions are usually not broadcast to other staff so that everyone can become more vigilant in terms of their own practices. Generally speaking, although lack of training can certainly result in serious transgressions, it tends to be less insidious than the remaining four factors. Errors in professional judgment, which can be attributed to gaps in the training of individual correctional educators, can also be easily corrected by providing better initial training and retraining on an ongoing basis.

The Influence of Groupthink

According to *The Canadian Oxford Dictionary* (1998), groupthink is, "the practice of thinking or making decisions as a group, often resulting in poor quality decision-making." Teaching in a prison environment often involves one correctional educator working with the same group of inmates for hours at a stretch, day after day, with limited interaction with other staff. A correctional educator who is working in isolation from his or her "non-criminal" colleagues and at the same time is immersed for prolonged periods with a group of inmates with "pro-criminal" attitudes may eventually absorb some of the values, outlooks and biases of the inmate group. Most correctional educators are capable of recognizing the belief systems that often permeate the inmate subculture. Professional correctional educators must, at the very least, work around those belief systems. In fact, the most accomplished correctional educators try to address and shift antisocial attitudes, which many inmates have, thereby disrupting the groupthink pattern that simply reinforces those attitudes among groups of inmates. Some correctional educators, however, seem to be inordinately susceptible to the influence of the group with which they spend large amounts of time. In certain prison work environments the "group of predominant influence" happens to be the group of inmates with whom a correctional educator spends prolonged periods of time. When a correctional educator who tends to be influenced by groupthink is then exposed to a work environment that involves spending prolonged time with a group of inmates, the attitudes prevalent within the inmate subculture may be absorbed by the teacher. The correctional educator, to a certain degree, viewing most prison officials as "the man" or agents of oppression. In other words, the correctional educator can start to develop attitudes demonizing the prison system and its employees. It is just a matter of time then before the teacher sees nothing wrong with "helping out" inmates by perhaps sneaking in contraband or providing advance notice to the inmates about upcoming prison searches.

Isolation

In examining the effects of social isolation on humans, Haythorn (1973) wrote, "It is generally recognized that man is a social animal whose behaviour is significantly determined by his need for other people and his reactions to other people" (p. 219).

This social aspect of existence is nowhere more evident than when persons are isolated. Sometimes people don't need to be influenced by others to come up with some pretty strange ideas. I believe that isolation is probably the least prevalent factor behind professional infractions that I have encountered in the past. In my opinion, however, it may have played a role in conjunction with other factors. In some prisons (particularly maximum security institutions), for a variety of reasons, teaching staff often end up spending large amounts of time by themselves. Often, the teacher is located in a classroom physically separated by locked barriers from other staff. Add to this working condition the effects of prisoner lockdowns, which can go on for weeks or months, and we can appreciate the isolated work environment of a correctional educator.

The impact of isolation on correctional educators can be twofold: They do not have the opportunities to interact with colleagues on an ongoing basis, and prisons tend to be monotonous places lacking the myriad of stimuli to which people "on the outside" are subjected (often to the opposite extreme).

Regularly interacting with colleagues at work not only provides a variety of external stimuli and idea exchanges; colleagues act as "mirrors" for a person's thoughts and behaviors. If a person's views and behavior are generally considered acceptable by the group, feedback to the individual tends to be positive or at least neutral. On the other hand, if an individual's views and behavior stray too far from what is considered "normal" or appropriate, the group tends to provide negative or "corrective" feedback to the individual. That corrective feedback can vary from subtle messages ("Well, that's certainly a different way of looking at things.") to direct confrontation ("You don't really believe that do you? I think you've had too much time by yourself.").

In the absence of regular social interaction in the workplace and the feedback provided via those interactions, any prison worker can develop some fairly distorted views of the world. For example, the teacher might become convinced that all inmates should be treated harshly because of the awful crimes they have perpetrated or, the other extreme, might conclude that all inmates are simply misunderstood individuals in need of boundless sympathy. The inappropriateness of both extremes would probably be detected by coworkers and feedback would be provided to any individual correctional educator who might espouse such views. Otherwise, if these or other similar beliefs were allowed to remain unchallenged due to lack of social feedback, a correctional educator's professional boundaries may become blurred. Each correctional educator relies on those boundaries to define which beliefs and behaviors are appropriate and, conversely, which beliefs and behaviors are inappropriate.

Two examples come to mind of prison teachers I have worked with who, in my opinion, may have spent too much time working in isolation. One teacher, who typically worked by himself in a locked office within a classroom where his students were locked in, openly expressed the view that all inmates are "a bunch of snot-drinking bastards who will never amount to anything." The second teacher, who typically worked in an almost identical isolated environment for several years, seemed to undergo a number of negative changes such as a decrease in motivation, a decrease in his ability to focus on specific projects or issues and a decline in his ability to interact effectively with both inmates and staff. Although I cannot say with any certainty that these two examples of apparent deterioration in professional behavior can be attributed to the effects of prolonged, ongoing isolation, it is my opinion that isolation may have been a factor.

In addition to the isolation that reduces social interaction and the "mirroring" that comes from those interactions, isolation can also take the form of working in a monotonous environment where routines are rigidly followed and various sensory stimuli can be deliberately muted. An environment with predictable schedules and muted stimuli is not inherently negative and possibly contributes to a calm atmosphere in a prison where inmates can easily become agitated. If a reduced-stimuli atmosphere is combined with a situation in which a correctional educator spends prolonged periods of time with minimal social interactions with coworkers, however, the impact of the isolation may be compounded. Charles Brownfield, who conducted significant research on the effects of isolation, used the term "monotonous, static sensory" to describe certain types of environments (Brownfield, 1972). Much of the research on the psychological impact of prolonged isolation has been applied to situations involving human space travel or people staying for long periods in the Antarctic. In remote locations where the environments are notably atypical or "exotic," it is obvious that people will be subjected to isolation and measures can be taken to deal with the stress produced by isolation or, at least the need for monitoring behavior is clearly recognized. Working in some maximum security prisons for example, where the isolation factor is less obvious, may subject both inmates and staff to the stress produced by prolonged exposure to "monotonous, static sensory environments."

Examining factors that may drive correctional educators to act in ways that are outside of their professional boundaries Harrison and Connors (1984) concluded that problems caused by isolation-induced stress may include a decline in motivation, mood changes, diminished morale and decreased attention. These factors could then contribute to some correctional educators— those who spend long periods of time working in relatively monotonous, static sensory environments—losing their sense of duty to rigorously adhere to the standards of the profession, especially if those correctional educators are, during the same time, deprived of regular, "normalizing" interactions with other correctional staff.

The Maverick Mindset

The end result of the "maverick mindset" is identical to the results attributable to both the "groupthink factor" and the "isolation factor." All three factors may result in "aberrant" belief systems, which may precipitate behaviors that fall outside the professional boundaries established for correctional educators. In the case of the groupthink factor, the teacher's attitudes become aligned with the attitudes of the inmate subculture through ongoing exposure to those attitudes with diminished exposure to attitudes of non-criminals. With the isolation factor, individuals spending too much time alone in a stimulus-poor environment may develop strange ideas or let their sense of professionalism slip to the point of engaging in behavior outside of professional boundaries. The maverick mindset, in contrast to the first two factors, is one in which the teacher already possesses certain highly individualistic, somewhat rebellious belief systems prior to actually working in a prison environment such as: "Rules can always be bent" or "It is understandable that society's 'have-nots' will take from the 'haves'" or "Inmates are just the socially disadvantaged 'have-nots' who were unlucky enough to get caught by the 'man.'" These are examples of sentiments which, by themselves or in the context of the community at large, are simply opinions. Within the prison environment, however, rules abound and individual staff behavior can have an enormous impact on the collective safety and security of everyone in the prison. If a staff member translates opinions similar to the ones expressed above into behaviors that overstep his or her professional boundaries, the consequences can be far-reaching.

In more extreme cases of maverick mindset, flaunting rules and taking risks can become an end in itself where the teacher engages in "outlaw" activities primarily for the thrill of engaging in risky behavior. As a manager, I have personally had to deal with a number of cases of inappropriate teacher behavior at work appears to have been the maverick mindset. These cases involved flirtations or outright affairs with inmates, bringing in contraband, conveying information to inmates about imminent prison searches, and making deals with inmates to obtain goods and services.

The maverick mindset, then, appears to be a significant factor in a number of cases involving correctional educators overstepping their professional boundaries. In some cases, the correctional educator had a perception that he or she was acting covertly to help society's disadvantaged while, in other cases the correctional educator enjoyed "living on the edge" when engaging in risky behavior.

Personal Vulnerabilities

In my opinion, personal vulnerability was probably the most prevalent factor behind professional infractions I have encountered in the past. An individual teacher whose behavior is driven by the maverick mindset is well aware that he or she is breaking the rules, but believes the rules are unreasonable or unfair or simply enjoys the experience of taking risks. On the other hand, an individual who is personally vulnerable may be psychologically manipulated by inmates to engage in behavior that oversteps the boundaries of the profession. As observed by Allen and Bosta (1981):

> The art of manipulating the human thought process to alter behavior is as old a man himself; yet people are as vulnerable to it today as they were in man's beginning. One of the reasons for this vulnerability is that people set idealistic goals for themselves, and in a reckless desire for goal achievement, they accept information without question when it appears to be consistent with their hopes and beliefs. (p. viii)

Allen and Bosta (1984) go on to say, "People heading to prison bring their survival trade of manipulation with them and adapt it to the prison environment" (p. ix).

In order to manipulate correctional educators as well as other correctional staff, some inmates can be very adept at meeting the psychological needs of vulnerable individuals. For example, most teachers in prisons understand the power of praise in motivating inmate students to do what the teacher wants. Likewise, many inmate students understand the power of praise in motivating certain teachers to do what the inmate wants.

No individual is completely immune to manipulative influences inside or outside of prisons. Different individuals appear to be susceptible to manipulation to varying degrees depending on a number of variables. Langone's (1996) research on what makes some people more receptive to the "sales pitches" of cults would appear to have broader applications in terms of why some people are easier to manipulate than others. Some of Langone's situational and developmental factors that (singly or in combination) contribute to a person's vulnerability are: A high level of stress or dissatisfaction; lack of self-confidence; non-assertiveness; gullibility; desire to belong to a group; low tolerance for ambiguity; and, naïve idealism.

Langone's clinical research findings regarding people's (variable) susceptibility to psychological manipulation are certainly consistent with the more "hands-on" conclusions drawn by Allen and Bosta regarding case studies of prison staff members who were manipulated by inmates.

Conclusion

There appear to be a variety of factors at play when correctional educators step outside of their professional boundaries. In some cases, transgressions may occur simply due to lack of training. In other cases they may be the result of a correctional educator coming under the influence of inmate groupthink, being susceptible to manipulation by inmates or spending too much time in an isolated, stimulus-poor environment. Finally, professional transgressions may be the result of individual correctional educators having belief systems, prior to entering correctional work, that are inherently incompatible with working in a prison environment. Usually, when correctional educators go astray in terms of overstepping their professional boundaries, it involves a combination of factors and an interaction among those factors. Fortunately, the majority of correctional educators do maintain rigorous professional standards throughout their careers. Only a small percentage strays from those standards. The impact of those few, however, can be powerful in terms of loss of individual employment, risk to the safety and security of both staff and inmates and damage to the reputation of the correctional education profession.

Chapter VIII

Push and Pull in Correctional Education

By Thom Gehring

Introduction

Correctional educators frequently work in environments that are hostile toward teaching and learning. To survive (perhaps even flourish) we are constantly assessing our abilities and weaknesses, identifying strategies that can be effective in the institutional setting, and working to diminish our vulnerability to anti-education influences. This chapter is about influences in our lives that are rarely discussed openly—the roles of purpose and intuition in our patterns of professional identity. It is based on the idea that every bit of clarity we can harness to our teaching and learning agenda can help us to (a) overcome, negotiate or transcend institutional constraints, or at least (b) navigate through them with minimal negative impact on students, the program and ourselves. The chapter begins by summarizing some of my earlier writings on the correctional education professional identity issue and then proceeds to propose that the most effective correctional educators apply both "an open mind" and "a warm heart" to their daily work. The last part is directed to a demystification of these intuitive influences and a tentative explanation of the telos that draws us into the future—our fate, destiny or purpose.

Beginning a Career in Correctional Education

I was prepared with a four-year degree from Trenton State College, New Jersey, to become a high school social studies teacher. The job market was depressed when I completed in 1972, so I sent resumés to each of the states, and was hired by a school in South Dakota. But my girlfriend protested, so I searched desperately for something closer to home. I did not understand that a job for which I applied was at a prison—Youth Correctional Institution, Bordentown. I thought it was some General Equivalency Diploma (GED) center. Anyway, I was hired and have since been a correctional educator.

That first assignment was difficult, mostly because the world "inside" was new to me. There were special challenges but also a number of nurturing experiences that impacted all my thought processes. It seemed that my head exploded when I wrote my first social education curriculum. Called *Work Energy* (WE), it emphasized how students could help each other in what I labeled collective activities; today, we call it cooperative learning. Working professionally at a place where intellectual capital was recognized seemed the best job anyone could have. I went on to write four or five small grants to help round out student learning opportunities at Bordentown. They were all funded, and the skills I learned through the process helped me relocate two years later, along with two of my colleagues, to Virginia, and a statewide management role.

Another very positive aspect of the work at Bordentown was the strong school leadership. The institutional education director had been trained by Dr. Tony Ryan and he had a strong pattern of professional identification with the field of correctional education. All the teachers were instructed that, despite any previous training or pattern of identification we had, we were now correctional educators. Second, the director had negotiated the work week so we were relieved from instructional responsibilities every Friday afternoon when we could engage in curriculum development and correctional education in-service, and sometimes even get caught up on our regular paperwork. Those Friday afternoons were a great blessing in my life, although my time at Bordentown was continually marked by terrible personal problems (I was getting socialized to an authoritarian work situation after a college career of resistance to authority). The Friday afternoon activities helped us all maximize our effectiveness on the job. Another result was that we were inclined to put in extra hours on key projects during our free time.

I left Bordentown for greater responsibilities in Richmond, Virginia. The shock of relocating was substantial. Along with two Bordentown colleagues, I had been hired by the Adult Education Program at Virginia Commonwealth University, which had the contract for delivering Title I, Elementary and Secondary Education services for neglected and delinquent youth in State of Virginia institutions. I experienced two profound changes and recognized some important things.

First, I was given an opportunity to obtain a master's degree in Adult Education through the university and my official hours were scaled to 75 percent to help me accomplish that educational goal. Second, I no longer had access to a community of professionals whose primary pattern of professional identification was correctional education, with the exception of the three of us from Bordentown. I became acutely aware of a terrible lack in my professional life: I was ignorant of the rich tradition of our field, to which I had access previously because of Tony Ryan's influence at Bordentown. I resolved to fill that lack through networking with like-minded colleagues, searching the literature and readings and writings, as reported in the following pages.

Brief Summaries of Some of My Early Articles

For this chapter's purposes I will focus on seven of my articles in *The Journal of Correctional Education* between 1981 and 2002. In all my writing, my primary goal is to learn about my topic—I write to gain clarity and a mature outlook. Writing is my primary vehicle for personal/professional maturation; without it, I would be ineffective in most of the complex skills our work requires.

The first article in this sequence was "The Correctional Education Professional Identity Issue" (March 1981). It established a context for the issue: (a) although our jobs each have specific dimensions, the fullness of our work can be summarized under the correctional education practitioner role; (b) ours is a developing field, at the forefront of modern education; and, (c) it is afflicted by a host of restrictive influences (few teacher education programs, no real repository of data, practitioners themselves often do not understand their careers). "We have a lot of work to do" (p. 9). The rest of the article compared and contrasted special and correctional education and introduced the concept that whatever "works" in our field will likely help solve problems of related fields. Near the article's end was a question: "Do you identify as a correctional educator?"

I was not very impressed by the essay at the time. Rather, I saw it as a necessary first approach to a complex series of problems. However, the Correctional Education Association (CEA) leaders were very impressed. They asked me to write a second essay with additional details and required the new article to have the same title as the first. So, I called the next piece, "The Correctional Education Professional Identity Issue, Part II," to keep the two distinct in my mind.

That second article appeared in the *Journal*'s September 1981 edition and set the pace for subsequent articles in our current sequence, because it introduced pervasive concepts that were poorly represented in the literature, along with concise terms to describe them. In current parlance, that article could be said to introduce a Theory of Everything, or TOE, for the correctional education professional identity issue; the rest would all be details. The September essay explained that none of us were properly prepared professionally for our work in correctional education, that our primary patterns of professional identification were, therefore, anchored to the related fields and that we tend to see ourselves as sojourners in institutional education. It proposed that the "knowledge, skills and attitudes" formula that drove local schools was properly reversed in our field—"attitudes, skills and knowledge"—and justified this with an implied life and death dimension of our work ("Correctional educators cannot afford the luxury of traditional content-oriented goals" [p. 20]). It stated this identification issue (with related fields or with content driven programs) exacerbated a whole constellation of related problems: "[A] general lack of standards, primitive curricula, domination by security-oriented personnel, and superficial needs assessments and evaluation" (p. 20). Further, it was the first article to name and describe what I called the "good-old-boy syndrome" in correctional education (pp. 21-22)—a term that has permeated our field since it appeared and probably needs no explanation today.

I was astonished at the response to this second article. I thought I would be fired or at least scorned and persecuted by my colleagues, but instead the CEA leaders encouraged me to write yet another piece in the same vein. I decided to write a leveraging piece to encourage CEA to address relevant issues and take initiatives to correct some of the problems. That article appeared in January 1982, "An Identified Need: The Development of a CEA Rationale Statement."

This time I began by voicing the need to articulate a concept of our field that would transcend "the theories of retribution, deterrence, rehabilitation, and reintegration," replacing them with a new theory based on education as "a self-help strategy, which is applied to help learners develop and pursue responsible life goals." Correctional education "is the only institutional program that parallels the identified interests of all community groups, both confined and free. Education is the most pro-social Institution on the American scene" (p. 4). The rest of the article explained MacCormick's nuanced definitions of nonsocial, antisocial, and social, and for the first time identified correctional education as a social activist movement: "The historical evolution of correctional education; the organized activities of correctional education advocates" (p. 4). I reviewed salient elements of a speech by Dr. Glenn Kendall, as reported in 1973 on "What Makes Correctional Education Correctional?" and combined all this with some widely accepted truths about our work. Then I began the process of introducing profound quotes from significant junctures of the correctional education movement. One was in 1930 at the founding of the American Prison Association Standing Committee on Education (which later became the CEA):

> Dr. Ellis: I have here a resolution presented by Mrs. La Du and Dr. Mary B. Harris.
>
> **Whereas**, education in the broadest sense has been found to be one of the most effective measures in the rehabilitation and reformation of delinquents, and
>
> **Whereas**, a program of education would do much toward ameliorating idleness in our correctional and penal institutions and also in greatly reducing the disciplinary problem thereof,
>
> **Be it Resolved**, that a Committee on Education of the American Prison Association [APA] be authorized and a Chairman be appointed [Austin MacCormick], for the purpose of promoting educational programs in institutions of that character. The resolution has the approval of the Committee on Resolutions and is recommended for the action of the [APA] Congress. (American Prison Association, 1930, p. 258)

Another was that this glorious sentiment actually built on a previous concept facilitated by Zebulon Brockway in 1870 at the first APA conference in Cincinnati. The sentiment was also expanded at the 1930 conference (they added the sentences on recreation to the 1870 principle that follows):

> Education is a vital force in the reformation of fallen men and women. Its tendency is to quicken the intellect, inspire self-respect, excite the higher aims, and afford a healthful substitute for low and vicious amusements. Recreation is considered to be an essential part of education. It has come to be recognized that recreation is an indispensable factor in human life. This principle is now heartily [endorsed] by prison administrators. Education

in its broadest sense is, therefore, a matter of primary importance in prisons. (American Prison Association, 1930, p. 250)

(Later I learned the 1930 version left out a primary part of the original 1870 statement—that education should be "carried out to the utmost extent consistent with the other purposes of such institutions" [Wines, 1871, p. 542]. If I had known this in 1982, I would have reported it.)

This article was received so well that the CEA leaders asked me to establish a new ad hoc Resolutions Committee to advance specific strategies to improve the association and the field of correctional education. Those resolutions are reported in two subsequent articles I wrote that are not in the sequence under immediate consideration: "Our Future is in Our Own Hands: Recognizing Common Goals to Develop a CEA 'Core Program'" (March 1983), and "CEA Executive Board Approves Resolutions, Begins Implementation" (December 1984).

Next in our current sequence was an article called, "Five Principles of Correctional Education" (December 1988). For convenience, we will couple this with "Five More Principles of Correctional Education" (March 1993), even though I wrote other articles that appeared between them. These two essays were inspired by my aspiration to learn and report on at least one new idea each year, for a manuscript in the series every five years. It seemed a modest goal. The reason for the series' discontinuation is that other concerns I considered more pressing impeded the report process.

The original 'Five Principles...' essay (1988) urged readers to (1) identify student learning as the professional priority; (2) use education to promote personal transformation; (3) hire only mature and qualified teacher candidates (instead of hoping teachers with mere paper credentials will grow up 'on the job'); (4) get educators installed as correctional education decision-makers; and, (5) remain open to the possibility of trusting offenders to do the right thing. The current (1993) essay is about how (1) theory informs practice; (2) knowledge can actually inhibit transformative learning; (3) culture inhibits crime; (4) teachers can be students and students can be teachers; and, (5) the Golden Rule. (Gehring, 1993, pp. 4-5)

There are obviously a lot of important details not included here— readers are urged to consult the original material. One of my most salient impressions about this series is that Bill Muth, who was principal of the school at the Federal Correctional Institution in Butner, North Carolina, asked me to present to the faculty there on the 1988 article. When he introduced me, he said I would be speaking about "The Five Principles of Correctional Education." But I was never that convinced I had found the Truth; these were merely five principles—there might be fifty others of which I was ignorant (and may still be). One of the enduring aspects of correctional education is that no one can

79

claim the Truth. We are all doing what we can to learn and grow through the terrible problems that afflict our field. That is why we formed a research-based center at San Bernardino—the Center for the Study of Correctional Education at California State University, San Bernardino—to remind ourselves and others that we were still studying the field and that much was still to be learned. We are all scrambling and stretching to learn about our field; anyone who holds otherwise is likely telling a mistruth or poorly informed.

Nevertheless, three external confirmations led me to put great emphasis on the next article in this series, "A Change in Our Way of Thinking," which appeared in the December 1989 issue of *The Journal of Correctional Education*. First, an important cluster our field's leading-edge thinkers helped me navigate through the issues reported in that piece: Steve Duguid, Carolyn Eggleston, David Werner, Bill Muth and others. Though I wrote the article, it was a statement of our perceptions of the field and its challenges. Second, the New Zealand prison education administrator was so impressed by the quality and usefulness of this group's thinking that he came to visit Carolyn and me in New York State in 1990 to discuss it and what it meant. As a result, a few years later Carolyn and I went to New Zealand to help establish an organization like the CEA. Third, an important adult educator from Holland also came to visit us after he read that article. He was influential in the thinking that helped forge the European Prison Education Association, which has since been on the cusp of progressive thinking in our field. There were many details in that article, but its core is presented in the following display, which was part of the larger chart on pages 169-170 of the original:

FIGURE 1: SOME CENTRAL PRINCIPLES AND ASPIRATIONS

WE ACCEPT THESE STRATEGIES	WE REJECT THESE STRATEGIES
Cultural literacy and critical thinking skills, along with basic and marketable skills, to address cognitive deficiencies and help students "think their way through life's problems."	Superficial literacy skills and the "hands-on only" approach to help students learn officially acceptable, compartmentalized knowledge that is separated from ethical implications.
Social education and learning in the humanities, which links human values, behavior, and individual responsibility.	The "basic and marketable skills only" approach, which can only result in "criminals with job skills."
Clarity for personal development and social responsibility, based on tolerance and reciprocity (treat others as you would have them treat you.)	Ambiguity, acquired through educational experiences that foster learned helplessness and self-indulgence (an ego-centered orientation).

FIGURE 1: SOME CENTRAL PRINCIPLES AND ASPIRATIONS, CONT'D.

WE ACCEPT THESE STRATEGIES	WE REJECT THESE STRATEGIES
Professionalization, based on good practice and research; preparation specifically for correctional education assignments and ongoing in-service applicable to education in institutional settings.	"Cult of the personality" and "good-old-boy" influence; diverse and local orientations, based on the inclinations of officials in each jurisdiction.
The empowerment of learners and teachers, and the prioritization of student learning.	Coercion and manipulation, which tend to make student learning an accidental by-product of education—if it occurs at all.
Participatory management, consistent with the ideals of good citizenship.	Authoritarianism, consistent with identified attributes of the criminal personality.
Integrity—consistency between values and behavior.	Opportunism—the sacrifice of long-term goals for short-term benefit.
A core program of regional, national, and international correctional education improvement.	Isolation of correctional education staff from colleagues in similar assignments, even at nearby facilities.
Correctional education as a function of prison reform (the effort to reform prisoners and prisons—to transform prisons into schools).	Correctional education as a function of prison management, or as "window dressing" for visitors and the entertainment of prisoners.
Class activities to help students discover the inherent meaning of everyday decisions.	Sophisticated technologies as a substitute for educating "the whole person."

The final article for *The Journal of Correctional Education* in this correctional education professional identity sequence was jointly authored with Teri Hollingsworth. It is "Coping and Beyond: Practical Suggestions for Correctional Educators" (September 2002). While perusing materials at the Center for the Study of Correctional Education, Teri found an unpublished manuscript I wrote in 1983 and urged me to update it She coordinated the improvements and the resultant essay was well received.

This "Coping..." article reiterated some of the themes of the six that were introduced above. For example:

1. The teaching profession is notorious for its special challenges and low salaries. Even in most teacher markets, however, correctional educators' salaries are not competitive.

2. Our students (devoted to them as we may be) are often the most disadvantaged, downtrodden, miserable, manipulative and resistant groups ever assembled.

3. We are asked to perform our noble duties in what are some of mankind's most depressing and dehumanizing settings.

4. Staff, whose main concern is security, manage the institutions in which we work; they often display blatant disregard toward the educational program.

5. Correctional education programs tend to be poorly planned/ staffed/implemented, and rarely evaluated systematically.

6. Correctional education is unable to compete for funds, even within the scope of local institutions, where its need is most evident. (Gehring & Hollingsworth, 2002, p. 89)

That essay went on to revisit the theme of anti-education institutional constraints and recommended professional growth as a strategy to "fight back," without getting the good-old boys' and girls' attention. "Nurture your professional identification as you improve your professional excellence. Keep your eyes on the big picture to improve each of the smaller ones" (p. 94). Readings from the history and literature of our field were recommended to help keep hope alive.

My Current Thinking on the Professional Identity Issue

Some book manuscripts helped me continue the learning I experienced while preparing those earlier articles. I observed the profound influence that can be experienced by correctional educators who open their minds and warm their hearts to the compelling literature of our field—especially, but not only, the work of John Henry Pestalozzi (Switzerland, early nineteenth century), Elizabeth Fry (England and Europe, early nineteenth century), Alexander Maconochie (South Pacific, early 1840s), Mary Carpenter (England, mid- to late-nineteenth century), Zebulon Brockway (esp. New York State, 1876-1900), William George (New York, 1895 to the 1930s), Thomas Mott Osborne (New York State and New Hampshire, 1913-1926), Austin MacCormick (nationwide U.S., 1915-1979), Anton Makarenko (U.S.S.R., 1920s to late 1930s), Kenyon Scudder (California, 1940s and 1950s), Tony Ryan (nationwide U.S., 1960s to the present), Stephen Duguid (esp. Canada, 1970s to the present), Robert Ross (esp. Canada, 1980s and 1990s), David Werner (California, 1980s to the present), Carolyn Eggleston (nationwide U.S., 1980s to the present), and Randall Wright (North America, 1980s to the present).

The effect of accessing the writings of these major contributors has been much like the effect I experienced during my first months at Bordentown. Appreciation of the cultural dimensions of our field produces an intense subjective effect that infuses the objective conditions of classroom interaction, suggesting new teaching and learning strategies and permeating traditional strategies with a wonderful new enthusiasm. And in programs blessed with enlightened administrators, there are real social outcomes that are realized as barriers to effective human and material resources break down. In short, acquaintance with the literature of correctional education and prison reform (a cultural experience) "jump starts" the practitioner's (subjective) rationale for being engaged in this work, the (objective) conditions of teaching and learning, and the (social) effect of intelligent resource use (see Figure 2 below.) Transcending the confused professional identity syndrome is therefore a low-cost, highly visible way to improve correctional education.

FIGURE 2: TASKS FOR CORRECTIONAL EDUCATORS IN THE NEW MILLENNIUM

SUBJECTIVE	OBJECTIVE
NAVIGATE: Steer the self system through constraints and supports, to accomplish one's life purpose.	PROFESSIONALIZE: Access useful information; study and learn, to support teaching and learning.
CULTURAL	**SOCIAL**
NETWORK: Mobilize professionals through their schools of thought.	STRUGGLE: For equality, democracy, and freedom; against predatory imperialism, racism, war, sexism, and genocide.

I am convinced that our correctional education/prison reform school of thought (SOT) is a powerful tool to improve our personal/professional lives. The SOT concept has so much universal application that I believe it should be adopted in the U.S. Constitution. The Founding Fathers operated within a mindset dominated by agriculture; since then we have been similarly dominated by industry and now by the information age. Yet our electoral scheme is still based on agricultural turf. I do not know the situation of others, but I have much more in common with teachers around the nation than I do with the person who lives across the street from me; more in common with correctional educators in Hawaii or Ohio than with the person who lives next door. I would feel even more comfortable if I could vote with correctional educators who tend to identify more with prison reform than with prison management. Imagine the political, economic, and cultural growth we would experience if our House and Senate jurisdictions corresponded with our SOTs. These are the kinds of questions that have accrued from my work on the articles reviewed to this point in the current chapter. The remainder of the chapter introduces an intuitive and fateful component that I think can enhance correctional education professional identity still further. It emerged from a rather earthy observation of two cats.

The Blues Brothers

My wife Carolyn and I recently got two male kittens from the local animal shelter. At first we named them Einstein and Tesla, but we soon realized those names were more sophisticated than the kittens themselves. So Carolyn renamed them Jake and Elwood, after the infamous Blues Brothers, two of the cultural heroes in our family pantheon.

I watched as Jake and Elwood tried to manipulate a plastic ink pen. They like pens because they are good toys: If they get a running start and jump on the pen on the kitchen tile floor, they can get a good six foot-slide—like a kitty skateboard. That is great fun.

This day the pen was on a table, right beside a round napkin holder. They both tried and tried, but were unable to manipulate the pen into a place where they could play with it. As I watched, I saw the problem: They were unable to push when the situation called for it, or to pull when that would accomplish their aim. Their push and pull motions were random and, ultimately, it turned out they lacked the discipline or dedication to continue their struggle to fruition. Jake and Elwood are not too smart—indeed, that is how they earned their names.

I wondered what the attributes of this push and pull problem would be if it afflicted humans. In Piaget's terminology, the kittens are clearly in the sensory motor stage. They have not even mastered concrete objects. By contrast, most mature humans would probably be in the formal operations stage, in which abstract ideas are at the forefront, or perhaps even in the post formal operations stage, which some have speculated stretches toward the mystical.

From the formal operations point of view, it seemed that the human analogy for the cats' push/pull confusion would be manifested in the confusion between causal and teleological influences. Most of us are familiar with causality; from this point of view it can be equated with "push." By that I mean that if I push a chair, it moves. The push is the cause, and the movement of the chair is the effect. Most Western thought, and almost the entire scientific movement, is a search for causal influences. North Americans are obsessed with causality, with the push.

By contrast, the telos can be thought of as fate, destiny, or a purpose that draws us forward. Sometimes events unfold in a way that we cannot or do not monitor at the time, but that later, in retrospect, seem best. I certainly do not pretend to be smart about all this. Rather, I simply know that there are often forces at work that are outside my comprehension. In this I suspect I am not alone. For example, who among us intended from an early age to work in correctional education? (My earliest career projections were to become a cowboy or a garbage man.) Yet here we all are, working to transform prisons and prisoners, and being transformed ourselves in the process. Is there a possibility that fate, destiny or telos is at work here, in addition to our own conscious initiatives and decisions? Of course there is. So, I propose the following assumptions.

Some Central Assumptions that Might Apply

Several salient parts of our world are rarely discussed, especially in the research and scholarship literature. For example, despite often grand self-concepts, scientists (and certainly those of us in the social and behavioral sciences) do not know everything—are not even on the verge of knowing everything. Physicians are stumped by the common cold, educators are stumped by the drop-out rate, correctional educators by the recidivism rate and so on. Biologists and chemists have been promising for centuries to find the reasons for crime in heredity, nutrition, brain chemistry, etc., but they have never made good on that promise. They keep designing tests to forecast what humans will do, but to date all their predictions are flawed. Despite the arrogance of the various professions, most of us are as ignorant as little children. Perhaps, first, we would do better to admit our ignorance so we could start off fresh and focus on learning our way through the problems we so frequently create.

Second, we should admit that most of us cannot even track with the things we do know. The complexity of our work can overwhelm, like simultaneous physical motions. Even when we know the facts, we are incapable of monitoring them simultaneously. For example, we move on the surface of the planet, which turns daily and moves seasonally and orbits around the Sun, shifting periodically. Our solar system moves within the galaxy, which travels through space as part of a cluster. Meanwhile, the universe is expanding—perhaps in a phasic "Big Bang/Big Crunch." There may be additional movements that have not yet been described. We cannot conceptualize all these motions rationally, despite our intellectual understanding of each separately. And it is likely that the same problem applies when we try to take stock of our professional work.

So third, we must subjectively interpret complex processes with reason plus intuition. Wilber (2000) called this approach "transrational," because it includes both rational "head" and intuitive "heart." Einstein's report can be considered a confirmation of transrationality: "I did not discover relativity by rational thinking alone" (in Goswami, 2001, p. 30).

Fourth, the best preparation for transrational operations would be to approach problems "with open minds and warm hearts." And experience suggests this is precisely how most correctional educators work—they employ both their cognitive and affective abilities to facilitate student learning in their classes. Folks in our SOT navigate these challenges with savvy effectiveness, although they rarely discuss their strategies in direct terms. Indeed, the entirety of our work is to help learners with concrete strategies, permeated with a nurturing, non-threatening personal tone. We are masters of transrationality, though the term itself seems new.

Fifth, despite our experiences in different fields and situations and our various aspirations for ourselves, students and things we would rather be doing—we are all here and now. Our "right now" work is correctional education, the organized effort to transform prisoners and prisons. So, we should apply our internal and external resources to the tasks at hand.

Sixth, once we settle in to this here and now agenda, we might become aware of certain blessings we enjoy. Some are large, often overlooked blessings: (a) our bodies are made of stuff that emerged billions of years ago in exploding stars; (b) during the last few centuries earth's climate has been unusually conducive to our species; and, (c) despite absurd wars instigated by dominator hierarchies, most North Americans have experienced a remarkable period of peace since the end of World War II. This list could go on and on. Readers will likely get the point—whether we acknowledge it or not—we have enjoyed abundantly favorable conditions.

Seventh, when we take the time to consider the fiercely independent, individualist, self-reliant lip service that constitutes Americans' most frequent rant, we become increasingly aware of the interconnection of all things. Even the ideologues attempting to convince themselves they are in charge of their own fate would experience extreme discomfort if their lives were truly structured according to their propaganda. The food they eat comes from a great distance, thanks to the work of others, as do the clothes they wear and the materials of which their homes are constructed. The dogma they defend came to these shores from distant imperialist societies; they learned its basic principles in extremely social universities, reading books that were printed far away by others, made of materials purchased in remote corners of the world. To update the old saw, despite our aspirations, "no person is an island." The "global economy" has actually been operational for centuries; we are dependent on others for much of the stuff that gives life and makes our lives pleasant.

Eighth, we are connected to the students in our classes in more ways than we normally consider. Teachers who are sincerely committed to teaching are also learners themselves (though usually at a different educational level than their students). And most of us (teachers) have our own versions of the attitude problems that afflict students. For example, while inmate students may be embittered learners, I frequently feel sorry for myself because I have more work to accomplish than time to accomplish it. And I share a deficit of patience with students. By almost any standard I apply, I have an attitude problem analogous to the documented affective deficits of most confined students—both of us are less than perfect. I suspect I am not alone in this. "But for the grace of God…" can be alternatively stated "they" as "us," except for situational differences.

Ninth, if we are honest we will admit that past practice is flawed—our systems have been in continual failure for more than 200 years. Institutions are an easily recognized negative exemplar: Prisons have failed as monasteries, factories, hospitals and warehouses. On this the philosopher Jean Rousseau and the important correctional educator Mary Carpenter agreed:

> Do precisely the opposite to what is usually done, and you will have hit on the right plan. (Rousseau in Quick, 1916, p. 241)

> Surely, then, if the present system has totally failed, there must be something radically wrong in it, and it ought to be changed. (Carpenter, 1864/1969, Vol. 2, p. 218)

The principle that we must work to have open minds (fourth point, above) is not merely a requirement for effectiveness in a complex world; it is rooted in our nearly complete individual and collective failure to improve the world (enjoy permanent peace, end brutality [racism, sexism, imperialism, genocide], and provide the necessities of life). In short, past practice is bad practice.

Finally, in the face of these realities rarely addressed by researchers and scholars, we might see the merit of humility over arrogance, of admitting how little we know rather than assuming we have all the answers. Instead of being well informed about the parameters of life, or even of correctional education, we all need to learn as much as we can. Or, in the language of Matthew 18:3 (KJV), "Except ye...become as little children..." we would do better to (a) admit that we only have the vaguest notion of what we are doing than to (b) pretend to be experts in this drama.

Indeed, these ten principles can be seen as corollaries of one orienting generalization: The world is a lot more mysterious than we normally admit. This generalization, and its ten corollaries, are presented in Figure 3.

FIGURE 3: A PRINCIPLE AND TEN COROLLARIES

Principle:	If we are honest with ourselves, we will admit that the world is much more mysterious than we acknowledge in our everyday interactions.
Corollary 1:	We do not know everything.
Corollary 2:	We cannot even monitor the things we do know.
Corollary 3:	Rationality and intuition ("head" and "heart") are more effective when combined than when either is used without the other.

FIGURE 3: A PRINCIPLE AND TEN COROLLARIES, CONT'D.

Corollary 4:	In the field of correctional education, we will do best when we combine an open mind with a warm heart.
Corollary 5:	Despite all our different life experiences and professional aspirations, we are correctional educators—we need a "here and now" agenda.
Corollary 6:	Even though it usually goes unrecognized, we each have enjoyed great blessings in our lives.
Corollary 7:	All things are interconnected, despite everyday perceptions and individual self-reliance aspirations.
Corollary 8:	The students in our classes are not the only ones who need a better attitude; most of what we hope to accomplish could be facilitated with enthusiasm.
Corollary 9:	Past practice is flawed.
Corollary 10:	We will do best to acknowledge how much we do not know, to be humble and admit we are like children.

"Push" and "Pull"

Having admitted that we are not as smart as we would like to be, we can get on with the central principle of this chapter. Remember, the "push" we experience in daily life is from cause and effect, of causality. We track external influences we encounter and our internal mobilization to accomplish our responsibilities. Most of us are familiar with the push; we spend our lives trying to develop "power" to overcome our "load." Power might include professional qualifications, skills, a livable income and a network of friends and colleagues to help us through the difficult times. Load might include resource inadequacy at work, muddled public perceptions of correctional education (for example, inmates are often perceived as either victimizers or victims, but rarely as both simultaneously), and anti-education institutional influences. These influences can be considered part of cause and effect relations, the "push."

The "pull" fits better with the mystery of life, at least at our current level of understanding. Again, this influence is the telos, a.k.a. fate or destiny, the purpose that is unfolding in the universe. Because this is a relatively unexplored topic for most of us, we may benefit from an examination of some rather concrete elements that contribute to teleological influences.

Elements of the "Pull"

One way to summarize the sequence of cognitive or cognitive-moral growth (outlined by Piaget, Kohlberg, Gilligan, Loevinger, etc.) is of ever-increasing ability to abstract the world and contain the abstraction within our minds. For example, I can discuss ideas because I have language and I can read and write—powers that the kittens Jake and Elwood lack. By contrast, Jake and Elwood appear to operate as if they can know everything about an object by sniffing or pawing it. So one result of cognitive development is an ability to contain more of the world within our minds than Jake and Elwood can imagine.

A second element of how the telos works in our daily lives is our aspirations. Tom Paine was a master at expressing aspirations; a result was the success of the American Revolution. Austin MacCormick was always writing and speaking about the "high aims" of correctional education; two results were the establishment of the Correctional Education Association and *The Journal of Correctional Education*. Alexander Maconochie began the correctional paradigm at a remote British penal colony in the South Pacific in the 1840s and Zebulon Brockway brought Maconochie's system to the U.S. in 1876. They both had high aims or aspirations. Consider how their lives were summarized. In 1851, Matthew Davenport Hill called Maconochie's "the noblest missionary cause that could be conceived. To raise the fallen—to rescue the lost—a higher and more interesting enterprise could not be devised" (Barry, 1958, p. 209). In 1894, Charles Dudley Warner praised Brockway similarly: "it...is scientific work...To rectify the bodies, to develop and train abnormal minds—this is glorious work" (Brockway, 1969/1912, p. 338).

The essence of correctional education is the organized effort to reform or transform prisoners and prisons, to transform prisons into schools. That is a high aspiration. The connection between known aspirations and the mysterious telos is simply expressed in the aspiration-based lyrics of Rogers and Hammerstein's "Happy Talk" song from the musical *South Pacific*: "You got to have a dream—if you don't have a dream, how you gonna make a dream come true?" (2000/1958)

A third element that draws us toward our purpose is our own professionalization. And as Hollingsworth and I explained in our "Coping..." article (2002), professionalization can be a way to "fight back" against institutional obstructionists (predatory, anti-education good-old-boys and girls). Because it is not based on domination, good-old-boys fail to notice the effects of professionalization. What should be our aspirations to professsionalize the field of correctional education? In a recent manuscript I introduced four professional aspirations for correctional educators in the third millennium. Those tasks were rooted in the idea that prisons and prisonization are part of a global, historic effort by a relatively small ruling class to dominate.

A fourth element that "drives" the telos is our uneven personal development. An example might be if I were very mature with regard to my reading habits but very immature when it came to financial planning and rather average with regard to my sense of community duty. Persons with whom I interacted would not encounter three personalities, but one—they would encounter my "center of gravity," my general functioning level, despite the intrapersonal differences in my ability set. Like the impact of my aspirations on my behavior (second element, above), my uneven personal development tends to facilitate growth in the direction of my "higher" self or selves.

A fifth element that contributes to teleological influence is evident when we reach a stage Wilber calls "second tier" (2000, p. 135). In a nutshell, second tier is a very mature level of cognitive or cognitive-moral functioning in which a person finally realizes that there are many potential strategies that can be pursued to accomplish any particular goal. First tier contains six different versions of "the Truth"; adherents to each believe only their version is appropriate or will work, so they deny the others and persecute the advocates of those respective ways of thinking. By contrast, second tier thinking finds some merit in each of the six approaches and accepts that any of them might work to attain the goal, so long as it is implemented in an effective and nurturing way. For our current purposes, second tier thinking is aligned with the telos because it opens up possibilities for action that would be inconceivable to persons operating at first tier.

A sixth element is what Wilber calls transrationality. It means that the formula discussed above (head and heart together) is more effective than either head or heart separately. Head can lead to a worldview that is cold or even brutal. Heart can lead to naïve gullibility. Head and heart can complement each other to better inform our problem-selection and decision-making. The "transrational" label is applied to acknowledge that we have more than two choices: rational or irrational. The third choice is transrational, in which rational decision-making is informed by intuition. Sorokin, an expert on issues social and cultural, proclaimed that "The only source of…self-evident…postulates and axioms is intuition" (1985, p. 684). Anyone who thinks about it will realize the truth of Sorokin's claim.

Consider: You never see the term *Eureka!* (I have found it!) without the exclamation point that signifies the intuitive "aha" experience. It transcends rationality, without negating rationality. Einstein was said to have conceived relativity while stepping on a trolley, when head and heart were working together.

Epiphany seems to come from nowhere or from everywhere—the important point for us is that it has an intuitive element. Wilber maintained that all people, regardless of their current level of maturation, are capable of epiphany (Wilber, 1999, p. 191). The trick, he maintained, is to interpret it in a mature fashion. Sorokin called it "mystic intuition" (1985, pp. 684, 688), exemplified by Mozart's experience in writing music.

What, you ask, is my method in writing and elaborating my large and lumbering things? I can in fact say nothing more about it than this: I do not know myself and can never find out. When I am in particularly good condition, perhaps riding in a carriage, or on a walk after a good meal, and in a sleepless night, then the thoughts come to me in a rush, and best of all. Whence and how—that I do not know and cannot learn. Those which please me I retain…. (in Sorokin, 1985, p. 687)

Similar was the philosopher Schelling's dictum:

Just as the man of destiny does not execute what he wills or intends, but what he is obliged to execute through an incomprehensible fate under whose influence he stands, so the artist…seems to stand under the influence of a power which…compels him to declare or represent things which he himself does not completely see through, and whose impact is infinite. (in Sorokin, 1985, p. 687)

After the first Russian Revolution of 1917, in preparation for the Bolshevik Revolution that would soon follow, Trotsky experienced the pull of the telos:

In these days…he established his platform in the Cirque Moderne, where almost every night he addressed enormous crowds. The amphitheatre was so densely packed that Trotsky was usually shuffled towards the platform over the heads of the audience, and from his elevation he would catch the excited eyes of the daughters of his first marriage, who attended the meetings. He spoke on the topics of the day and the aims of the revolution with his usual piercing logic, but he also absorbed the spirit of the crowd, its harsh sense of justice, its desire to see things in sharp and clear outline, its suspense, and its great expectations. Later he recollected how at the mere sight of the multitude, words and arguments he had prepared well in advance receded and dispersed in his mind and other words and arguments, unexpected by himself but meeting a need in his listeners, rushed up as if from his subconscious. He then listened to his own voice as if to that of a stranger, trying to keep pace with the tumultuous rush of his own ideas and phrases and afraid lest like a sleepwalker he might suddenly wake and break down. Here his politics ceased to be the distillation of individual reflection or of debates in small circles of professional politicians. He merged emotionally with the warm, dark human mass in front of him, and became its medium. (Deutscher, 2003, pp. 216-217)

Sorokin proposed how our lives would be shattered if we suddenly lacked this intuitive capability.

If, for a moment, one can imagine all artistic, religious, philosophical, ethical values eliminated, and all our knowledge reduced to strictly 'scientific discoveries,' formulated in dry propositions, how greatly our cognition of the world and reality would be impoverished and diminished! From millionaires we would be turned into beggars. (1985, p. 689; emphasis in original)

Thus there is hardly any doubt that intuition is the real source of real knowledge, different from the role of the senses and reason... The organs of the senses, not controlled by reason or intuition, can give us but a chaotic mass of impressions, perceptions, sensations, incapable of supplying any integrated knowledge...meaningless 'facts,' without any coherence, relevance, and comprehension... For thousands of years many empirical uniformities of natural phenomena were lying under their nose; and yet they were unable to see, to hear, to smell, to touch these sensory forms of reality...When they were 'discovered,'... [it was] only through the co-operation of other sources of cognition: logic and intuition. (pp. 690-691)

Interested readers should consult Sorokin's great book (pp. 684-692) for additional examples. To identify how this principle applies in correctional education, we turn to exemplars William George and Thomas Mott Osborne, who became aware intuitively that democratic management principles could be applied "inside."

Suddenly George was jolted...he later wrote 'Our Glorious Republic' in miniature—a Junior Republic—and I recall shouting at the top of my voice, I have it—I have it—I have it; and like a school boy I ran as fast as my legs could carry me, and told my mother. I felt it to have been a God-given idea. (George, in Holl, 1971, p. 100)

Osborne's sentiment about prison democracy was similar:

...*the thing works...the thing works*...In Auburn prison for more than two years, in Sing Sing prison for more than a year, the new system has been in operation and *the thing works...it works*. (Osborne, 1975/1916, pp. 222-233 [emphases in original])

I have not a single theory or idea about this prison game that I am not ready to alter or throw away the moment it bumps up against a fact. (Osborne, 1924, pp. 44-45)

Perhaps one of the biggest impediments to our realization of our own innate intuitive capabilities and of their potential alignment with rationality, is the teaching models we apply. In education the medical model is called the diagnostic-prescriptive method. Both focus on the professional's perceived function: diagnosing the problems of others, prescribing remedial activities, monitoring the "cure." At least two concerns should be evident. First, for good reason correctional educators frequently criticize the medical model in its applications. But then the same educators advocate the diagnostic-prescriptive model for classroom applications. That is a double standard. Second, in the medical model/diagnostic-prescriptive method the change agent is not supposed to be impacted by the change process. All the engineered changes are to be experienced by the client; the professional/teacher is thought not to need change; all interactions are one way—and that is another double standard. Our whole concern about the correctional education professional identity issue is precisely because we ourselves need to change in part through the interactions with students, and through our identification with our school of thought (SOT).

A seventh element is that, despite our lip service to the contrary, most correctional educators apply their gut understandings—their hearts—all the time. For example, despite the emphasis on computers and digital instruction, most of us intuitively know that machines cannot turn people's lives around; only people can do that. And despite all we were taught about incremental learning and individually prescribed instruction, we know that (a) most relevant learning occurs in leaps of consciousness after ideas or feelings have "cooked" in students and, (b) social learning opportunities fit better than individualization with the identified needs of offender students. We know that, even when appearances suggest no learning progress is being made, progress is in fact being experienced but not expressed.

Without understanding these learning dynamics, we might be unable to stand up to all the "shuckin' and jivin'" of the criminal justice politics. Most correctional educators also intuitively understand that academic diagnostic tests and risk assessment inventories are impotent when used to predict what a confined student will do who has finally decided to improve his or her life. This is why we often discuss students as if they were "late bloomers" and are so invested in the "readiness to learn" principle.

An eighth element is that anyone who works in the intense prison setting and is alert to the human condition will intuitively grasp that—despite all the outward impressions of conditions as monolithic and eternal—there is nothing more certain than change itself. All institutional employees accept this possibility of "a change in the weather;" it is why we work so hard (anticipating positive change) and why the officers are so tense about potential riots (anticipating negative change).

Finally (and ninth) is that the pull experienced as telos can help liberate us from the push of causal relationships, consistent with the overall pattern of human growth. In 1970 Knowles summarized Overstreet's 1949 findings on maturation and one of the prime dimensions he referenced was the shift from dependence toward autonomy (p. 25). We recognize parallel findings from the theories that drive our everyday work with offenders—Maslow's emphasis on self-actualization and the general goal of moving from an external locus of control (push) to an internal locus of control (pull). Why would a (teleological) pull be more liberating than a (causal) push? Precisely because, as told and retold in the narrative above about the elements that explain the telos, its direction is regulated by our aspirations, our "higher selves" (in the case of our uneven development). These nine mechanisms that account for the telos are summarized in Figure 4. The reader is cautioned, because I cannot claim to catalogue all the ways the telos plays out in our personal/professional lives. There might be seventy-five more applications of which I am ignorant. My purpose in this presentation is merely to demystify the telos, based on my own limited experience, and hopefully increase access to this robust concept for correctional educators. Secondly and almost as an aside, readers should note that researchers engaged in quantitative studies, which typically express their findings in numbers with statistics, tend to define their role as a search for causal influences (the push). By contrast, researchers engaged in qualitative studies, which typically express their findings in words or narrative, tend to be more open to persons' perceptions of teleological influences (the pull) because they help explain the profound meaning inherent in everyday life.

FIGURE 4: SUMMARIZING THE TELOS' PULL TOWARD HUMAN PROGRESS

1. The human ability to abstract things to ideas inclines us naturally toward growth, development and maturation.

2. Personal and shared aspirations, even politically correct lip service, can set the pace for how progress will unfold.

3. The professionalization of correctional education can drive and expand the progress we attain in our field of education.

4. The uneven personal/professional growth that we all experience allows us to imagine and articulate progress.

5. Second-tier thinking, an effect of maturation that allows us to pursue goals through various approaches instead of relying solely on one, enhances our opportunities for success by expanding our repertoire of effective strategies.

6. Transrationality—the combination of "head" and "heart" to improve problem selection and decision-making—can be a potent tool for manifesting progress.

7. We all apply transrationality whenever we are alert to our "gut feelings," our "common sense."

8. Despite appearances, change is inevitable, so progress is possible.

9. The direction of the telos is consistent with our perception of growth: from dependence toward autonomy, self-actualization and readiness to learn.

How can one know whether the telos is operational in one's life? The current writer does not have all the answers. However, Figure 5 outlines attributes I have experienced, which are contrary to logical expectations—I believe they indicate teleological influence.

FIGURE 5: SUGGESTED INDICATORS OF THE TELOS IN ACTION, BASED ON PERSONAL EXPERIENCE

1. Loss of tine sense when working toward one's mission (tendency to neglect time passing).

2. Useful information becomes available through dreams or intuitive leaps.

3. Profound sense of joy or accomplishment ("following your bliss"), even when there are no real events or trends to report.

4. Intense, unaccountable feelings of well-being.

5. Repeated experience of epiphany; direct appreciation of how all things are connected.

6. Diminished sense of being victimized by others or by conditions.

7. Lessened awareness of having to rush throughout the day's activities.

8. Diminished relation between inputs and outputs—some tasks get accomplished expeditiously; some long-standing or pressing problem(s) seem to solve themselves, often in ways that are dramatically complex, or dramatically simple, efficient or effective.

9. Personal responses very different from one's own earlier responses to the same stimuli.

10. Generalized sense of thankfulness/gratefulness/appreciation.

11. New or especially intense willingness to forgive the flaws of others.

12. Increased attachment to/identification with the struggles and accomplishments of all life forms.

13. Surprising, unaccountable urge to help a person or a cause.

14. General sensitivity to or awareness of the telos' pull on us toward a specific task or outcome.

The Pull Toward Correctional Education Professional Identity

Why should we be concerned about the telos when we already have so many responsibilities. In part, because we seek a single rather than a double standard—one that applies for example, to both students and teachers. We are accustomed to applying the "external/internal" locus of control concept to inmate students, but not necessarily to ourselves or to correctional educators in general. We describe students as impetuous and lacking in goal-setting or planning skills. Yet the "student as teacher and teacher as student" formula (which allows teachers to be human and accounts for our own development) suggests the truth in this application. In this regard, how would correctional educators with an internal locus of control be different from those with an external locus?

Figure 6: Locus of Control

External	Internal
Behaves passively	Behaves with engagement, from an activist perspective
Consumes without thinking	Contributes consciously
Tends to assimilate in any social context	Tends to be rooted in a discrete SOT
Maintains existing systems (conventional)	Innovates, to improve the world (transformative)
Consumes emotional energy	Radiates emotional energy
Identifies self as an accident of the universe	Identifies self as a purpose of the universe
Is fragmented, in response to many perceived struggles	Applies internal resources
Is conflicted or confused about issues	Acts out of strong sense of commitment
Experiences interpersonal insecurity and impotence	Is dedicated/disciplined, with unity of purpose
Identifies as a victim	Experiences security; feels interpersonally empowered

FIGURE 6: LOCUS OF CONTROL, CONT'D

EXTERNAL	INTERNAL
Feels socially invisible	Acts with self-determination
Feels alien in most settings (a stranger in any land)	Feels confident
Acts individually	Feels part of the fabric of the universe
Seeks (but never finds) meaning and confirmation	Acts individually, but also socially, culturally
Is driven by exterior events	Finds meaning and confirmation in everyday events. Is driven by interior purpose.
Experiences interpersonal insecurity and impotence	Experiences security; feels interpersonally empowered

Herein lies the heart of the correctional education movement. To participate actively in a part of the human drama that unfolds under intense pressures in a closed, extremely complex social environment, one should be able, willing and open—aligned with the telos. And the telos is aligned with our highest aspirations, our own subjective, objective, social and cultural selves. What alternative do we really have but to acknowledge that we are impacted by forces of the mysterious universe? It is therefore our duty to let ourselves take that required leap of consciousness, that act of faith that will be supported by a purposeful universe. In other words, we must develop a proactive pattern of professional identity. In the parlance of *Star Wars*, "May the Force [telos] be with you."

The standard we apply to inmate student growth is "attitudes, skills and knowledge," in that order. We prepare them for gainful employment not because a job is inherently good, but because employed persons tend to have more, to be more, than non-employed persons—and they are therefore better citizens, neighbors and individuals. Correctional education's program of improvement is not about external but internal things; that is why we focus on attitudes.

And so the same must apply to ourselves, educators, as well as to students. Any different standard would be a double standard. Our effort to improve and consolidate the program reflects our aspiration to improve and consolidate ourselves, our interior and individual (subjective) selves and our interior and shared (cultural) selves. The measure of progress is not whether we access the most recent high-tech gadget or even whether we have enough texts and desks in our classrooms. Rather, it is whether—or the extent to which—we acquire integrity (intrapersonally), credibility (interpersonally) and effectiveness (personally, as representatives of the correctional education SOT). To what extent can we articulate useful principles that others find compelling? To what extent can we navigate through life's obstructions and resources? Resist the dehumanization that institutions foster? Unite with other correctional educators to advocate for effective programming? Become effective ourselves?

The most appropriate measure of our work has more to do with the internal resources we can bring to bear to relevant tasks (leadership) than about the external resources we can mobilize (funding, equipment and so forth). Stated alternatively, you are the most important resource students can access; your effectiveness in this work depends on your ability to interact with students in a way that stimulates them to self-improvement. Any obsession with technology, equipment, budget, etc. can distract if you pursue it without also pursuing your own self-improvement.

Our task (students and teachers alike; my task and your task) is to develop into better people (to master ourselves), not to become masters of inanimate things or systems of things. To be a good teacher, one has to be a good person: able and willing, nurturing and disciplined, dedicated to learning and teaching, and effective as both an individual and as a team member.

The powerful tug of the telos suggests that (a) our brains are wired, and our minds designed to function, more like antennae than as the current "personal, stand-alone computer" paradigm would suggest, and (b) the current "interpersonal" model of communication should be replaced with one that is both interpersonal and intrapersonal. In other words, teleological communication between our everyday selves and our higher selves is at least as important as communication with each other. If our minds operate like antennae, the connections between and among them might allow us to function collectively, just as we can function independently. It all comes down to mediation, the sequencing and explanation of learning. In cognitive theory mediation is the theme of Vygotsky (in his ZPD concept—zone of proximal development), Feuerstein (in his MLE model—mediated learning experience), and even Piaget (in his self-mediation model). We need to mediate our own activities, to maximize our own learning. The work of mediating learning is part and parcel of all religions, spiritual traditions and practices (it is the work of the Holy Spirit, the prophets, angels and saints, as well as exemplars and sages).

Most North Americans are monotheists—they believe in the One. From this perspective, an accurate way to describe life is that we are here to represent the One who sent us. Yet how will we align ourselves, our thinking and action, with the One if we do not try to hear the One voice?

Although some historical periods seemed characterized by unity, ours is clearly fragmented. Shall we align ourselves with the fragmented influences of the causal "pushes," or with the One purpose of the telos? If we are serious about accepting the work that is given to us, it is our duty to try to get past the many influences that propel us through our days, resulting in conflict and confusion. Rather we must become alert to the One voice of the telos. The difference between confusion (as in the correctional education professional identity problem) and unity of purpose is merely a state of mind. Consider Mary Carpenter's approach, articulated in 1852, which largely accounts for her great accomplishments in transforming English juvenile facilities: "Let me only humbly and earnestly go on with the work in which I have been abundantly 'blessed'" (in Carpenter, 1974/1881, p. 131). Ultimately such unity of purpose does not require extensive skill development or learning over a protracted period—it requires only dedication and the discipline that accrues from our practice of being alert to one's function or purpose.

Wilber wrote that the direction of what we are calling push is from the One toward the many. This is the direction of the sensuous (the path based on data from the five senses—how uplifting a sunset can be, or the sight of a woodland stream). He also addressed what we call the pull, with its direction from the many toward the One (the sometimes ascetic path of personal growth and development). He wrote that we are all capable of each, but that reliance on one to the exclusion of the other puts our social and emotional selves out of balance. Both paths have merit. From a spiritual perspective, each of us always has choices (free agency). We can either be pushed by the many (fragmented/conflicted) or pulled by the One (toward unity of purpose).

The point of this chapter is that North Americans tend to be out of balance—we tend to emphasize the push and limit or exclude the pull from our daily lives. In my mainstream Foundations of Education courses the students respond to an essay question: Why are we all crazy? I am amazed at how rarely anyone protests the question's assumption. Almost to a person they admit that they are crazy: chasing too many agendas, hurrying through tasks, overworked, harried and out of balance. One can either be harried/conflicted/confused or have unity of purpose; it is not possible to experience both simultaneously. To regain balance, we need to focus for a time on the teleological pull, to find peace of mind. Real insight about our school of thought can only be found away from the cacophony of screaming voices, in line with our own personal/professional purpose.

Summary and Conclusion

For more than three decades I have felt drawn to articulate and clarify problems and possibilities associated with the correctional education professional identity issue. The resultant articles addressed topics such as (a) professional preparation of correctional educators; (b) the history of our field, and the emergence of the Correctional Education Association; (c) relationships between correctional education and the related fields of education and criminal justice; and; (d) relationships between the struggle to teach and learn in institutions and the political, economic and cultural constraints we so frequently encounter.

After reviewing attributes of seven articles I wrote since 1981 on professional identity for *The Journal of Correctional Education*, I find there are still many aspects that need to be explored. For example, I believe that (a) increased access to the history and literature of correctional education can fuel identification with our field and (b) the school of thought (SOT) phenomenon can be applied to vastly improve life in the U.S.

This chapter then introduced the possibility that there are influences in our personal/professional lives that we rarely acknowledge, largely because they seem mysterious. One way of making use of this reservoir of untapped direction is to demystify the telos (fate, destiny, the transformational purpose that draws us into the future). So, although I admitted a lack of complete understanding, I discussed concrete ways in which the telos operates in our daily lives, how that influence can be identified and how it might be nurtured. It is interesting that, if the influence of the telos is real, it does not matter whether we believe or accept it.

I hope that this chapter encourages correctional educators in their difficult work and provides some hope that was not previously available. We need to mobilize all available resources for our goal of transforming prisoners and prisons—internal and external; subjective, objective, social and cultural. With regard to understanding the telos, most of us are as incompetent as the kittens Jake and Elwood when they tried to move the pen. But by opening up to the possibility of teleological influence, we might better align our actions with our own aspirations and emergent future conditions.

Gehring and Eggleston at a California youth facility.

Chapter IX

My Story

by Teri Hollingsworth

Introduction

In the *Help Wanted* section of the June 1990, Lake Elsinore, California newspaper, I spotted an ad for the ideal employment: instructional aide in a juvenile detention facility. I immediately added up my qualifications. There were three years experience as an instructional assistant at the elementary school level, some functional experience with juvenile facilities that could easily be considered a hindrance, and an inherent desire to teach. My experience with juvenile facilities drew from my incarceration as a teenager in a facility much like the one described in the ad. The fact was, I had experience that no other applicant had. As a matter of fact (though I didn't know it at the time), I was more perfect than most applicants, because as Stigler and Hiebert (1999) explained, teachers learn from the educational culture in which they themselves were taught. In other words, teachers teach as they were taught.

I was taught inside a facility, so I was uniquely qualified.

Could it be that former correction students make the most effective teachers in correctional facilities? There are numerous stories of people who turned their lives around and then decided to go back and help others in similar situations. Alcoholics Anonymous would never exist without recovered mentors. Whether or not this is a valid theory, it does open up questions I want to address such as: What makes a highly qualified correctional educator? Should we require special credentials for this decidedly specific set of skills?

As I endeavor to answer these questions, I review some of the correctional education literature, but before we dig into that, let us hear the voices of others who teach in alternative or correctional programs. Through a qualitative survey of my coworkers, I explored the question of what brings correctional educators to the field and have gathered for the reader the experiences that educators bring to the correctional classroom. Although the term "correctional educator" applies to countless teaching positions such as prison educators, alternative day school teachers, or community transitions specialists, for our purpose "correctional educator" means juvenile educators in alternative and correctional settings.

My Story: Learning to Be a Correctional Educator

As you can probably surmise from the above, I did manage to obtain the position as an instructional aide for Los Pinos High School, a juvenile camp school for Orange County Juvenile Court Schools. That was in 1990, and I have been working as a correctional educator ever since. Because of my lack of pre-service training and little education, I struggled with my new position. Yet I remember telling my friends and family that it was a breeze, because I had a captive audience. I spent my first couple of years trying to control classroom behaviors through the curriculum. I still believe that good curriculum reduces classroom behavior problems, yet at the time "curriculum" to me meant making sure that everyone had plenty of busy work. Obviously there was much more to it than that. I was very aware that I had much to learn, so I took every training seminar the department offered. I also began and quickly completed the requirements for junior college and next transferred to the California State University system. The seminars offered by the Orange County Department of Education (OCDE) along with the courses I took at California State University, San Bernardino (CSUSB) eventually led me to CSUSB's Center for the Study of Correctional Education. Through the center (the only one in the country I might add), I met other correctional educators and joined the Correctional Education Association (CEA).

I remained at Los Pinos High School as an instructional aide (paraprofessional is the current term) until I received my credential in 1996 and became one of the few correctional educators to hold a certificate in correctional education. I attended the Alternative and Correctional Education Academy (ACEA)—one of the only programs of its kind—through the Center for the Study of Correctional Education at CSUSB and was named Graduate of the Year (an indication of my passion for correctional education). It was this certification experience that propelled me to simultaneously accept the position of president of the local CEA chapter (Tri-County CEA) and enter the master's program offered at CSUSB. Although I am unaware of any program that offers a master's degree in correctional education, the program at CSUSB was created specifically to integrate one's passion for any aspect of education into the program of study. I therefore was able to pursue my passion: the study of correctional education.

The master's program was a tremendous help to me in the classroom as I discovered and explored curriculum methods and theories. Nevertheless it also produced many questions about the correctional education field. The pursuit of answers prompted me to enroll in the doctorate program at Claremont Graduate University (CGU). The doctorate program allowed me to pursue my correctional education studies at a more academic and professional level.

Even now, I continue to experiment and research my theories in classrooms and with my coworkers.

My personal story was not the typical correctional educator story, but it is not unusual in that most correctional educators do not plan to become correctional educators and, therefore, are not prepared to teach in a correctional facility.

What Brought You To Alternative Community Correctional Education School Services?

In California where I currently study and practice, juveniles in alternative and correctional facilities obtain education through county-operated programs. This is unlike other states. Wolford, Purnell, and Brooks (1998) discovered in their national survey that in 63 percent of responding states, the primary agency responsible for the education in juvenile facilities was the juvenile justice agency. Because California's juvenile correctional educators fall under the supervision of county districts, correctional educators fall under credentialing requirements set by the California Department of Education.

All correctional educators in county programs are required to hold a California Teaching Credential. Therefore, California correctional educators are qualified to teach in any district school within the state. This is a big advantage over many other state juvenile corrections programs. Yet even in California, correctional educators are not specially or specifically prepared to teach in alternative or correctional facilities or programs. The educators I discuss here are also correctional educators in ACCESS (OCDE's Alternative, Community and Correctional Education Schools and Services Division of Alternative Education [ACCESS]). They are teachers or administrators in Orange County juvenile camp schools programs, alternative day schools, contract learning schools, homeless outreach program schools and/or group home classrooms.

To examine my claim that correctional educators come to the position without specific training, I sent an email to 112 of my colleagues whose names I recognized on the ACCESS email list. The selection of names was not random; these names were chosen because I knew they would recognize my name and be more likely to respond. I asked them to reply with "a couple sentences telling how they came to teach for ACCESS." I specified that I was not in search of their whole story but was interested in how they came to ACCESS. I wanted just a few words that explained whether they followed the normal "straight from college to classroom" path or the "ended up here as a surprise" path. The survey was not empirically structured with a control group or even a specific questionnaire. It was more a casual conversation with some coworkers, intended to provide qualitative evidence for my point.

Of the fifty-four responses I received, three respondents had landed in alternative education straight from college. Of those three, only one had intended to teach in alternative education; the other two came to it as instructional aides strictly for wages to sustain them until they finished university classes. Both stayed, however, and eventually obtained teaching positions.

Twelve of the respondents began as I did, with the county as classified staff and then went on to obtain their credential. Another observation, pointed out by one of the respondents, was that many correctional educators are drawn to the profession by friends or family already in the field. Out of the fifty-four respondents, eleven mentioned knowing someone who worked for and recommended the ACCESS program.

Other important information was ascertained from the responses. For example, twenty-nine (more than half) of the fifty-four respondents had taught in regular education before shifting to correctional/alternative education and seven of those twenty-nine mentioned special education experience. Eleven respondents expressed they had stayed home to raise their children before working for the county. Other prior careers included jobs in banking, health care, social service, data analysis, law enforcement, probation, public relations, radio, television, fashion and advertising.

Although the survey was not empirical, I surmise that my theory is correct: Most correctional educators do not come to the field intentionally. Consequently, correctional educators have not prepared for the specific challenges of teaching in correctional or alternative settings or for the special needs of correctional or alternative students. Although I did not ask their personal reasons for entering the alternative or correctional education field, many included such statements. More than a quarter of the statements were describing the passion for the work. Here are their words:

- I love working for ACCESS. I would have loved rolling out of college and into a career like this back in 1980.

- Irvine (school district) called…I told them that I had died and gone to teacher heaven I loved this job so much! When you salvage these kids, you not only save them from themselves, you also save all the victims that these potential predators would have had. To me, it is really meaningful and important work. My theory…anybody can teach regular kids, but it takes a really tremendous teacher to teach these kids.

- I always knew I wanted to have a career that made a difference. I couldn't stand the thought of working a job that brought me no inner satisfaction.

- …I've been thrilled to work here ever since. It is the perfect blend of teaching and social work….

- Got in an argument with the principal who thought alternative kids were losers and when another principal heard this, he hired me on the spot.

- I quit my job and started working in ACCESS. I see this as a mission field for my faith and a place where I can change lives.

- I have never looked back. Alternative Education is where I needed to be.

- I love working with these kids and I do not plan on leaving.

- I wanted to work with an at-risk population where I would feel more useful.

- …this career change was definitely a surprise, and a very good fit. I like to live a little outside the box. What a great job I have!

- I wanted to teach the ones that were left out so that I could give them an environment where they would feel they belonged. I wanted to teach those who were troubled or neglected by the school system. I was inspired by the words of Jesus about the importance of seemingly unimportant people: "Inasmuch as you have done it unto one of the least of these thy brethren, you have done it unto me." I wanted to work with "the least of these."

- I love the students we serve.

- My feeling was that the students I taught were largely programmed to succeed…meaning that they would succeed whether they had great teachers or lousy ones. It bored me. What attracted me to alternative education, which for many would seem to be degradation from teaching college, was that I was…potentially…a major component in the success or failure of my students. My favorite analogy is comparing alternative education to the work done by doctors in triage settings…we are not hospitals…or cosmetic surgeons…we are lifesavers….

The evidence presented here is significant. Correctional educators come to corrections through alternate paths and have significant passion for what they do. This could answer my question: What makes a highly qualified correctional educator? But when I conducted a review of the literature in search of correctional education's professionalization, I discovered that although correctional educators bring passion, they are still not equipped with a proper association between theory and practice. I provide the following review of the correctional education literature as evidence.

Literature Review: Disconnected Curriculum

Professionalism protects the status quo of a profession and prescribes how to promote or reform it. In this section I explore a need for professionalization of the correctional education field. I also search for further clarity of the specific characteristics of this specialty. The subject is significant since studies of incarcerated adult inmates have correlated education with reduced recidivism, the rate that inmates re-offend and return to prison (Steurer & Smith, 2003). Sound social policy, such as that used to direct our actions as they apply to correctional education, requires analysis. Yet little empirical data has demonstrated that the current educational practices within correctional facilities have been effective at reducing recidivism.

The case for the relation of theory to practice is evident in the general education literature. Stigler and Heibert (2000) for example, argue that teacher quality directly influences student learning; therefore, it belongs high on educational reform platforms. Quality correctional educators are important because America incarcerates large numbers of juveniles, with the hope that they will change their behavior and not re-offend. In addition, academic research of the general education field could inform professionalization of correctional education.

Current theory and practice in juvenile correctional classrooms follow a linear, prescriptive, behaviorist format that, based upon high recidivism rates, has not demonstrated effectiveness (Abramson, 1991). Through content analysis of fifty-four peer-reviewed articles found in *The Journal of Correctional Education*, Abramson discovered that an empirical-analytic approach was the principal theoretical foundation of curriculum used in the correctional classroom. Empirical-analytical theorists understand curriculum in a limited, linear, prescriptive and controlled way. A curriculum of behaviorist control fits within the status quo of most correctional facilities' cultures.

Abramson (1991) recommended a re-examination of the curriculum in terms of critical theory, which could address the "disconnect" between behaviorist curricula and teaching juveniles to think critically and act socially, by utilizing unrepressed curriculum in an otherwise controlled environment. Abramson's recommendation supports Osborne's (1975) statement made in 1916:

> The prison system endeavors to make men industrious by driving them to work; to make them virtuous by removing temptation; to make them respect the law by forcing them to obey the edicts of an autocrat; to make them farsighted by allowing them no chance to exercise foresight; to give them individual initiative by treating them in large groups; in short, to prepare them again for society by placing them in conditions as unlike real society as then could well be made. (p. 153)

Abramson (1991) maintained that more reliance upon a socially based curriculum theory should provide a way out of the conundrum presented by Osborne so long ago. A similar "disconnect" between goals and practice was found in boot camp facilities by Kilgore and Meade (2004), who conducted an institutional ethnography of seventeen juveniles in a boot camp facility. The researchers described the camp as a place where juveniles are subjected to highly structured and challenging vocational, educational, physical and therapeutic programming meant to shock and rehabilitate offenders. They found inconsistencies, a "disconnect," between the goals of the facility and the actual outcomes. Kilgore and Meade argued that the curriculum grounded in the behaviorist theory used at the camp resulted in short-term learning results. For example, they stated that juveniles were required to memorize a large quantity of information when arriving at camp and not permitted to progress in the program until they accomplished the task. The researchers found the tasks were always completed; however, no juvenile could remember the information upon exit from the camp; confirming, therefore, that the information was not retained in long-term memory and as a result did not affect behaviors.

Kilgore and Meade (2004) pointed out that long-term lessons, those obviously not intended by camp staff, occurred for juveniles instead. Their research revealed that juveniles retained those lessons such as how to avoid punishment or that awards are for a few accomplished juveniles and not worth the effort for most juveniles. The researchers also found that these juveniles learned to intentionally misbehave in order to attain desired breaks from work. Kilgore and Meade found that lessons learned socially remained in long-term memory, yet those learned by memorization—a method supported by empirical-analytical behaviorist curriculum theory—never made it to long-term memory. Their conclusions support curricula and methodologies associated with constructivist theory. The "get tough" policies at the boot camp do not reduce recidivism. Kilgore and Meade (2004) stated that nearly 75 percent of juveniles in one juvenile boot camp institution returned within one year.

Correctional research has shown that behaviorist curriculum theory has not resulted in the designated outcome goals for long-term change (Abramson, 1991; Kilgore & Meade, 2004). Yet control, a behaviorist method, is the primary tactic for bringing about changed behaviors in correctional facilities. Correctional education researchers found that issues of control originate from corrections staff, judges and society and have a direct effect upon the restrictive curriculum (Gehring & Hollingsworth, 2002). For example, according to Gehring and Hollingsworth, correctional educators encounter directives from correctional staff that establish a top-down, military type authority. Traditional teacher education programs do not address the control issues found in correctional facilities beyond the typical classroom behavior lesson on how to establish classroom rules. The research results of Abramson, Kilgore and Meade are significant given that, as stated earlier, Wolford, Purnell and Brooks (1998) pointed out that in 63 percent of responding states, the primary agency responsible for the education in juvenile justice facilities was the juvenile justice agency.

Drakeford's (2002) qualitative case study of six residents of a Maryland juvenile facility utilized a behaviorist method. His results proved positive for each intervention in reading fluency and attitude, showing that intensive literacy programming positively affected oral reading fluency of incarcerated youth. Although Drakeford's study demonstrated incremental progress, he was not looking for evidence of long-term learning. Significant for our purposes were the challenges Drakeford encountered during the study. He found inconsistent cooperation by administrators and correctional officers and recurring student absences due to court dates, lock downs, meetings with lawyers, cell searches and even fires in the units. Drakeford also stated that correctional officers' attitudes towards the literacy program were negative and asserted that an adjustment in institutional culture, principles, behaviors and incentives as they relate to education must arise if literacy initiatives were to succeed.

Authority and control issues were embedded in the phenomenological survey-dialogue that Wright (2004) conducted with Canadian prison educators on the subject of care. His study speculated how caring educators resisted the schismatic prison culture that treats prisoners as objects. Although Wright's work was limited because only six women participated, it informs this review as it raised a specific skill required of correctional educators. Wright expressed that most correctional educators experienced the dilemma and conflict that arose from their need to "get 'close' or 'near' enough to them as students in order to teach—while also keeping their emotional and social 'distance' from them [prisoners]" (p. 201). This important issue which is specific to correctional educators is not addressed in California's teacher credentialing program nor in the Beginning Teacher Support and Assessment (BTSA) program literature (California Commission on Teacher Credentialing, 2001).

Foley and Gao (2002), in their description of instructional practices and assessment in correctional settings, discovered that about two-thirds of the correctional educators they surveyed reported using individualized one-to-one instruction in their classrooms and that less than half of the respondents reported using group work. The researchers implied that one-to-one instruction was not an effective method for instructing correctional students since, depending upon teacher-student ratio and instructional period length, students were likely to receive instruction for only a few minutes a day. Again the research uncovers a "disconnect" between classroom practice and effective teaching.

The findings of researchers Abramson (1991), Foley and Gao (2002), Gehring and Hollingsworth (2002), Kilgore and Meade (2004) and Wright (2004) offered evidence supporting a need for correctional curriculum revision and correctional educator preparation, as did Moody's (2003) who established that 30 percent to 70 percent of juveniles in correctional facilities qualified for special education; however, most educators working in those facilities have not been trained in special education procedure or interventions. All of these researchers' work implied a need to prepare correctional educators for classroom instruction methods that are implicit in the special characteristics of corrections students and all agreed that more empirical studies were needed.

Given that correctional educators earn no specific credential, no empirical data was expected to be uncovered in the literature that examined the effectiveness of credentialed teachers on quality of prison programs or student outcomes. It was therefore necessary to look to other education research for some illumination about teacher preparation and credentialing. According to Stigler and Heibert (1999), improvement of teaching was limited because teaching is a culture that has evolved over long time periods. The researchers explain that changing one or two parts of a system simply caused the other parts to adjust to return the system to the status quo. Teachers gained knowledge of the teaching culture, Stigler and Heibert asserted, from classroom experiences as a child and teach as they were taught, which continues the system's balance. Stigler and Heibert's findings have implications for correctional educators since most correctional educators were not taught in correctional classrooms. The study of correctional education provides fertile ground for studying just how to change the foundational culture of teaching, inside and out.

The unfamiliar ground correctional educators find when entering a classroom is vastly dissimilar to the one in which they were taught and could possibly cause teachers to revert to a curriculum that is easier to control in the classroom, one based on behaviorist principles. This could possibly explain the "disconnect" found by researchers (Abramson, 1991; Kilgore & Meade, 2004) between the goal of changed behaviors and outcomes resulting from current correctional classroom teaching. Another implication possibly drawn from Stigler and Heibert's (1999) findings may be that teacher preparation would have a larger impact upon correctional educators even though Stigler and Heibert contended that teachers learn little from formal training (p. 83). In their survey of all fifty state departments of education, Wolford, Purnell and Brooks (1998) suggested that researchers and educators continued to ask for instruction and special certification. Educators remained interested in professional development to such an extent that, according to the Wolford, Purnell and Brooks' survey, its lack was one of the ten most significant barriers to the delivery of quality education in correctional settings.

Other barriers, described by Thomas (1990), that could possibly explain the slow change in professionalization of correctional education, were the shifts in societal goals. Thomas found that political climate had an effect on educational goals, as did changes such as shifts in political control, economic crisis and popularization of a new educational philosophy or even the discovery of a new technological innovation. Could Thomas' findings explain why, even though Osborne (1916) called for democratic educational reform in America's prisons almost a century ago, the political climate of the time pressured him to end his successful experiment in prison social democracy? Osborne successfully brought democratic governance to three major prisons. Under his management, prisoners ran most of the day-to-day functions in New York's Sing Sing, and Auburn prisons, as well as at the U.S. Naval Prison at Portsmouth. Holl (1971) asserted that the politics of the progressive era and the subsequent social reform were responsible for the creation and eventual demise of the democratic experiment. The political climate that facilitated passing of three-strikes laws in California and similar laws nationwide, may possibly contribute to the slow change in correctional education theory and practice.

Although the research revealed several possible explanations for the slow change in correctional education professionalization, one exception was found in the program described by McKibbin (1999) in *Kappa Delta Pi Record*

The article described a California program that could possibly have a positive effect on the preparation of correctional educators in that state. It described an alternative certification program that created internships for teachers in possession of emergency credentials and those already teaching but whom, for varying reasons, were not able to obtain credentials. McKibbin noted that the internship programs were established as a result of a remarkable cooperation between university teacher preparation programs and school districts. She noted the programs have successfully resulted in qualified teachers with classroom experience.

The purpose of teacher internships, according to McKibbin (1999), was to recruit nontraditional and traditionally underrepresented applicants to the teaching field in order to fill hard-to-fill positions in classrooms where California teachers customarily had chosen not to teach, such as inner city schools or isolated rural schools. The program allowed teachers to continue teaching and earning a paycheck while attaining their credential, which McKibbin stated, resulted in including previously excluded hopefuls from the field who could not afford university credential programs. Components, according to the article, were 60 to 200 hours of pre-service preparation before entering classrooms followed by extensive instructional sequences offered in cohort classes, which met on weekends or evenings. Some classes were co-taught by teams of university professors and seasoned classroom teachers and, according to McKibbin, the retention rate for teachers certified through intern programs was 87 percent over a five-year period. That figure compares to the state retention rate of 84 percent and the national retention rate of 67 percent as reported by the Preliminary Report on Teacher Retention in California (2002).

Summary

This literature review revealed a need for specific professional preparation for correctional educators who teach in juvenile correctional institutions. Although many correctional educators were prepared and granted credentials through certification programs designed for teachers in regular K-12 classrooms (Wolford, Purnell & Brooks, 1998), the correctional education field comprises specific skills and knowledge exclusive to the correctional education field (Abramson, 1991; Foley & Gao, 2002; Gehring and Hollingsworth, 2002; Kilgore & Meade, 2004; Moody, 2003; Wolford, Purnell & Brooks, 1998; and Wright, 2004). Even though Stigler and Heibert (1999) contended that teachers learn little from formal training (p. 83) because they reproduce the cultures of teaching in which they were taught, this may not apply to correctional educators since they were not themselves taught in a correctional classroom. Research should be conducted to provide evidence as to whether correctional education preparation would be effective for the field. This research should benefit K-12 education as well. A study of how educators who must learn to teach in a different way than they were taught would provide an eye into the important school reform movement at large.

Educators who work with juvenile offenders have special personal and professionally related needs that are not addressed in current certification programs. Some of these specific, correctional education needs were issues of care and control, methods for effective classroom instruction, special education training, and access to relevant curriculum (Abramson, 1991; Drakeford, 2002; Foley & Gao, 2002; Kilgore & Meade, 2004; and Wright, 2004). Additionally, research has uncovered a shortage of studies that examined current theory and practice in the correctional classroom that informed teaching and learning in the unique correctional culture.

Given that the recidivism rate for juveniles was high (Kilgore & Meade, 2004), research on the influence correctional education had upon recidivism rates of juveniles in correctional facilities should provide insight into further practice. Since there were no specific correctional credentialing programs in place, studying their effectiveness would prove difficult; therefore, a study that examined the current in-service programs specific to correctional education may inform the field. Research aimed at ascertaining the effectiveness of these programs upon the correctional educator would inform future goals.

Abramson (1991) saw a need for enhanced student voice through critical curriculum because active student participation "has been associated with an increase in the goal-directed behavior incompatible with self-defeating, anti-social activity" (p. 91). Furthermore, Kilgore and Meade (2004) saw a need for correctional programs to bring social activities to the classroom supported by social constructivist theory. To realize these recommendations, preparation for correctional educators would need to promote methods associated with critical theory and social constructivist theory rather than the current empirical-analytical theory based curriculum. Critical theory would also enhance the voice of the correctional educator by bringing the expert—the educator who has the experience in the correction classroom—to the table to inform decisions made about the field. Additional research analyzing the effects of America's political climate on correctional education theory and practice would inform future correctional education policy decisions.

A possible solution to the problem of correctional educator preparation was found in the teacher interns program described by McKibbin (1999). Since California provides credentials for correctional educators through the same paths as regular K-12 classrooms and education in state juvenile facilities through county offices of education, it follows that correctional educators have already been prepared and credentialed in teacher intern programs and, therefore, research conducted on these educators would benefit the field. Although further study would confirm the assertion, the solutions would still require many added components that the internship program is missing along with components such as a foundational history of the profession. Correctional educators prepared through teaching intern programs could receive specific support that would include seasoned correctional educators' voices. However, few trained professional correctional educators are available to conduct these programs. Therefore an academic field of study resulting in postgraduate degrees (taught by experienced correctional educators?) seems appropriate.

Some Concluding Remarks

California Commission on Teacher Credentialing (1997) confirms "if teachers' expertise, capabilities, and accomplishments are to be enriched over time, the teachers must become reflective practitioners who actively seek to strengthen and augment their professional skills, knowledge and perspectives throughout their careers" (2). This quote, along with the other evidence presented in this chapter, provokes the question: What makes a highly qualified correctional educator? As for the second question; yes, the correctional education profession should require special credentials for this decidedly specific set of skills.

As part of the movement to professionalize the field of correctional education, I conduct a one- to two-hour workshop with teachers new to our department. I do reading exercises with them that introduce them to the history of their new field. I show them the web sites where they can glean the important information required for professional growth in their field. And, I tell them the story of one of my favorite heroes in correctional education history, William George of the George Junior Republic. I believe one of the most important contributions we can make to society is the professionalization of the correctional education field, because high-quality correctional education reduces recidivism. The path to high-quality correctional education is through high-quality programs that address curriculum theory issues, bring correctional education foundational history to educators, address the control and behavior issues that are found in most facilities and, above all, create a community of and give a voice to high-quality correctional educators.

By the way, I am glad I applied for that correctional education position!

CHAPTER X

THE PROFESSOR IN PRISON: REFLECTIONS

by Stephen Duguid

The point of intersection between biography and professional practice is a slippery one, shifting as the actor changes over time (i.e. accumulates more "biography") and as the context for practice evolves. In my case the engagement with prison education lasted well over twenty years and, during that time, the ground on which that engagement took place shifted from classroom to program to research to administration and back again. And now, some distance from any real presence in prisons or in the professional field of prison education, my engagement is mostly reflection.

I entered prison in September 1973. It was not a professional choice. I was a graduate student in the midst of a doctorate program designed to secure me a career as a historian. But, like so many of the students I was to encounter, I was driven to prison by financial need. Two young children, a sudden evaporation of job opportunities and a general lack of practical skills had me applying for jobs in the strangest of places, prison seeming at the time—in a very real sense—the end of the line.

Unlike many university types with prison teaching experience, I did not just "drop in" to teach a course or two. I was hired full time by the University of Victoria's brand new Correctional Education Program at the British Columbia Penitentiary and at the Matsqui Medium Security Institution. After a year as an itinerant history instructor bouncing between the two prisons every other day, I became the local administrator/teacher at the Matsqui site and remained in that position until 1980.

I was a classic "product of the sixties" (which really lasted until at least 1972) and was fortunate in many ways to miss the 1970s altogether. An anti-war activist, student radical, early tree-hugger, small-is-beautiful advocate and budding Marxist, I would have been a prison administrator's worst nightmare (if they had ever bothered to look). But people were more tolerant then, even in prison. In that claustrophobic and timeless world of the prison, my teacher peers and I were able to prolong the cultural and political world of the 1960s well after it had passed in the real world, or "the street" as the prisoners called it.

So here, then, is the first intersection point between biography and professional practice, the imposition of a specific set of beliefs and assumptions that were biographically derived from a completely foreign realm of professional practice. The prisoner-students had, by and large, missed the 1960s, being too busy, too imprisoned or too drug-addled to notice the "revolution." And since we had been so singularly unsuccessful at bringing about a cooperative, peaceful and progressive change on "the street," this seemed a golden opportunity to try again, but in a more confined and manageable space.

But, of course, we did not see it quite so clearly, our primary interest being teaching and earning a living. In retrospect it seems clear that in the early 1970s we carried into the prison education program a varied but still coherent agenda based on some fundamental principles, which in turn shaped the assumptions from which we worked. So what were some of those key assumptions that I brought with me into the prison in 1973, and how did they become part of the prison education program? I can identify three:

1. Based on a critique of existing institutions in the wider society and influenced by the work of Michel Foucault, I was easily persuaded that the function and form of prisons are much the same everywhere, consisting of some combination of punishment, deterrence and rehabilitation. Between the prison and the prisoner there is then a fundamentally unbridgeable antagonistic relationship. Anything the prison attempts to do with or to the imprisoned will be greeted with fear, skepticism or loathing. Therefore, any hope for individual change on the part of the imprisoned individuals must come from interaction with "outsiders," individuals and organizations not linked to the prison or to the correctional enterprise. It seemed crucial to me that to offer a critique of crime to the prisoner, one also had to maintain a critical stance toward the criminal justice system.

2. Much of the energy of the 1960s had originated in a rejection of patterns, domino theories and other "forces of history" arguments, insisting instead that one could choose to follow different paths. In confronting the prison, then, I argued from the start that most criminal activity has a strong element of choice in its origin. That is, most criminals are not helplessly "driven" to crime by poverty, ignorance or illness. Choices involve decisions, which in turn engage both reason (critical thinking) and ethics (moral assessments). And as an educator I was convinced that the most direct and powerful way to enhance critical thinking and become more cognizant of moral issues was via education, particularly education in the humanities and social sciences.

3. Thanks to imbibing the ideas of Herbert Marcuse, Saul Alinsky, Noam Chomsky and other activist intellectuals and being enamored (unwisely, as it turned out) of the politics of Maoist China, it was clear to me that for new ideas, perspectives or stages in personal development genuinely to take root in an individual, there must be a connection between education and action. New ways of thinking and new moral values must be linked to opportunities in which they can be tried, tested and modified to fit. There must, then, be a social and even a political dimension to any prison education program that attempts to address cognitive and moral change.

There were no doubt others, but thinking in threes is always a good idea and these were the assumptions that had the most profound effect on the model post-secondary prison education program that I participated in building in Canada from 1973 to 1993.

That model, formally constructed around certain theories of cognitive and moral development, provided a dynamic and flexible framework within which individual educators could work. And while the teachers and administrators of the University of Victoria/Simon Fraser University program (1973-1993) each brought their own assumptions, skills and talents to the program, it was my job, first at Matsqui Institution and then later as director of the program at all four prisons, to try to keep the model vibrant, organic and coherent. Reflecting on this process now, I can appreciate more fully the role that these assumptions played in making this happen, in keeping the overall program both innovative and consistent.

My initial assumption that there were irreconcilable conflicts between prisoner and prison meant that, for good or ill, we went to great lengths in the operation of each of our programs to ensure our students perceived us to be distinct from the prison. Of course, we had to simultaneously maintain relations with prison staff and the correctional system *per se* that were at least civil, and certainly cooperative if not cordial. Our insistence on a separation from the correctional enterprise, therefore, had to have a basis in a theory, a rationale beyond mere preference or prejudice. Hence we developed, or rather borrowed, the idea of the "just community" from the work of Lawrence Kohlberg and Peter Scharf at Harvard and even at times veered somewhat dangerously toward the more well-known theories supporting therapeutic communities. Our version, the "democratic community," could only operate in a kind of "splendid isolation" from the necessarily authoritarian prison community.

Basing our desire for self-governing school units, for the privacy of student transcripts (when little else of the prisoner's possessions were private), for "academic freedom" in terms of courses, texts and staff, and for non-interference by custody staff on an established theory enabled us to argue that our relative independence or autonomy was an essential component of the program itself. Indeed we argued that it was a key element in the rehabilitative hope that the program (and the correctional service) saw as the basis for its presence in the prison. And since we tended to attract some of the most "difficult" prisoners in the prisons, correctional staff were generally quite willing to give us the rope by which we might end up hanging ourselves.

My second assumption, that choice or decision-making is a more likely foundation for human action than social determinations such as class or ethnicity, placed us at the center of some very controversial issues in criminology and corrections. A strong case can be made that most people in prison are, to varying degrees, products or victims of their life circumstances. It seemed obvious, however, that nothing that took place during imprisonment—which involved a complete removal from those circumstances—could affect the social, economic, ethnic or gender dimensions of their lives. What could be affected, however, was the manner in which they thought about these circumstances and the moral guidelines they could employ in responding to them after release. Faith in the potential for making better and more socially progressive choices in the future was perhaps a slender reed upon which to base our hopes for lowering recidivism, but it was the best to which we had access.

So we amplified the role of choice in human affairs, making it—perhaps unrealistically—more powerful than the forces that so often restrict or stifle choice. We were careful, however, to avoid the medical, psychological or illness approach, which placed the cause for poor choices squarely on the individual. Instead, responding to our own analyses of the political struggles of the 1960s, we argued that even if we are often unable to choose the circumstances within which we must make decisions, we remain active decision-makers. Our task was to find ways to use education, specifically courses in literature, history, philosophy, psychology and related disciplines, as a means of exploring the concept of choice and the choices of others.

But—and this is where the third assumption entered the model—a simple awareness of options or of the mechanics of decision-making or critical thinking was not necessarily going to lead to action in the world. The educational model we were intent on creating came out of an activist, dynamic tradition of social change. We were convinced that for ideas to take hold, for new values to be internalized, there had to be a way to employ them in real (not simulated or paper-and-pencil) situations. And so we began the most difficult task of all: creating situations within the prison education program in which the students could exercise decision-making.

I have written about this "just community" or "democratic community" at some length and there is no need to retell all those stories here, but instead I refer the reader to the references below. Obviously this objective was never easy to implement, whether in maximum- or medium-security institutions. The withdrawal of decision-making is one of the hallmarks of incarceration and we went to great lengths both to create situations and to convince the students to utilize them. It was in the struggle to create functioning democratic communities within the prison programs that I gained important insights about institutions and individuals. On the one hand, I was impressed at the ability of authoritarian institutions not just to compel obedience, but also to transform the objects of their authority into authoritarians themselves—the prisoners understood the system and accepted, even admired it. On the other hand, I was even more impressed by the students' eagerness to try cooperative and democratic practices even when severely limited in scope and power, in effect focusing on the "local" when larger areas of power remained out of bounds.

Interestingly, the research on the effectiveness of the program showed the theater activities—sponsored by or spun off from the university program— had perhaps the greatest impact. Each of the program sites had an active theater program that often included putting on performances for an "outside" audience. Theater productions are a cooperative, ostensibly democratic and crisis-ridden process and it was men who were involved in those theater productions that showed the most remarkable post-release transformations (Duguid, 1998b). This was, in a classic research term, an "unintended outcome" and testament to the importance of avoiding the "one-size-fits-all" approach to prison programming.

These "transformations," or at least improvements over expectations, were explored in a major assessment of the effectiveness of the British Columbia university prison education program carried out from 1993-96, thanks to a major research grant from the Federal government in 1998. Unfortunately, the Correctional Service of Canada, an arm of the same Federal government, decided to cancel the program's funding as part of a series of budget cuts and shifting programming priorities (Duguid, 1998a).

I was already employed full time at the university and involved with many other projects and my engagement with prison education since 1996 had been more reflective than proactive. My assessment of the British Columbia twenty-year program is that, successful as it was, the most difficult task in initiatives like this is renewal. Sad as I was—and even angry for a while—to see the program disappear, I had to acknowledge that it had become stale, ossified and taken for granted by students and staff. There had been a vibrant early period of creation and development, an energy boost during an earlier (1983) attempt at closure, and a dynamic period of expansion in programming and in "presence." But by the early 1990s, much of the energy and innovative spirit was ebbing. The staff meeting minutes are dominated by arguments about salaries and "time off," the key players were beginning to look elsewhere for personal satisfaction and the students increasingly saw the program as a "right" and a "given."

Even more important, the prison itself and the correctional professionals linked to it were no longer willing to tolerate a free-standing, almost alien body within their world. Program bits and pieces were borrowed and molded into competitive activities like "cognitive skills" that subsequently became mandatory. And so it was, perhaps, time to leave.

In the meantime, it is fair to ask in turn what kind of impact the prison experience had on me. It was transformative to be sure. I entered the prison in 1973 as a narrowly trained historian and emerged wedded forever to interdisciplinary teaching and research. As in so many small, off-campus programs, I worked closely with colleagues in other disciplines and learned to appreciate the importance of breadth and depth of knowledge. And, I watched how students chose to be attracted to different subject areas and how each could work its own magic. I learned a lot about collegiality and the value-added possibilities of learning within a community. My democratic instincts were affirmed, but with a strong dose of realism as I saw how difficult it was to persuade people to exercise their rights and how seductive and attractive authoritarian structures can be, even to their victims.

Having entered the prison in 1973 thinking I had reached the "end of the line" in terms of teaching possibilities, I quickly discovered the reality was quite different. I often shock even my current graduate students by telling them they are almost as good as the men I taught in prison. I suspect our prisons do not reflect a true cross-section of the population, but rather are weighted toward the top and the bottom in terms of skills, ability and intelligence. I encountered some very bright people who challenged me at every turn and I am sure I learned as much as they did in the experience. Certainly I learned how to teach.

I also came away from the experience with a commitment to accountability. Prison education may indeed fall under the rubric of "good works," but as long as tax dollars are paying for it, the public and their government is entitled to know if it is effective, and also what "effectiveness" means. I have over the years taken a lot of "heat" for trying to show that education, properly conceived and delivered, can have a positive impact on rates of recidivism. I am grateful that our students delivered the goods.

Inmates at New York's Auburn prison under Thomas Mott Osborne's influence there in 1914. Note the Mutual Welfare League banners, a symbol of the inmates' democratic organization. In some ways, League activities demonstrated that the principles underlying the British Columbia Postsecondary program could be effective.

CHAPTER XI

FROM OUTSIDE TO INSIDE:
PEDAGOGY WITHIN PRISON WALLS

by Cormac Behan

Introduction

This chapter explores how educators working in prison might achieve their goals. As imprisonment becomes wider, longer and deeper, we should reflect on the concept of imprisonment as a political construct. I will argue that our goals as educators can be realized only if we locate our pedagogy within the adult education tradition. This theoretical framework seeks to locate learning in its social context. We must constantly explore ways to circumvent the negative aspects of imprisonment. It is, therefore, essential to analyze the prison in its social, cultural and political context if we are to create the space, as both educators and learners, for a positive pedagogical experience.

Prison Damages People

Prison damages people. It damages those who are committed there, those who send them there, those who guard them, and those who work in the various social and educational services. Society suffers by using it as a method to punish those who have transgressed accepted norms. Those who enter prison will find an environment, architecture, regime and a stultifying atmosphere that is alien to the human condition. It is an unnatural place. It is a horrific institution but one which society seems incapable of doing without. It is a confused institution with little overall direction or sense of its place in society. The prison regime is regimented yet chaotic, structured yet undisciplined, aimless yet full of regulation, ideologically driven yet unsure of its direction.

There is little public debate about the nature of prison, its usefulness, its aims or alternative methods of punishing those who violate social codes. Despite this, the prison population throughout the world is increasing as the policy of "Prison Works" is more widely adopted. In the U.S. over the past twenty years, the numbers incarcerated have nearly quadrupled, reaching two million in 2002 (U.S. Department of Justice, 2003).

Great Britain shares a similar story. Between 1992 and 2000 it experienced a 50 percent increase in the numbers sent to prison, rising from 40,600 in 1992 to 63,000 in 2000 (James, 2001). By February 2004, the prison population had reached nearly 75,000 (Morris, 2004).

The situation in Ireland is also alarming. There the number of prisoners increased from 2,210 in 1995 to 3,200 by 2003, nearly a 50 percent increase in less than ten years (Irish Prison Service, 2004). We should remember that the size of the prison population "is neither determined by, nor determines the level of crime. It is largely a symbolic gesture, politically decided" (Morgan, 1997, p. 1184).

Mountjoy Prison, opened in 1850, which originally held prisoners awaiting transportation to Van Diemen's Land, is being phased out as this book is in press.

The penal system is a social and political construction, a reflection of society. As the Irish Criminologist Paul O'Mahony has written:

> A nation's prison system is a cultural product, shaped by prevailing social, political and moral values and attitudes. How a nation defines crime and reacts to it and specifically, how it punishes or fails to punish criminals is a question of central importance, which reflects the core values of a society and is definitive in its essential character. (O'Mahony, 1997, p. 152)

Despite near universal acceptance of an institution that represents our society, we know relatively little about the reality of prison life or the effect it has on the individual.

> The ordinary citizen, with his own home, free to come and go as he pleases, able to choose his company and pastimes, finds it difficult to visualize the lot of a prisoner, confined within a forbidding perimeter and bleak environment, shut up alone in a cell for sixteen hours of everyday, his movement restricted at every turn by locks and bars, his daily regime one of utter predictability and barely tolerable monotony, under constant observation and

thus enjoying no privacy, his correspondence censored, his visits regulated and supervised, no time in private with loved ones. (Department of Justice, 1985, p. 38)

The penal system and the prison regime are the context in which prison educators operate. Education is not a neutral technology that can be removed from the situation in which it finds itself (Thomas, 1995, p. 3). As correctional educators, we should not only reflect on prison as an institution but also give ourselves the space and opportunity to explore how education can achieve a positive transformation in a place that one inmate claimed can "change you for the worst...that gets inside you and eats away at you like a cancer" (National Economic and Social Forum, 2002, p. 41). Drawing on my teaching experience in prison and examining Irish and European prison education policy, this chapter will inquire how we might achieve, for both educator and learner, a positive pedagogical experience. It will examine the prison regime, explore its effects on the individual and suggest that locating our practice within an adult education framework is essential to create conditions where education might be successful behind prison walls. As a practitioner in prison education, I am convinced we must look beyond our role as educators and challenge the current orthodoxy of penal policy. We should engage in a vigorous and challenging debate about our position within the prison system and how educators and students might become reflective agents for change within the educational sphere, the penal system and throughout wider society.

According to Paulo Freire, the objective of adult educators is to "fight alongside the people for the recovery of the people's stolen humanity" (Freire, 1970, p. 75-76). Those who end up in prison have usually hurt others and also harmed themselves. Those who convict them have been adversely affected, as are those who work within the prison walls. Society has been damaged by the need for such a bizarre, strange and abnormal institution as a prison. Therefore, the challenge for educators is to try to recover the humanity of the individual who has caused suffering, those they have hurt and those who work in such abominable places. We should try also to stimulate debate in society on the continued use of imprisonment as a form of punishment.

Architecture, Routine and Regime

The objectives of prison include punishment, retribution, deterrence and reformation. Erving Goffman's study of what he termed "Total Institutions," including prisons, concluded it is widely accepted that they "fall considerably short of their official aims" (Goffman, 1961, p. 80-81). Prison deprives freedom yet seeks to transform the individual, usually overlooking the fact that the former is essential to achieve the latter. The prison system creates a regime that is concerned primarily with security. It is an institutionalized bureaucracy, which takes little account of the subtleties of the individual. Despite the best intentions of the most well-meaning staff, the individual needs, desires and wants of the incarcerated are subsumed in an attempt to normalize the deprivation of liberty.

Architecture can be creative or destructive. Prison architecture is rarely the former. Prisons are designed to discourage, not promote independence. However, prisons are merely a physical outgrowth of the political, social and cultural construction of the penal system. The earlier Irish and British prisons were based on the Benthamite Panopticon model of Pentonville Prison in London, built in 1842. The Benthamite Panopticon or "all seeing eye" should allow perfect vision into every cell, to keep a watchful eye on the prisoner and oversee his/her reformation. While most prisons did not follow exactly this model, many were built around wings, each observable from a control unit, which contains the officers' administrative area. A large window in the circle's roof was to allow the light of moral goodness to shine on the darkness below.

Advocates of this new form of punishment had found their utopia in one single structure. "The theme of the Panopticon–at once surveillance and observation, security and knowledge, individualization and tantalization, isolation and transparence–is found in the prison, its privileged locus of realization" (Foucault, 1977, p. 249). The prisons built during this period in the United Kingdom (including Ireland) "stand as monuments to an age in which they existed both to deter the rising urban proletariat from crime and as models of muscular Christian punishment" (Glancey, 2002, p. 16). While the Christian ethos may no longer dominate, the objective of using prison to deter the urban proletariat from crime still exists. The form of the prison as an all-encompassing, inward-looking space leaves no doubt about its function. Punishment and retribution triumph over reformation and transformation in the design. The architecture constantly reminds one that prison is for punishment, not transformation.

It is characteristic of total institutions that "all phases of the day's activities are tightly scheduled, with one activity leading at a prearranged time into the next" (Goffman, 1961, p. 17). Foucault, writing about the 1830s prison system noted how the regime:

> ...not only in a day, but in the succession of days and even years, may regulate for the man the time of waking and sleeping, of activity and rest, the number and duration of meals, the quality and ration of food, the nature and product of labor, the time of prayer...It takes possession of man as a whole, of all the physical and moral faculties that are in him and of the time in which he is himself. (Foucault, 1977, p. 236)

This daily routine contrasts significantly with a prisoner's previous lifestyle, which has usually been chaotic and unregulated. Many inmates never attended school regularly and few held a job for a prolonged period. "From the terror, boredom and ecstasy of the criminal lifestyle, the state prescribes, indeed demands, a transition to the 'silent heroism of daily living'" (Duguid, 2000, p. 17). The pattern of daily life in prison has changed remarkably little over the last century. Irish prisoners still spend up to two-thirds of their day in cells leaving little time to carry out their daily activities. Erwin James, the prison correspondent for *The Guardian*, recorded his thoughts on the daily routine seventeen years into his life sentence:

> Prison life is mostly a continuous repetition of the same day over and over again. Finding a purpose beyond 'punishment' can be a struggle. Often people are not in long enough to discover anything worthwhile beyond a new set of criminal alliances. Or people end up inside for so long that any good that might have been achieved along the way is undermined by bitterness and resentment. (James, 2001, p. 3)

This daily routine of imprisonment works against prisoners taking responsibility, deciding to take control of their lives, as all aspects of their day are set out by the institution. Inside the total institution there is lifestyle disruption and rejection of the idea that one is an adult with self-determination, autonomy and freedom of action (Goffman, 1961, p. 47). Foucault described the prison as the "darkest region in the apparatus of justice...it silently organizes a field of objectivity in which punishment will be able to function openly as treatment and the sentence be inscribed among the discourses of knowledge" (Foucault, 1977, p. 256). However, individuals at the center of what is called the rehabilitative process are rarely asked what may be best for them. The subjectivity of the individual is rarely considered. The prisoners' subjective sense of self, including their ideas, beliefs and emotions that are essential for education, are ignored by the institutionalized bureaucracy that claims to know what is best for the individual. Upon sentencing, the mortification process of the individual begins.

> The recruit comes into the establishment with a conception of himself made possible by certain stable social arrangements in his home world. Upon entrance, he is immediately stripped of the support provided by these arrangements. In the accurate language of some of our oldest total institutions, he begins a series of abasements, degradations, humiliations, and profanations of self. He is systematically, if often unintentionally, mortified. (Goffman, 1961, p. 69)

The prison regime dehumanizes the individual. It is a bureaucratic apparatus for the maintenance of an institution. It can radically alter the perception of one's self as supports and networks are removed. Conditions are so different from those prevailing in the outside world that they make it extremely difficult to prepare for life outside the prison. "Everything the inmate encounters is a substitute for reality—artificial friends, superficial work, artificial education, artificial relationships, no proper privacy, no proper identity, no proper time of day" (Department of Justice, 1985, p. 91). Prison creates an artificial individual with a created subjectivity. Living in this artificial world, the self:

...is not the property of the person to whom it is attributed, but dwells rather in the pattern of social control that is exerted in connection with the person by himself and those around him. This special kind of institutional arrangement does not so much support the self as constitute it. (Goffman, 1997, p. 69)

A virtual prison industry has arisen with specialists seeking to understand and gain insight into the mind of the prisoner. We are led to believe this is necessary, as we cannot easily understand the prisoner in the same light as the non-prison population. Their previous self destroyed, we try to understand the new self created by the institution. One researcher, having examined the files in various prisons, was "struck by the repetition of the word 'insight' (as in lack thereof) and by its apparent multiple meanings as it is deployed by psychologists, psychiatrists, core management officers, parole officers, counselors, parole board members and prisoners themselves" (Duguid, 2000, p. 48). If we had an insight into the mind of the prisoner then we could rehabilitate her or him and make the individual conform to society. We might be able to destroy the deviancy in the individual. Unfortunately the prison regime, in setting out to destroy the deviancy in the individual, can end up destroying the individuality of the deviant. To understand the subjectivity of an individual, it is essential to listen. All those involved in this prison industry are keen to have their understanding, observation and characterization of the individual recorded. Yet while we try to understand the individual, we can neglect to appreciate the effect the regime has on the self. Prison peels back the layers of self and leaves the individual naked. It can strip the individual of all responsibility, dignity and humanity. It is impossible for one who has not been incarcerated to understand the reality of prison life. An American inmate explains:

To describe what it means to be a prisoner, how it feels to be confined is impossible for one who has not experienced it. The psychological state of complete passivity and dependence on the decisions of the guards and officers must be included among the pains of imprisonment, along with the restriction of physical liberty, the possession of goods and services and heterosexual relations...The imprisoned criminal finds his picture of himself as a self-determining individual being destroyed by the regime of the custodian. (Duguid, 2000, p. 83)

After arriving in prison many years previously, Erwin James wrote how, after an inquiry into prison riots, he began to reflect on what society thought of prisoners:

Prison was no doubt necessary. But it was unsettling that prison life was such a mystery to society. There seemed an assumption among the outside world that people in prison were inherently different. Prisoners were not individuals but a collective, with the same crude standards, values and culture—a sub-race almost. (James, 2001, p. 3)

Human beings are sent to prison. They are transformed from people into prisoners. They are given labels: prisoner and, upon release, ex-prisoner. "The automatic identification of the inmate is not merely name calling; it is at the center of a basic means of social control" (Goffman, 1961, p. 81). Their individuality destroyed, they are made something apart. Not only are they inside the prison, they are also now outside society. We now redefine them. The person becomes the label we have given them. It is an extraordinary label. Even to reflect on the word "prison" can be a powerful experience. All the labels are weapons in the dehumanizing process. When persons are committed to prison they become prisoners. When they are released, they become ex-prisoners. If they are allowed out temporarily, they are still a prisoner on TR, temporary release. If they flee, they are escaped prisoners. The governor of the institution is a prison governor; those who guard them are prison officers. Those who teach them are prison teachers. Those who wish to reform the system are prison reformers. Prison becomes the defining characteristic of the new imprisoned individual and everybody that is concerned with the place.

The labeling of prisoners is a very determined action in the process of humiliation. It is another step in removing the human being's individuality. Although typically examined in the context of how it will affect their employment, housing prospects and life chances, labeling's impact is far more serious. This branding can remain with the individual throughout his or her life, both officially and unofficially. Labeling damages self-esteem and takes away individuality, further mortifying their being. Even the Irish government's report conceded that denial of liberty is not the only punishment a prisoner must endure.

> Such deprivations and constraints are not all a prisoner suffers. They are usually accompanied by social stigmatization for life, a lowering of dignity and self-esteem, reinforcement of feelings of inadequacy, diminished scope for moral responsibility, loss of self-confidence, depression, a stronger inclination towards the criminal sub-culture and towards institutionalization and, in many cases irretrievable breakdown in family life and relationships. (Department of Justice, 1985, p. 38)

Prison disables the individual, taking from the person attributes necessary for critical reflection. In many cases the individual is cut off from the social supports necessary for humanity to survive. The daily routine is stifling, the architecture is claustrophobic and the regime at times so harmful that it becomes difficult to overcome. The characteristics which imprisonment denies are essential for a positive educational experience. To enter a classroom each day when the regime, the atmosphere and the system are so negative, one must question whether education can achieve any positive results in such an institution. Learning involves "the integrated functioning of the total organism—thinking, feeling, perceiving and behaving" (Kolb, 1993, p. 148). As Kolb noted:

> Learning is the major process of human adaptation. This concept of learning is considerably broader than that commonly associated with the school classroom. It occurs in all human settings, from schools to the workplace, from the research laboratory to the management boardroom, in personal relationships and the aisles of the local grocery store. (Kolb, 1993, p. 149)

Achievement of this total organism of thinking, feeling, perceiving and behaving becomes all the more difficult in such a stultifying regime. To suggest that merely attending school daily will achieve a positive educational experience fails to take account of the regime's negative aspects. To merely provide a school and teachers will not necessarily create the opportunity for a constructive learning experience. It, therefore, challenges us as educators to explore how to foster a positive learning environment in such an institution.

Discourse, Dialogue and Co-operation

As prison educators we need to reflect on our role by trying to define the philosophical ideas that underpin our practice. Prison educators should strive to create a theoretical framework that informs their thinking. We must be especially careful of the pitfalls of working within the penal system and avoid being subsumed into the agenda of the correctional and justice departments. As educators in prison, we must define our own agenda, located in the integrity of our profession. We must distinguish our practice from the criminogenic courses provided by the justice departments and also reject the banking concept of education (Freire, 1970) that seeks to promote the mere accumulation of knowledge or the acquisition of skills. The traditional education system has generally failed to fulfill our learners' needs. Therefore we must devise new curricula, create new methods of determining success, move away from the traditional educational structure and strive to achieve something new. We can explore ways to achieve these goals in the adult education tradition.

Prison education should take the best adult education practices from outside and bring them into prison. The adult education approach takes a holistic attitude toward education as it aims to respond to the needs of the whole person; promotes a wide and varied curriculum; develops flexible and adaptable programs; creates a needs-based learning plan for students; and, strives for a free space where critical thinking is promoted on the basis of mutuality, trust, respect and equality. Educators in prison should promote the concept of Mezirow's Transformative Learning, encouraging practitioners to strive for the conditions to achieve dialogue that is open, free and equal.

Some examples of this adult education approach that might inspire our theoretical framework can be found in the Irish and European policy documents. Irish prison education policy is largely based on *Education in Prison* (Council of Europe, 1990), *The Management of Offenders* (Department of Justice, 1994) and the *Strategy Statement of the Prison Education Service 2003-2007* (Irish Prison Education Service, 2004).

The Council of Europe policy document *Education in Prison* (1990) argues that "the education of prisoners must in its philosophy, methods and content, be brought as close as possible to the best adult education in society outside" (Council of Europe, 1990, p. 14). The educators who drafted the Council of Europe policies on inmate education recognized that prison "by its very nature is abnormal and destructive of the personality in a number of ways" (Council of Europe, 1990, p. 15). However, they argued that education has the "capacity to render the situation less abnormal, to limit somewhat the damage done to men and women through prison" (Council of Europe, 1990, p. 13). Every effort shall be made to ensure that the regimes of the institutions are designed and managed so as "the conditions of life are compatible with human dignity and acceptable standards in the community" (Council of Europe, 1987, p. 20).

The Council of Europe,
created after WW II to promote human rights, meets in Strasbourg, France.

The Irish Prison Education Service's *Strategy Statement* (2004) outlined the aims of the education service. These include a commitment "to provide a high quality, broad and flexible program of education that meets the needs of those in custody" (p. 4). Education in prison should help prisoners to "cope with their sentence; achieve personal development; prepare for life after release and establish the appetite and capacity for lifelong learning" (Irish Prison Education Service, 2004, p. 20). Mezirow's concept of Transformative

Learning provides a framework that may help us pursue our pedagogy in a prison environment.

Transformation theory (Mezirow & Associates, 1990) is a theoretical model that suggests adults learn as a result of transforming frames of reference. A frame of reference is the structure of assumptions within which sense perceptions are interpreted and by so doing, experience is created. Assumptions are beliefs about reality that are taken for granted and usually unquestioned. A more fully developed frame of reference is one that is more inclusive, differentiating, more integrative of experience and more open to alternative perspectives.

> Transformative learning is the process of becoming aware through critical reflection of the frame of reference in which one thinks, feels, and acts. It involves becoming aware of its genesis in one's individual history and/or culture, the search for a new more developed frame, and acting on the basis of the new frame of reference. (Fleming 2002, pp. 3-4)

Brookfield (1987) argues that critical thinking can only develop when we accept that the experience will be uncomfortable, ambiguous, tentative, uncertain and evolving. A key element in any transformative learning experience is that individuals must decide to seek change, to challenge their frame of reference and their assumptions, and to take responsibility for their actions. The prison regime dulls the senses and can create a comfort zone, which goes against the opportunity for critical reflection. Mezirow (1999) has written that the process of transforming frames of reference begins with critical reflection, with assessing one's own assumptions and presuppositions. To engage in critical reflection should leave one uncomfortable and challenged. The prison creates an environment that works against this. Ironically, the lack of responsibility provides safety in the comfort zone. There is little opportunity for ambiguity, uncertainty or feelings of insecurity in such a stifling routine.

Educators are constantly seeking opportunities and places for domination-free discourse. Learners and educators must have trust and empathic solidarity with those participating in discourse; freedom from coercion, equal opportunity to participate in discussion and all must have the opportunity to have their voices heard (Mezirow, 1996, 1999). There are few places in the total institution where the regime does not interfere, where students can be themselves, free from coercion. However, if the regime has not fully destroyed the self, the school or classroom might provide an opportunity for discourse because "in order to have full, free participation in discourse there must be freedom, equality, tolerance, justice and a valuing of rationality" (Fleming, 1998, p. 10). And there are always possibilities, because even in coercive institutions there are free spaces.

Goffman believed that total institutions have places of vulnerability. Space—to discuss, challenge and survive by undermining the regime's

128

monotony using what he calls removal activities—can be found in the most unlikely places. These are activities where individuals can get lost, experiencing a temporary blotting out of a sense of the environment in which they live (Goffman, 1977, p. 84).

> The study of Total Institutions also suggests that formal organizations have standard places of vulnerability, such as supply rooms, sick bays, kitchens, or scenes of highly technical labor. These are the damp corners where secondary adjustments breed and start to infest the establishment. (Goffman, 1997, p. 82).

The prison school can be a place of vulnerability as the classroom environment is one of the few areas of the prison where prisoners have the ultimate freedom to express themselves. It is a legitimate way to overcome the establishment. The creation of an autonomous educational space gives the learner the freedom to engage in critical enquiry. This encourages enquiry of the self as well as society, even going as far as challenging the whole penal system. The Council of Europe recognized this when it reminded prison educators that while criminal activity should not be condoned:

> There are aspects of the prisoner's culture, which the adult educator must respect, or at least accept. These aspects may include a critical view of authority, anger at social injustice, solidarity with one another in the face of adversity etc. As in the field of adult education, respect and acceptance of the students and potential students are crucial to their motivation and participation. (Council of Europe, 1990, p. 127)

The Council of Europe's *Education in Prison* (1990) and the Irish Prison Education Services' *Strategy Statement* (2004), written by educators, promote access to education as a fundamental human right. The stress on education as a human right poses the question: How to promote and safeguard those rights? This might be achieved through a transformative learning process where rights are guaranteed, not by governments or more specifically by justice departments and prison authorities, but by a full development of a human rights perspective from the student themselves. In a participative democracy and a learning society, the people are the ultimate guarantors of human rights both inside and outside prison. Encouraging students to become agents for change, both inside school and throughout the penal system, is the best way to promote human dignity. We, as adult educators working in a prison environment, have roles to play in this process. As Mezirow noted:

> Although adult educators do not become leaders, advocates or organizers of collective social action, they may help learners learn how to assume these roles, to anticipate and plan to overcome constraining situational factors, to deal with emotional resistance

to taking action or to find relevant information needed to act. The social context is of great importance in determining whether transformative learning will result in collective social action. (Mezirow, 1996, p. 12)

While prison attempts to normalize the deprivation of liberty, we should endeavor to create autonomy for students within the school environment. It is essential that as educators we bring our practice from the outside into the prison to try to create pedagogy within prison walls. Drawing on our professional integrity we should try to create a positive learning space similar to our attempts to achieve this in any pedagogical environment in the community. In his analysis of the 1987 *European Prison Rules*, Tulkens reminded us not only of the limitations of imprisonment but also of the possibilities.

If you go on using imprisonment you have to at least try hard to make it as harmless as possible for the prisoners. Therefore; listen to them, take account of their opinions, make them co-operate and assume responsibilities; on the other hand, do not be over ambitious as to what can be achieved or what can be promised, but offer prisoners consequently realistic and attainable opportunities, chances, activities and help which meet their needs and stimulate their interest. (Tulkens, in Warner, 2002b, pp. 34-35)

From the Personal to the Theoretical

There are a number of ways I have encouraged students to take responsibility in the school/classroom. Allowing them to present a class on a topic of their choice is one method. Initially students are hesitant because of a lack of confidence and experience. But a successful outcome to this class can be transformative for students as they receive a confidence boost and positive peer affirmation. The recognition of their potential can start the process of self-belief, leading them toward the concept of human agency. As the Council of Europe (1990) notes, we should not hesitate to take on controversial social and political issues in the learning space, as these are issues that inform our learners' lifeworld. Discussions on a range of issues can be facilitated; even reflection on the concept of imprisonment and the social and political context of the prison is possible, while remaining critical of a prisoner's activities.

Bringing the outside into the prison can be a very empowering experience for a group. Students can organize this activity by inviting in a public speaker/visitor of their choice. There are certain constraints to this activity (i.e. contacting an individual directly) but once these are overcome, students can take control of the process. They can decide the agenda, write a leaflet to be distributed to each cell and design a poster for the various parts of the prison. They can also prepare resources for the visitor and other students. A student can chair the meeting. This can be a very empowering experience, creating independence not only for the students who organize the event but for all the students who leave behind their surroundings for a period in an autonomous learning space. It gives students the opportunity to take responsibility, stimulates their interest and encourages them to reflect on their capacity as independent individuals regardless of the institution.

Another method of trying to achieve autonomy in the learning space is organizing debates with outside schools/universities. This can be an ideal opportunity for prisoner students to interact with other students, while gaining recognition for their academic abilities. Students can take control of preparations for their team with the teacher acting as facilitator. They can decide the topic, divide up the various aspects to be covered, discuss tactics, create their own agenda and elect a captain for their team. During the debate, they are in control. It usually attracts other non-students to the school to support their team in a spirit of healthy competition. It is a positive method of empowering students and creating equality with students from the community. The process, especially if the home team wins, brings a positive "feel-good" atmosphere to the school and the whole prison. It also gives validity to the educational achievements of the students in a non-conventional process, which challenges from traditional methods of assessment.

Teachers as Organic Intellectuals

A sense of awareness of a student's present position and future possibilities is essential in any adult education experience. Activities that recognize this and empower students are especially welcome within prison. Teachers should also strive to encourage students to believe in their capability to embrace education to its fullest and achieve their potential. Gramsci believed that by a variety of activities, including the exercise of a skill or knowledge of a language, every individual demonstrates the capacity for intellectual activity (Joll, 1977, p. 91). He argued that the intellectual realm should not be conceived as specialized functions confined to the narrow elite, but as an integral part of political struggle grounded in everyday life. Based on the work of Gramsci, Boggs developed the concept of the Organic Intellectuals, which he argued, must be an organic part of and come from their community (Boggs, 1976, p. 76). Organic Intellectuals in prison are powerful in drawing others to the school. A prisoner who has been successful in an examination or has had an inspirational learning experience is a more positive advocate for the school than any advertisement by a dynamic teacher or an outstanding program. A belief in oneself is a liberating experience for a student and all our activities should be designed to realize that potential. We should believe in and speak the language of possibility with our students.

This positive dynamic within the school environment may seep into other aspects of the prison regime. In Goffman's words, it might begin to infest the establishment. The school should act as a beacon, a ray of light not only to attract people but also to shine into the other, darker parts of the regime.

Goffman believes a common feature of closed institutions is the practice of reserving something of oneself from the clutches of the institution. He argues that this "recalcitrance is not an incidental mechanism of defense but rather an essential constituent of the self" (Goffman, 1977, p. 89). Despite the structural constraints of Goffman's total institution, there is always space over which the institution has no control. There is always some part of the individual the institutions cannot dominate.

> Our sense of being a person can come from being drawn into a wider social unit, our sense of selfhood can arise through the little ways in which we can resist the pull. Our status is backed by the solid buildings of the world, while our sense of identity resides within the cracks. (Goffman, 1997, p. 90)

It is within the cracks that real democratic educational space might survive and grow. In this way, for a session in the classroom, inmates might lose themselves in removal activities. They exist not because they are in the institution, but because they are removed from it. Despite the regime having charge of the body, it is difficult to control the mind. The school can provide the opportunity for free, unencumbered discourse, where frames of reference can be examined and subjectivities challenged. It is there where prisoners should be encouraged to engage in an intelligent riot (Davidson, 1995, p. 9) of the mind and inquiry based on freedom, mutuality and respect.

We should be conscious that there may be a contrast between this type of learning and that promoted by the prison authorities and justice departments. They seek to change the individual; we should set out to challenge the individual. The justice departments are usually critical of the individual; we seek to promote critical thinking in the individual. Adult education promotes autonomy; the authorities seek to deny autonomy. We should be cautious about the courses that the prison authorities might desire, designed to promote a change in a prisoner's behavior.

> For all their proclamations about seeking behavioral change, many 'criminogenic'-focused courses, I suspect, lead to superficial change: prisoners jump through hoops because life is more bearable for them if they do so. What adult education as envisaged by Mezirow is about is a process that leads to genuine change in the fundamental assumptions a person holds...My guess is that because it is more respectful, more genuinely participative and works with people on a wider, deeper level—such adult education approaches beat the 'criminogenic' ones even on the latter's terms. (Warner, 1998, p. 128)

Instead of prisoners challenging their frame of reference, Warner warns of the possibility of role dispossession (Goffman, 1961, p. 24). A reconstituted institutionalized self is created either to get on with authorities or get out early.

132

This approach by the prison authorities will not encourage learners to challenge their frames of reference. It is designed to change a learner's behavior to conform to the norms of society. While there are certain types of harmful behavior that are unacceptable to human beings, transformative learning must promote critical thinking and provide the opportunity for individuals to challenge their own assumptions and come to their own conclusions. As Freire pointed out, "it is not our role to speak to people about our own view of the world nor to attempt to impose that view on them, but rather to dialogue with the people about their views and ours" (Freire, 1970, p. 77).

The type of education promoted in prison should encourage the search for critical inquiry. If the philosophy is firmly rooted in the adult education movement, then education in prison should encourage people to think about their lives, and thus their whole frame of reference can be challenged. Freire reminded us that liberating education through "the methods of dialogical education draw us into the intimacy of society, the *raison d'être* of every object of study" (Freire, 1987, p. 13). Prison authorities may not see the importance of an adult education approach and the promotion of transformative learning. The natural home for adult education is in the cracks and on the margins; this might be the best place for it to survive if the regime becomes more punitive. However, we would be in noble and illustrious company:

> The history of social movements is a history of people operating in cracks and superstructures...of exercising considerable imagination, critical thinking, subversion and undutiful behavior to destabilize and deconstruct the authority of the inevitable. All of them ways of 'taking back control' based on the inter-relationship between consciousness and courage, between theory and practice. Taking back control and joining with others in collective action to achieve change is at the root of concepts like participation and democracy. (Thompson, 1996, p. 21)

Understanding the constraints in which learners and educators engage in pedagogy and making appropriate provision for them is essential. If this is done, then schools in total institutions might also be "sites of opposition" "perhaps no less and no more constrained than other cultural and educational formations" (Davidson, 1995, p. 10).

Conclusion

Prison remains the mainstay of the penal system internationally. It seems the solution to some types of criminal activity is incarceration. Imprisonment is becoming wider, longer and deeper. As prison educators we must take a position on the conditions of our learners and the social, cultural and political context of the penal system. Freire has pointed out that all education and educators are political. An educator in a critically reflective educational experience cannot be neutral; neutrality merely propagates the status quo (Freire, 1987). As one of the authors of the Council of Europe's *Education in Prison* (1990) noted, "Prison or correctional educators cannot remain isolated or neutral in the current debates about penal policies" (Warner, 1998, p. 131). This would excuse the economic, social and political system, which is mirrored in the prison system.

One important aspect of radical adult education is that actors in any particular environment would be reflective agents of change. While conscious that the greatest impetus for change within the penal system must come from prisoners and ex-prisoners, those working within the system must provide resistance to the dominant penal ideology. As human beings we should be concerned about the treatment of other human beings. As professional educators, if our objectives include helping people cope with their sentence, we should be concerned about the prison regime, architecture and environment and our students' living conditions. "If you are talking about developing the whole person, things that inhibit the development of people, like appalling conditions, like cruelty, like psychological torture or other types of torture are obviously working against that development" (Warner, personal communication, 5 April, 2002). The position of those working and living within the prison system gives us an opportunity to work as agents for change.

> If you say your main objective is rehabilitation then you have got to modify security objectives. You have got to take risks; you have got to give people space...So if the regimes are working against education, that is part of the larger picture. Sometimes, the deepening of imprisonment is working against the objective of resettlement, rehabilitation, helping people get beyond the prison. (Warner, 2002, pp. 15-16).

However, we should bear in mind that "the greatest single obstacle to the personal development of prisoners is the nature of prison itself" (Department of Justice, 1985, p. 90).

> There is simply no humane way that one human being can lock up another human being. Humane intentions are no guarantee of humane results and even among the best motivated of professional staff, there is a tendency to see the inmate as prisoner first and as a patient, a student, an apprentice or a client, second. (Department of Justice, 1985, p. 91)

The educationalist Germanotta, echoed this sentiment in his examination of education in American penal institutions: "Coercive institutions destroy the aspiration of the human spirit by definition" (Germanotta, 1995, p. 119). To ignore the social and structural dimension of our students' lives overlooks a key aspect of our role as adult educators.

Educators within the prison must always be conscious of the context in which we work. They cannot be seen to be providing "value free" education.

Instead we must strive for space that encourages critical thinking in an attempt to understand society, provide an alternative educational experience and support the needs of those who have been imprisoned. Thomas concludes his examination of schooling in a total institution by arguing that progressive prison educators should "stop talking about reforming programs and begin to work to reform prisons" (Thomas, 1995, p. 40). Reformation programs have failed. "Prison education cannot be fully implemented without a transformation of the philosophy of punishment in North America and without rethinking how, as a society we ought to define and respond to criminal offence" (Thomas, 1995, p. 39). We should constantly remind ourselves and the public of the limitations on the use of imprisonment. Prison as we know it today is rarely a solution to society's problems.

> Prisoners are people who have been failed. Many have had a long history of failure at home, at school, at work, and at establishing human relationships. It is unrealistic to expect that prison can achieve what better-placed institutions in society have failed to do. Neither are prisons like laundries where what is wrong, personally and socially, can be washed away. (Department of Justice, 1985, p. 91)

While prison damages people, education provides opportunities to overcome that harm. Trying to create conditions for critical thinking can be difficult. Recognizing the constraints of prison is the beginning and attempting to understand the context in which educators and learners operate is essential. Education can be domesticating or liberating and there is no formulaic way we can create ideal conditions for liberating education. It is rare that there will be a perfect learning space, either within or without the prison walls. However, while recognizing the difficulties that exist within prison we should also appreciate the positives. There is much to give us hope. The greatest resource within the prison education system is the people, both educators and learners. It is as agents for change engaged in discourse, that we will overcome the constraints of an institution that is punitive, dehumanizing and has failed in its objectives. The potential for prison education, as with all adult education, lies not within the walls of the prison or the structural context, but within the human spirit. It is as human beings that we enter into dialogue and strive to co-operate with the desire to promote human dignity and the belief that real freedom will exist for one only when it exists for all.

Chapter XII

Beyond Offending Behavior:
The Wider Perspectives of Adult Education and the European Prison Rules

by Anne Costelloe and Kevin Warner

This is a revised version of a paper first presented to the Ninth EPEA International Conference on Prison Education, Langesund, Norway, June 2003.

Introduction

This chapter questions a rhetoric that appears to have become increasingly pervasive in many prison systems. It is a rhetoric based on a one-dimensional view that sees prisoners just as "offenders." At its heart lies the taken-for-granted assumption that the sole or overriding purpose of prison is to rehabilitate. The rhetoric is manifest most clearly in programs that seek to address offending behavior and in similar offense-focused work. Our misgivings lie not just with the rhetoric but perhaps more importantly with its unquestioned acceptance. We are suggesting that unless it is subjected to critique and thorough debate a suspiciously unchallengeable consensus will take hold. This chapter is an attempt to generate some debate on the matter.

The basic premise on which this chapter is based is our view that the rhetoric to which we refer is in fact more than that. It is a discourse (Foucault, 1972), which is a language system that has developed socially to make sense of and give meaning to our lives. Those sections of society that create the discourse and shape meaning work ideologically to "naturalize" them into common sense. In other words, a discourse is a historically, socially and institutionally specific structure of statements, beliefs, habits and practices that construct the way people think, talk about and respond to daily life. It produces positions that people automatically take because they assume them to be natural or normal.

A clear example of a dominant discourse that has come to be embedded in our public psyche is that of counseling. If somebody suffered bereavement or marital breakdown thirty years ago in Ireland, there was never any suggestion that they should talk to a professional counselor about it; in fact, there was scarcely such a profession. Instead they looked to their family, friends or clergy for guidance and support. Today, counseling is almost forced on those unfortunate enough to suffer personal tragedy. Victims who suggest they do not need counseling can be accused of "being in denial" or "not coping." Furthermore, there is a counseling industry fueling the discourse of counseling and in turn ensuring its continued dominance. In this chapter we are suggesting that the rhetoric of offending behavior programs is similarly becoming the dominant and entrenched discourse of prison regime management.

This concerns us because the power of discourse resides in its exclusions. A discourse defines what is appropriate and that which is deemed inappropriate is then systematically marginalized, silenced and repressed. We are worried that alternative prison regime discourses are being sidelined, in particular those that give a more central role to prison education and those grounded in the central tenets of Council of Europe policy, as expressed in the *European Prison Rules* (EPR) published in 1987. Thus we argue that critical perspective be maintained and the possibilities afforded by other viewpoints elucidated.

It is our concern that education, like many other professions and activities in prison, is now expected to give priority attention to the new discourse and its advocacy of programs that are presumed to address directly the "criminogenic factors" in the prisoner. Typically these are in areas such as addiction, anger-management, thinking skills, preparation for release, etc. It would seem to us that the dominance of this discourse has shifted the ground rules. Prison education, like all other activities, must now defend itself primarily in response to the question: How is it addressing offending behavior? It is no longer deemed acceptable or apt to suggest that perhaps the question is itself misguided. As a result, evaluation of prison education tends to be based on whether its courses can be seen to reduce recidivism.

We wish to stress that we regard encouraging and enabling people to turn away from crime to be of the utmost importance. Our concern is that "over-focusing" on so-called criminogenic factors, and on the prisoner's shortcomings, is a limiting and negative approach. Such an approach views the prisoner primarily as something broken in need of fixing or as an object in need of treatment. It appears to us to be a regressive concept reminiscent of the now discredited medical model of imprisonment. We are particularly wary of how the new discourse frames attempts to change the inmate while ignoring the wider context from which they came and to which they will return. This framing serves to highlight the significantly different social outlooks behind the offending behavior approach and the traditional Council of Europe approach. The former fits very well with (even if it is not synonymous with) a political mood that negatively stereotypes prisoners, that says "prison works," that wants to "get tough on crime" and thus lock up more people. It fits in part because it deflects attention from the social dimensions to the causes of crime "entirely" onto individual responsibility. Also, it deflects from how the larger prison system inherently damages people. In contrast, the Council of Europe outlook is based on the assumptions that (a) the prisoner is a citizen, and (b) prison alienates further the person from society and thus hampers their development, so that prison should be used only as a last resort.

Our premise challenges this narrowing of perspective and draws attention to what we feel is being lost or neglected. What is being lost is the fundamental philosophy of the Council of Europe and its awareness of what prisons are and should be doing as delineated in the *European Prison Rules (EPR)* (1987). What is being neglected is the adult education perspective that lies at the core of another Council of Europe document, *Education in Prison* (1990). In this chapter, we look at both adult education and "European" penal policy in an attempt to widen the focus once more.

Kilmainham Gaol played an important part in Irish history before being decommissioned in 1924. It now houses a museum of Irish Nationalism.

Adult Education

One of the more tangible impacts of the new discourse is that it has forced many prison educators to question exactly what it is they are doing. This is a positive move as sometimes we can become complacent, falling into the trap of viewing prison education as an inherently good thing, which as such requires little or no further justification. Instead we are now being asked to rationalize both practice and policy. We are being asked why and how we are educating prisoners. The traditional response to the first half of that question from European prison educators is that prison education is a moral right that meets a basic human need. This response sees education as a key element of human development, and is the perspective that lies at the heart of *Education in Prison* (1990). This approach to prison education is applied, in particular, in Nordic countries and Ireland (Nordic Council of Ministers, 2005; Warner, 2002; Prison Education Service, 2003; Prison Education Service, 2004; Behan, 2006).

In essence this perspective considers personal development to be an aim, a process and a result of adult learning. It is concerned with the development of the whole person through the process of self-actualization and can be best achieved by providing a liberal education within a broad curriculum. In applying this perspective to the prison context Morin (1981) claims, "for the inmate, this vision is full of hope and promise. It introduces him to the search for life's meaning, it allows him to grope with the fundamental why and wherefores, with the what for and what questions, for the idea which he has of himself will justify his existence, give meaning to his life and determine, in large measure, his conduct and behaviors." Accordingly, we can see that it has much to offer any adult learner, within or beyond the prison walls. However, the second half of the question—how do we educate prisoners?—deserves more attention.

It is accepted widely, and rightly so, that in terms of methodology and curriculum, prison education must mirror the best practice available in the community. However, that context of prison education is more problematic. But before tackling that, we should outline the generally accepted principles of adult learning. In any adult learning situation, teaching and learning are considered to be dynamic and, to a large extent, interchangeable. Learners participate on a voluntary basis and take active responsibility for their learning. The educator can facilitate this by creating the climate for learning and in many cases "teach" the learner how to learn, but the learning must be always self-directed. The learner, in dialogue with the teacher, sets the agenda in terms of goals, self-appraisal, curriculum and evaluation. A particular example from Ireland of this approach is the way adults develop their literacy, based explicitly on the work of Freire, Mezirow and Rogers (National Adult Literacy Agency, 2005); these tried and tested methods are replicated in literacy work in Irish prisons (Prison Education Service, 2002).

Similarly the ideals of collaborative learning, particularly small groups engaged in supportive discussion and problem solving, are relevant as is a constructivist view of learning. Rather than the teacher being the only giver of knowledge and the guiding force in learning, in constructivism the learners construct their own meaning, because it is believed that knowledge cannot be passed from one individual to another but is for each individual to process. Constructivism stresses learner inquiry, natural curiosity, engaging in dialogue with other students and the teacher to help provide multiple representations, cooperative learning, real-world situations in context and authentic life experiences. Acknowledging learners' past experiences and applying these to the construction and consideration of new knowledge and skills is important. The approach is inherently student-centered; people and processes are considered to be more important than the subject taught.

That is not to say that the curriculum is unimportant in adult education. A broad curriculum is especially important in the prison context, particularly if the following quotation from John McVickar (a heavy-duty English criminal who became an academic) is any indication of the impact of education on a prisoner's life. McVickar claims "nowadays it is not so much that I find crime repugnant as that I am more interested in other things" (Duguid, 2000, p. 92). The fundamental appeal of a broad curriculum for prison education lies in widening the interests and choices available to the student by providing them with the opportunity to become "interested in other things." We feel this open-ended approach is one of the strengths of Irish prison education (Warner, 2002). It is also in line with the philosophy and good practice of adult education in the community and, of course, this wide concept of education is a key feature of the Council of Europe's *Education in Prisons* (1990).

Returning to the issue of context and prison education, we should consider Caffarella and Merriam's (1999) contention that "learning cannot be separated from the context in which it takes place." The necessity to contextualize learning makes it incumbent on prison students and educators to be critical and reflective about the type of education provided in their particular situation. It is no longer good enough to suggest that prison education is just adult education in a different setting. While the principles must mirror best practice on the outside, its rationale must be appraised within the prison context. We must do this because, if we do not, others will do it for us and, as alluded to earlier on, they may set an inappropriate framework against which prison education is evaluated. More importantly, this call for the adult education principle of critical reflection is echoed in progressive penal policy, as expressed by Hans Tulkens (1998), the former Head of the Prison Service in The Netherlands. He said in relation to the *EPR*:

> What comes to the fore in particular is that prisoners should be listened to and their agreement or willingness should be sought in connection with decisions. This means that...the prisoner should no longer be seen as an object of treatment but as a responsible subject. (p. 8)

If we accept prisoners as reflective beings, then prison education must develop and promote reflection among the student body and education staff. The necessity for this type of reflection is embedded in several progressive paradigms of adult education, in particular critical education as buttressed by such concepts as "really useful knowledge" (Thompson, 1997), critical thinking (Brookfield, 2001, 1987), conscientization (Freire, 1972; Mayo, 1999) and perspective transformation (Mezirow, 2000). While it is not practical to delve into these concepts in any great depth here, they are referenced to signify not only the theoretical framework within which our view of adult learning is based but also the broad strand of adult education that we feel most applicable to prison education.

Critical education is not concerned merely with skills acquisition and the upgrading of qualifications but with a significant change in understanding and worldview. It is based on the ideals of critical theory as associated with the Frankfork School and interpreted via Habermas (1987). It is concerned primarily with three interrelated processes: (a) the process by which adults question and then replace an assumption that up to then had been uncritically accepted; (b) the process through which adults develop alternative perspectives on previously taken-for-granted ideas and beliefs; and, (c) the process by which adults come to recognize and reframe their culturally induced dependency roles and relationships. In short, it is the process of assessing our assumptions and presuppositions and understanding their development. As a result, it is focused on learners making things happen rather than believing that things happen to them. In this way it challenges the prisoners' preconceptions, prejudices, indoctrinations and fatalism. Because of this deep potential, it may facilitate a far greater degree of change in people and their lives than offense-focused work.

In concluding this part of the chapter, it is essential to remember that, in one very important aspect, prison education is not like adult education on the outside. It lacks that independence. It operates within the shadow of a penal system more subject to the whims and caprices of populist rhetoric and other sections of society. It is more vulnerable to "moral panics" in media and political spheres and to the negative stereotyping of our students than any other adult learning opportunity. This is why prison educators must be very aware of how we view our students, what it is we are doing, why we are doing it and how best to do it. Fortunately, the Council of Europe can answer some of these questions.

Penal Policy

The Council of Europe can suffer from confusion with the European Union (EU), or at least be overshadowed by it. Yet, it is a far older, larger and, one might argue, wiser institution than the EU, having underpinned human rights and democracy in Europe since World War II. It has been called "the democratic conscience of Europe" due to its concern with the advancement of social and democratic issues through political, legislative and constitutional reform. With forty-six members, it involves nearly all European countries. It exerts significant influence over European prison systems through the European Convention on Human Rights, the European Court of Human Rights, the *European Prison Rules*, other recommendations and via an inspection body known as the CPT—the European Committee for the Prevention of Torture and Inhumane and Degrading Treatment or Punishment.

Consequently, a sense of human rights underpins *Education in Prison* (1990)—people held in prison are citizens; citizens are entitled to lifelong education to ensure their full development, therefore prisoners should be offered meaningful education. Likewise, seeing the prisoner as a citizen is at the heart of the *EPR* (1987), as is some hardheaded realism about the nature of prisons and prisoners. The *EPR* is essentially the Council of Europe's "policy document" on prisons and was formulated and agreed by the member states in 1987, as an adaptation "to European conditions and aspirations" of the United Nations' Standard Minimum Rules for the Treatment of Prisoners. They are important as "rules" or standards against which prisons, prison systems and countries can be, and are, judged. But they are perhaps most important for their underlying philosophy, what they tell us about prisons and prisoners.

The *EPR* concept of what prison regimes should seek to do is probably best encapsulated in Rule 65. We will examine this rule and critique the offense–focused approach against the objectives set out in it. Rule 65 states:

Every effort shall be made to ensure that the regimes of the institutions are designed and managed so as:

(a) to ensure that the conditions of life are compatible with human dignity and acceptable standards in the community;

(b) to minimise the detrimental effects of imprisonment and the differences between prison life and life at liberty which tend to diminish the self-respect or sense of personal responsibility of prisoners;

(c) to sustain and strengthen those links with relatives and the outside community that will promote the best interests of prisoners and their families;

(d) to provide opportunities for prisoners to develop skills and aptitudes that will improve their prospects of successful resettlement after release.

In the first objective (a), the sense of the prisoner as citizen, entitled to the human rights and conditions they should have on the outside, is evident. This sees the person in prison, not initially or primarily as an offender, but as a person to whom dignity and respect are due and as a member of the larger society. Quite simply, a key problem of offense-focused work is the focus on the offense. The person tends to be seen one-dimensionally, entirely or mainly as an offender, with the rest of his or her life, personality, talents and problems pushed aside. This goes against the grain of the *EPR*

The second objective (b), challenges the idea that "prison works" by recognizing the "detrimental effects of imprisonment." This objective also recognizes the prison itself plays a role in diminishing the sense of personal responsibility of prisoners—a fact often conveniently ignored by many of the approaches that are focused on the prisoner "taking responsibility" and "making choices."

The reality is that prisons themselves are "criminogenic." They are major contributors to recidivism because they institutionalize people and further inculcate them in a criminal culture. A Rand Corporation study in California for the U.S. Department of Justice showed prison as less effective than probation in a study of matched offenders because of the detrimental effect of prison that tends to be ignored in the recidivism debates (Irwin & Austin, 1993, p. 119). Like surgery, prison is a radical intervention into someone's life; it is necessary at times, but its serious negative side effects should be recognized and minimized. Thus, prison should be a last resort. Education and other programs are only a small part of prison regimes and of the impact of prisons on those held in custody. While programs may be beneficial, many other things may be happening that work in the opposite direction: Abuse by other prisoners? Humiliation or degradation by staff? Inhumane conditions? Further alienation from society? Barriers to work, housing and other forms of integration, upon release? The "detrimental effects of imprisonment" are ignored in most offense-focused work in prisons and in most prison strategy statements that prioritize "rehabilitation."

The third objective (c), also attempts to counteract a negative side effect of prison—the further alienation of the person in prison from any positive influence of family and the community in general. Might not a supportive family member or an employer who keeps in contact and a door to work open, or a sports instructor who stays in touch be more crucial to resettlement than a course geared to addressing offender behavior? Might not allowing the vote in elections be an important "link with the outside community," sometimes as valuable as a session designed to ensure insight?

What is striking about the first three of the four objectives outlined above is that they are all "defensive," focused, quite properly, on recognizing and attempting to undo or minimize the negative effects of imprisonment itself. This is a long way from the confidence of much offense-focused work, which asserts it can intervene and improve people while ignoring the counter-influences inherent in the prison system. The fourth objective implies programs not geared narrowly to the offense and "rehabilitation," but to the much wider goal of "resettlement"—a term that implies adjustment may be needed in the world outside, and within the man or woman coming from prison.

Such a wider perspective on penal policy leads to a far wider role for education in prison than is derived from a perspective fixated on addressing offender behavior. We stated earlier that the logic of adult learning in a prison context is to widen the curriculum. The policy perspective of the Council of Europe in relation to prisons and prisoners, as conveyed in Rule 65 of the *EPR*, has similar implications for education. Education has crucial roles to play in the lives of prisoners: (a) in supporting the dignity of the person in prison; (b) in helping that person "cope" with the sentence ("minimizing the detrimental effects of imprisonment"); (c) in strengthening the links with family and community; and, (d) in preparing the person for release and resettlement in a variety of ways.

As suggested earlier, education's greatest contribution to combating crime may well be significant but indirect, getting people "interested in other things." That would seem to be the thinking also of Austin MacCormick, one of the pioneers of prison education in the U.S., who wrote in 1931:

> Education of prisoners is fundamentally a problem of adult education, taking the term in its European sense...Its philosophy is to consider the prisoner as primarily an adult in need of education and only secondarily as a criminal in need of reform. Its aim is to extend to prisoners as individuals every type of educational opportunity that experience or sound reasoning shows may be of benefit or of interest to them. (pp. 9-12)

It is ironic then, more than seventy years later, that huge openness to possibilities from multiple directions should be so severely narrowed in the current outlook and practice of prison education in North America. Similar restriction is now evident in parts of Europe. Yet, some of the clearest voices countering that narrowing come from North America, in particular Stephen Duguid in Vancouver, Canada.

A recent book by Duguid (2000), *Can Prisons Work: The Prisoner as Object and Subject in Modern Corrections*, supports much of the argument of this chapter. It is, among many other things, a powerful argument for the provision of education in prisons along adult education lines or, in Duguid's terms, for the teaching of "Humanities" in prison. He details research on twenty years of college courses in British Columbia prisons that indicates how they were influential in decreasing recidivism, effectively beating the offense-focused work at its own game. He is devastatingly critical also of the massive shifting of resources within Canadian prisons to "cognitive skills" and other courses that target "criminogenic needs." He notes "education programs were neutralized, eliminated or transformed into service programs for cognitive skills." Proof perhaps that the warnings outlined in our introduction should not be dismissed.

Duguid reports how Robert Ross, the key originator of cognitive skills, insisted that it was not a panacea; its real strength lay in preventing delinquency rather than rehabilitation. Yet it holds great attraction for the prison system, being taught by prison staff after only brief training and built via "packages." (Perhaps also this kind of "deficit" model averts the need to look beyond the faults in the prisoner to those in the prison and the wider society). Duguid argues that, though claiming to offer the prisoner self-understanding, the real aim is to have the prisoner "adopt the understanding of self that has been prescribed by the examiner." Clearly, the self thus projected by officialdom over-concentrates on criminality and neglects larger, and possibly more positive, aspects of the "whole person." Duguid claims "the deception is both transparent and despised. Only the weakest willed take on the self suggested by the state, the clever wear it only as a veil, and the stubborn resist it as best they can." (This brings to mind the running joke among British prisoners who frequently refer to their enhanced thinking skills programs as entranced thinking skills.)

There are two other ways in which the offense-focused approach and the narrow rehabilitative discourse are being oversold. First, there seems to be a high degree of selectivity in terms of the number of prisoners who are, in the end, "addressed;" and, second and perhaps more importantly, the claim that this approach presents "choices" to prisoners tends to be hugely exaggerated. In relation to selectivity, authorities often target only limited categories of prisoners and, in addition, prisoners themselves opt out of these programs in great numbers—points emphasized by Duguid in relation to Canada. Giving offense-focused work a central part in policy or strategy should at least imply some universality in application. All prisoners should be envisaged and offered at least some of the programs in question, but this seldom seems to be the case.

The second oversell lies in maintaining that such programs offer real choice to prisoners, enabling them to choose paths away from crime. While it is always possible in a theoretical way to assert that choice is available, in practice the options facing ex-prisoners are enormously grim. Aside from prisoners' own personal pressures and problems, society as a whole places a multitude of barriers and obstacles in their paths. Problems with income, housing, employment, acceptance by the larger community and adaptation to a changed world can be overwhelming. A discourse that takes so little cognizance of the impact and restrictions social environments and economic realities place on the choices open to individuals is unlikely to succeed. It would seem that the underlying presupposition of many of these courses is that prisoners frequently make bad choices or the wrong choice due to an underdevelopment of certain cognitive and moral abilities. The solution offered is to dwell on the undeveloped cognitive ability that is presumed to distort the thinking in the first place. Yet this seems rather simplistic, particularly if one is of the view that choice is not freely available to all. After all, few prisoners can access the vast range of socio-economic, political and cultural choices freely available to "ordinary citizens."

Conclusion

Again we must stress that we do not question in any way the seriousness of crime—for the victim, society, or perpetrator. Nor are we inherently critical of attempts to address offending behavior and the reflection of these attempts in policy statements and targets. We accept that courses and activities that directly target "criminogenic" factors can be appropriate at times "as part of a wider goal." For example, such offense-focused work may be particularly relevant where "denial" is likely to be involved, as is often the case in relation to sex offenses. Our concern is that the overriding emphasis on addressing offender behavior represents too narrow an approach. Furthermore, we are concerned that the unchecked rise of the new discourse and its insidious inculcation of "medical model" language may depict all prisoners as in need of treatment. Language is never neutral or value-free, it has the power to establish a new ideology and rationalize its primacy on the grounds of common sense. This is why we have attempted to generate debate on the changing language of regime management and critique the new discourse evident in many prison systems.

Our intention has been to point out that the new limiting discourse represents a loss of possibilities and direction. As we have seen, the great potential of adult learning coupled with a realistic awareness of the nature of prisons and prisoners is in danger of being superseded by the emergent discourse. Accordingly, alternative and critical perspectives need to be maintained—though it seems a little strange that what European countries in their better moments had agreed to in the *European Prison Rules* should now have the badge of an "alternative" outlook.

Finally, one essential element is missing here, that of the voice of the prison student. All too often those who decide what is best for prisoners ignore their views and experiences. It is perhaps appropriate then to leave the last word to a prisoner. Someone who, in response to the question, "Why are you undertaking a higher education course while in prison?" eloquently encapsulated the reality of prison life and the typical reasons why anyone might avail of education while in custody:

The panopticon prison, designed by Bentham to enable total surveillance and made notorious by Foucault. Examples include Pelican Bay State Prison in California and Pentonville Prison in London.

My reasons for studying in prison are many; the combination of boredom, wanting to please others and restore some of their pride in you, an awareness that your offspring may someday look to you for assistance with their studies, being conscious of your own ignorance and lack of knowledge, a stubborn streak which keeps you going in the face of adversity or when told you're not capable or good enough, wanting to keep your head down and get on with things quietly, as a means of escape, anything to keep your mind focused and as far removed from reality as possible, to promote a sense of self-confidence, to experience the pleasure of learning and gaining knowledge simply for its own sake, not to mention costing the authorities money! ("Student" in Costelloe, 2003, p. 140)

We wonder what his response would be if asked, "Why are you undertaking a course addressing your offending behavior?"

Chapter XIII

Borderland Negotiations
Re Presentation of Identity as a Prison Educator

By Susan Yantz

Introduction

I did not plan to become a prison educator. I had never even considered it as a possibility. Yet on a crisp September morning, after a chance encounter with a colleague, I found myself walking through the prison gates and into the prison classroom. As I met and talked with many other prison educators during my eight-year term there, I was surprised how closely their stories about how they came to teach in prison resembled my own.

I taught adults in a prison classroom that in many ways resembled countless other adult education classrooms, but the adults I taught were serving time in prison. This chapter is about the invisible, unexpected and personal aspects of that prison teaching experience and about my quest to make sense of my teaching practice within the prison system and my identity as a correctional educator.

Lost in the Prison Landscape

There is a sense of secrecy surrounding teaching experiences within a classroom, particularly within a prison classroom. The prison, in its physical and psychological separation from the community, is an isolating institution. The prison classroom also isolates. Since teaching and corrections are typically private practices, I am segregated from adult educators in the community, as well as from other prison educators.

The dilemma and confusion surrounding the understanding of my professional identity is countered by naming and claiming my identity and voice as a correctional educator. The construction, or informing, of identity through narrative is itself an act of agency: "Our narrative identities determine our social action as agents of history and the constraints we place on the identities of others.... Narratives can become politically enabling of social transformation..." (McLaren, 1995, p. 89). The telling of my story, incomplete and messy as it is, is part of the reflection and voicing process.

Differences between the prison classroom and the adult education classroom located outside the prison walls cause prison educators to exist outside the typically defined category of school teachers and adult educators. Even within the prison classroom, prison educators' practices fall outside of normal prison practices. Therefore, prison educators are not only inside and outside at once, but also neither inside nor outside: "Within is not, has never been, a unitary place and space..." (Stanley, 1997, p. 203).

Discussion with a colleague:

Colleague: As a prison educator, do you find that you are generally received well in the community?

Susan: I find that my professional and social communities express curiosity about my work, questioning me about the sensational aspects of teaching in prison. But they have very little knowledge about adult education in prison and about prisons in general. They ask questions such as: "Why would you want to do that?" or "Wouldn't you rather teach in a regular school?" Some people express surprise, or anger, that education in prison even exists. But the most troubling reaction I have experienced personally within the community is one of being overlooked entirely in a discussion within a circle of educators. It was as if I was absent, or invisible, outside the margins of the group.

Colleague: Other teachers didn't include you in their discussion?

Susan: Initially they didn't. Then, when they realized they had excluded me, said, "Oh yes, you're a teacher too, in prison. What is that like?" I was left feeling unsure as to the level of genuine interest behind this question. I experienced their question as an after-attempt to include me once they realized their oversight.

Borderland Spaces

A borderland is symbolic of the landscape of my prison classroom. It is the place from which my practice originates within the prison: "It is not always easy to negotiate this in-betweenness, but it is something that I confront and consider daily" (Kothari, 1997, p. 162). Borderlands are suspended states of isolation, locations of struggle. Stanley (1997) explains the concept of a borderland space as follows:

The notion of borderlands signifies that there is also a territory between, on the borders of—precisely a state and a space of liminality, the in-between.... A borderland is a contested zone, if not always politically, ...then certainly socially in terms of the re/construction and re/negotiation of identities and biographies and thus also of knowledges. (p. 2)

Stanley further claims that borderlands "create people whose everyday ontological condition is one of constant liminality, of constant 'crossing over' between two states of being" (p. 2). Not only does this suspended state describe the institutional position of the prison teacher, it also describes the position of the prisoner-student.

148

Discussion with a colleague:

> **Colleague:** *How do you know where the school ends and the rest of the institution begins, both physically and psychologically?*

> **Susan:** *Well, the physical boundary, although sometimes vague, is more easily defined than the psychological boundary. The psychological boundary is messy and undefined, like a contested border or borderland.*

The borderland space of a prison classroom is a marginalized location full of obscure contradictions for the powerful and the powerless, for the insiders and the outsiders. It is a borderland also of dominant and subordinate identifications. To which group do correctional educators belong—insider or outsider? I wondered if I could belong to both groups at the same time? In my experience, I was both insider and outsider at once. I participated in both inside and outside worlds. My classroom consisted of complex and confusing interconnections between the prison and the outside world. The multiplicity of borders and border-crossings experienced by the prison educator occur not in some located place or space, but instead from within a borderland where borders and border-crossings are difficult to name and claim.

The prison educator's role has been described as ambiguous, not only within the community, but also within correctional systems, where prison education is "marginal to the overall corrections function rather than central to it" (Collins, 1988b, p. 24). That ambiguity places prison educators and their practices in liminal locations, as "others" within correctional systems, where they teach marginalized prisoner-students in those in-between spaces.

Journal entry and reflections:

> *The topic of personal teaching experiences arose in a discussion I had with a group of my peers. I was asked to describe my teaching experiences as a prison educator. My description of that experience led to questions about the prison environment and my prison classroom environment. Through the questions that were asked of me during this discussion, I was led to not only transform my understanding of my practice, but also to feel a sense of fraudulence. It was an extremely uncomfortable feeling.*

> *During this discussion, I explained that my prison classroom operated as a community unto itself, away from the watchful power of the prison institution. This was what I had believed and claimed since I began teaching there. I attributed this separation to the physical absence of security devices such as cameras and radios and to the absence of security staff in the classroom. I believed the absence of those surveillance mechanisms also contributed to the classroom's positive atmosphere of psychological separation from the rest of the institution.*

> But as I described the physical space, it suddenly occurred to me that the workspace area, with one staff member sitting "at the helm" in the office bubble, was in actuality a panopticon, an "architectural design which results in prisoners and staff being under continuous observation from a central location." (Collins, 1998, p. 59)

> I experienced an immediate flashback to a few months before when a new student asked if the staff member sitting in the office "bubble" was the "boss lady" (correctional officer). The student viewed the school as just another controlled prison location, complete with security staff. As I connected the pieces, I realized that my standard claims of a classroom "oasis" away from the "powers that be" were in fact false, that my classroom mirrored and supported the prison's defining feature as a mechanism of surveillance and control. I wondered how many of my students thought I was attempting to deceive them with my claims of a separate environment. Or did they realize that I was instead deceiving myself? My feeling of self-deception alarmed me, altering both my perspective on my teaching practice and my self-perception of my identity as a prison educator.

It is from within this undefined place that prison educators experience dilemmas of knowing and self through their attempts to construct knowledge from the experience of teaching within a borderland location. Yet prison educators' experiences of identity questions and professional confusion within their teaching practice bear resemblance to other educators' experiences outside the prison walls. Teachers on the outside also speak of professional and personal tensions and dilemmas created by conflicts between institutional practices and their own values or beliefs (Craig, 1995).

Journal entry and reflections:

> I remember reading in a journal article on prison education words to the effect that "adult education in prison is really no different than adult education on the outside." At least that was my impression of the author's statement, although that impression was likely not an accurate representation of the author's meaning. The following direct quotation from the article offers a more realistic account of meaning, in the context of the author's argument for using a critical perspective to examine prisons as mirrors of society: "Teachers of adult literacy in prisons share a common vocation with their counterparts working on the outside.... It is fallacious, then, to imply that the differences between teaching literacy in prison and teaching literacy on the outside completely outweigh the similarities." (Collins, 1995c, pp. 49-50)

I felt unbalanced by this statement, but could not put my finger on the cause of my discomfort, other than an understanding that some incongruity existed in the statement. I later realized the cause of my discomfort was twofold: (a) I sensed the absence of the prison educator's experience and voice within the statement and (b) recognized its connection to my confusion about my personal and professional identity.

Negotiating Identity

I am reminded of Lather's (1991) comment as I begin this section: "Identities are continually displaced / replaced. The subject is neither unified nor fixed" (p. 118). I recall too, my journal entry: "Outside of the ordinary is a confusing place to be, from inside the prison walls."

How do correctional educators negotiate that place of in-betweenness? I found I could not straddle the border between insider and outsider, between teacher and correctional educator. So, I needed to imagine an alternative to that border. I began to appreciate the complexities and contradictions within my identity as a correctional educator.

Identity conflicts often arise under conditions of difference in which we find ourselves outside of normalized positions. For example, as a correctional educator, I found myself outside of the normalized position of school teacher, or even adult educator. That positioning offered opportunities for questioning relationships of domination. According to Kothari (1997), "We are constantly negotiating the positions that we occupy...we adopt different strategies in order to manage the contradictions of identity and to move within and across borderlands of inclusion and exclusion" (p. 162). The negotiation of identity from within borderland locations allows for the creation of different identity perspectives from which to view those in-between spaces of marginality.

Discussion with a colleague:

Colleague: Much of what I hear teachers say about working in prisons is about working through the dividing practices of their locations. Those practices take place along the inside lines of a "we/they" maxim, a sort of insider/outsider mentality. Teachers seem to resist those practices that make them into outsiders.

Susan: I think my problem with my identity initially began from trying to struggle against the dividing practices instead of trying to understand and work through them. Of course difference exists, as does similarity. So, too, do the dividing practices. I was left feeling unbalanced and threatened.

Colleague: As you experienced the tension of the dividing practices, you became divided in your self?

Susan: Over the past few years, I felt dislocated from my identity as a teacher. I couldn't seem to connect that identity with my identity as a prison educator. And I experienced that inability to make the connection as a loss of identity. Remember when I asked if I could be two people at the same time? At the time I asked the question, I thought that was not possible.

Colleague: *I've learned that power not only establishes identity, but also erodes identities by presenting other, sometimes confusing, stories for teachers to live by. Confusing stories produce confused identities. How did you reconnect your two selves?*

Susan: *Change is an interesting phenomenon. Through a process of reflection on experience and dialogue with colleagues, I have re-evaluated my relationship to the system in which I work. I realize that I am not either/ or, that my identity isn't either correctional educator or adult educator. As I learned that my identity was not one-dimensional, I also learned it was not static, but changed over time and through space. In a sense, I renegotiated (with myself) my ideas about identity and its construction.*

Colleague: *Identity is a complex concept.*

No doubt, the concept of identity as constant is a myth. As a teacher, my identity has been formed by my teaching experiences, but also by my experiences from early childhood within educational systems that display the image of the "completed teacher self as the one who is in charge" (Schick, 1998, p. 124). Yet from within my experience and practice, the imagining of identities as unchanging causes tension when I am faced with conflicting roles and contradictory teaching practices. Stanley (1997) defines the nature of identity as follows: "Identity is emergent, subtly shifting and changing with the accumulation of experiences and years" (p. 174). Identities contain a multiplicity of selves and evolve across time. A refusal to limit identity through time, and in place and space, allows for the complexities of experience to influence identity re/construction.

In her struggle to understand her identity as a university professor, Overall (1998) challenges the cultural assumption that "identities—particularly subordinated and disadvantaged identities—are totalizing; that is, that they are assumed to define or constitute the totality of what one is" (p. 163). The turn away from a view of representations of identity as fixed and stable toward re-presentations of identity as evolving and tentative has been attributed to feminist theory and its deconstruction tendencies (Butler, 1992). The principles of indeterminacy in feminist thought allow us to examine the contradictions in binary oppositions, turning them back upon themselves to show how each forms the other and depends upon the other for that opposition (Eagleton, 1983, pp. 132-133). In an explanation of feminist theory's project of deconstructing the subject of feminism itself, Butler (1992) claims that in order to challenge tendencies to categorize (and limit) identity, deconstruction of identity categories allows for a "future of multiple significations..." (p. 16). In the absence of simplified defining categories, identities are allowed to regain their complex, evolving, multiply-layered character.

Journal entry and reflections:

A prisoner walked through my classroom door and wished to gain my attention. He hesitantly spoke: "Excuse me, ma'am." I cringed at the address. For some reason I have always disliked it. (I think I am reminded of the term "school-marm," or perhaps even "lady.") Well, at least he didn't call me Miss.... He enrolled in school and proceeded to name me 'teacher' (very respectfully, mind you) for a number of weeks. Finally, I began to tease him by calling him "student" instead of using his given name. He sheepishly asked me my name, even though I had mentioned it previously on multiple occasions in the hope that he would use it. He did call me by name for the remainder of the day. But the next day, we were back to "teacher" again.

A few days later, I asked him why he insisted on naming me "teacher." He replied that he had always called his teachers "teacher." ("It just seems right," he said.) We had a long discussion about some of his former teachers and he remembered many of them by name (Miss or Mrs...) and referred to them by name during our discussion. He had evidently liked a number of them. At first, I thought I preferred for him to call me by my given name. I had always felt that to be named "teacher" was so impersonal. But as we conversed, I began to realize that I was no longer so uncomfortable with "teacher" for a name. The student used the name as a name of respect rather than as an impersonal label. I also understood that to this student, I was not a "prison educator" or a "correctional educator," or even an "adult educator." I was simply a teacher.

The name "teacher" feels more comfortable to me now. ("Simply" can be a misleading concept. If I am honest, I must also ask myself whether or not I sense that the "respectful" name of teacher also confers some recognition of power, authority and dominance. Is that "sense" then, the source of my comfort?)

Working within totalizing systems of power relations, prison educators may find they are at risk of losing their identities to the totalizing identity of the systems. More likely, they are at risk of aligning their identity with that of the system without questioning the effects of that alignment. Those powerful systematized effects tend to essentialize identity into binary categories of either/or—either correctional educators or adult educators. Furthermore, the essentialization of identity disallows the multiple, complex and negotiated characteristics of identities. Yet Brown (1997) cautions us about the effects of claiming evolving, multiple-sited identities from within institutionalized settings: "The gatekeepers of...professional practice and nation states demand identity papers that offer unambiguous explanations as either/or, not both/and.... In advocating the indefiniteness and indeterminacy of the latter, we risk exclusion and inevitably encounter conflict and tension" (p. 142). It is an individual decision whether or not the risk is worthwhile.

Instead of adopting the concept of a fixed and unified identity, McLaren (1995) advises the following: "It is important to acknowledge that identities are never completed but always in the process of negotiation; they are continually struggled over..." (p. 99). More importantly, Weiler (1995) discusses the value of conceptions of identity as non-essentialized: "If we view individual selves as being constructed and negotiated, then we can begin to consider what exactly those forces are in which individuals shape themselves and by which they are shaped" (p. 38). Carlson and Apple (1998) attribute the re-presentation of identity (as nonessential) to the postmodern conception of a self that is "understood to have no meaning apart from the power relations it constitutes and is constituted by..." (p. 14). The self, in its infinite complexity, is involved in all power relations existing in its environment. As a prison educator, I am gaining an awareness of my identity as being formed through, and impacted by, my position of dominance. That growing awareness allows me to recognize that my identity is formed in part by the power of the prison system, at the expense of my students' identities. I refer to my journal again and read:

> As I continually re-negotiate my identity from the borderland of my practice, I am forced to analyze the aspects of the prison system that affect the shaping of my identity. The personal becomes the political.

Negotiating Across Differences

My colleague writes:

Dilemmas, contradictions, complexity, conflict; these are the story lines that shape the territory of the educator who chooses to walk through the prison gates. It is a rough terrain, but also one full of interpretive and generative possibilities. Our contradictory experiences surface in the space between being correctional and being educators. (Wright, 1998, pp. 52-53)

Journal entry and reflections:

> In my practice, I feel that I am caught in a position between assistance and control. I am not a correctional officer, nor am I simply an educator, or even an adult educator. Instead, I am a "correctional educator." It is not surprising then that I find myself as "other" within a system of power and control, marginalized from my fellow coworkers, as well as from educators and adult educators on the "outside." I am left feeling unsure of my identity inside the prison walls. I am marked as "different," by myself, by the "system" in which I work, by teachers on the outside and by theorists within the fields of corrections, education and adult education. Although I would like to imagine I am simply an adult educator, my experience, my heart and the correctional system tell me otherwise. In reality, I work in a prison, an environment defined by

characteristics of power and control. Those aspects of the prison greatly affect and influence my teaching practice and my self.

The complexities of the prison and the prison culture that influence my teaching practice and my identity as a teacher are in many ways unique to that location. While my experience has led me to believe that my educational practice is different from adult education outside the prison walls, I have also felt compelled to search for similarities between these seemingly different locations. From my space in the borderland between the correctional community and the outside educational community, I find I must continuously negotiate and redefine both my identity as a prison educator and the boundaries of my practice within the prison system.

Journal entry and reflections:

> *My confused sense of identity has been replaced with an acceptance that my identity is multiply-situated. I am teacher and prison educator at once. I am aware of some other presence, of a certainty that I am involved in shaping my own identity. I conclude that I previously allowed my experiences within my location to shape my identity in my absence.*

The recognition of difference within a community can lead to accountability, to correctional educators acknowledging their own positions of authority within their prison teaching practice and understanding the implications of that authority for their practice. As a correctional educator, I am in a position of power and authority over my students. The correctional system places me in that position, although a teacher in any community is in a somewhat similar position. Although there are many factors that impact the degree of my relative privilege, power and authority over my students, my ability to leave the prison at night is the greatest distinguishing feature of difference. That circumstance determines that I can never really be "other" than "outsider."

As a prison teacher who is an outsider within the prison, I am granted power and authority by the prison system. As a white prison teacher, my identity ensures my power and authority over my prisoner-students. Whether or not I acknowledge, understand or enact that power and authority does not influence the fact of its existence. If I claim to be uncomfortable with the power and authority of my position and privilege, I find I then must consider if I wish to surrender them. Honestly, that scenario also makes me uncomfortable.

Within my prison classroom, I attempt to recognize the power of my authority, as well as my responsibility in questioning my position of power. It is a challenging undertaking, one that is linked to feelings of inadequacy and agency. I remind myself daily that from within my prison classroom, I may impact the futures of others. In fact, I know that I have done so. The enormity of that position frightens me.

From my position in the prison classroom, I refuse to locate myself as either/or within this system of surveillance and control. I share with Alberti (1997) the following sentiment: "I have an appreciation of the possibilities inherent in outsider status, with its comparative freedom from the playing of institutional politics" (p. 146). I experiment with curriculum rather than following a prescribed course of study. I can attempt to make my classroom environment inviting and relaxed instead of tense and cold. I challenge my students to consider ideas from multiple perspectives rather than defining one "right" perspective for them. And I question the system from a position that is partially outside it. I also claim my position as both/and—not simply an adult educator, but neither simply a correctional educator. I have discovered a freedom to name my position and my practice as complex and multiply-situated. From that perspective in the uncertain and undefined borderland of the prison classroom, I am both "on the outside looking in" and "on the inside looking out." At the same time, I am also neither inside nor outside, but in a borderland zone with undetermined borders "To survive the Borderlands / you must live *sin fronteras* (without borders) / be a crossroads" (Anzaldua, 1987, p. 195).

Chapter XIV

The Issue of Voice and Validity in Prison Education Research

by Anne Costelloe

As a prison teacher carrying out academic research into prison education I was faced with a dilemma. On the one hand, I wanted my research findings to represent accurately my students' experiences and beliefs. On the other hand, I believe firmly in postmodernist research notions that there is no such thing as an accurate reflection of the truth. By this I am referring to views like those of Denzin and Lincoln that there is "no clear window into the inner life of an individual, any gaze is always filtered through the lens of language, gender, social class, race, and ethnicity" (2000, p. 19). My dilemma was compounded further by my agreement with the view that any research carried out on behalf of somebody else is ineffective. So, what was I to do? How was I going to resolve these seemingly conflicting issues? In other words, how was I to realize my research objective of "giving voice to the voiceless" while simultaneously stressing that in any research project there is a world of difference between the text being collected and the text being created? In terms of research ethics, this was the major quandary I faced.But first, a little background information.

The research to which I refer was carried out as part of a thesis for a doctorate in education entitled, *Third Level Education in Irish Prisons: Who Participates and Why?* As the title suggests, I wanted to establish a pattern of participation for prisoners undertaking degree courses while in prison. Furthermore, I wanted to provide an ethnography of the experiences and motivations of these university-level prison students. The rationale behind the two-pronged approach was because I believe patterns of participation in adult learning are largely meaningless unless accompanied by a shared understanding of what motivates the learners to participate or self-exclude. As a teacher in Ireland's largest prison for more than fifteen years, I was interested in exploring and documenting why any prisoner would undertake such intensive study and I was also keen to see if one could typify this particular group of prison students. I felt these questions were important as prison educators have much to learn from students who choose to participate in higher education simply because they are imprisoned. Similarly, we have much to learn from those who self-exclude. It should be noted that in Ireland participation in all prison education programs is voluntary, as befits an educational service based on the ideologies and principles of adult education.

Returning to the research, I think it necessary to provide an outline of the varying theoretical and methodological presuppositions that have influenced me as a teacher and an educational researcher and, ultimately, provided the foundations for theory formation throughout the research process. While drafting my research I was eager to highlight these presuppositions. I felt this recognition and identification of my belief systems was necessary in light of Denzin and Lincoln's (2000, p. 18) claim that "the gendered, multiculturally situated researcher approaches the world with a set of ideas" that predefine and configure each aspect of the research process. Undoubtedly, as a researcher my belief systems would influence strongly my judgments on research validity, reliability and generalization, as well as my choice of research tools. The importance of this position lies in Oppenheim's (1992) assertion that the quality of research design will depend frequently on the quality of research conceptualization. By outlining what I perceived to be my set of ideas, my beliefs on ontology (the nature of reality), epistemology (theories of knowledge) and research methodology, I was attempting to ensure the research process was subjected to critique in order to fulfill my belief that critical reflexivity should be an essential element of educational research. Of course, by attempting to identify my set of research beliefs I was locating my study firmly within the critical research paradigm and outing its postmodernist stance. On a more fundamental level I was hoping the identification of my methodological assumptions would help conceptualize the entire research process.

Having worked as a prison teacher, my research was influenced by those ideologies and viewpoints that reflect my understanding of adult and prison education. Just as no researcher can be completely detached from their subjects, communities or culture (Hitchcock & Hughes, 1995), neither can a teacher remain completely detached. Theorists such as Freire (1972) and Mezirow (2000, 1998, 1997) are examples of adult educators who have influenced me through the years. Freire's (1972, 1987) ideas on education as conscientization, as a possible agent for change and transformative action, tie in nicely with my postmodern views of knowledge and its potential to influence change. Furthermore, his ideas on the power relationships perpetuated in and by the dominant educational discourse reflect in a similar manner my views not only on educational content but also educational relationships and power struggles. Mezirow's (2000, 1998, 1997) view that the educational process is best understood by examining how those involved perceive and understand the process and their relationship to that process had a direct bearing on my choice of research paradigm. His conception of transformative learning emerging from critical reflection by developing thoughtful awareness of how presuppositions constrain the way we perceive, understand and react to our experiences and the world had as much to offer the educational researcher as the prison student. As an educator I was interested in encouraging reflection and reflexivity among my students. My research and narrative attempted to mirror that reflexivity.

Cultivated within the framework of the critical learning tradition, my view of adult and prison learning is one that acknowledges the concept of teacher as facilitator. Facilitators do not direct; rather, they assist learners to attain a state of self-actualization by fostering a spirit of critical reflection based on praxis. My understanding of praxis is closely related to that of Carr (1993) who proposes, "...it is a form of reflective action which can itself transform the theory which guides it." McNiff et al., (1996) also provide a salient conception of my view of praxis:

> Praxis is informed, committed action that gives rise to knowledge rather than just successful action. It is informed because other people's views are taken into account. It is committed and intentional in terms of values that have been examined and can be argued. It leads to knowledge from and about educational practice. (p. 8)

Thus facilitators and learners collaborate in a continual process of action, reflection on action, collaborative analysis of action, new action and further reflection along the lines attributed to Schon (1987). Surely such views would be automatically subsumed into my views on how to proceed with the research process? Such perceptions of the educator and the educational researcher in turn provides the foundations for Kemmis' (1993) view of "informed, committed action: praxis," and action research as "an embodiment of democratic principles in research" applied to praxis. He concludes that such intuitive insights are essential and must form the basis of action research (Kemmis, 1993). By buying into such views, should I not just proceed with an action research project? For me, the weakness of this argument lies in the proposition that while the accumulated intuitive insights would indeed be of immense benefit to those seeking to offer or develop a similar program, the criteria used for making evaluative judgments are likely to have limited potential for replication because they are the product of individual preferences and contextual variables. Thus by being overly situational, I feel the validity of much action research can be called into question. Consequently, the limitations of such a research process for my study lay with my desire to compare the prison context with the mainstream and I felt that a purely action research study would unduly shift that focus. So, if action research was out, what was in?

Returning to my educational perspectives, if we concede that the teachers' aim in fostering critical reflection is the nurturing of self-directed, empowered adults then their objective is to generate a realization in their learners that the bodies of knowledge, accepted truths, commonly held values and customary behavior that comprise their world are contextually and culturally constructed. As this ideology influences my practice as a teacher, it would inevitably influence my practice as an educational researcher. Although Hammersley (1993) expresses doubt as to the feasibility and applicability of this view of "learning as inquiry," I felt it had much to offer me as a practitioner. He contests the view of the teacher as facilitator by highlighting the difficulty in minimizing the role difference between teacher and learner; likewise, he believes teachers are automatically "an authority" in that they control the parameters of the learning process and thus he goes on to question the openness and democratic nature of inquiry learning. In the same way, he is resistant to critical research as being similarly ideologically biased in its treatment of data among other things (Hammersley, 1993). Even so, my observations and experiences forced me to favor emancipatory research with its basis in ideology critique. This approach spreads ownership and control of praxis and research across the participant group. It is emancipatory in that it allows the group to free themselves from the restrictions and dictates of outside influences and irrelevant contexts. This allows the researcher and the subject to become equal and active members and creates the conditions for collaborative research. Thus I felt that some form of critical (if not emancipatory) research could resolve the dilemma mentioned earlier and construe the theoretical paradigms and perspective influencing this research process.

Many would suggest that emancipatory research is the solution to the dilemma of voice and validity. Its acknowledgment of context, its emphasis on allowing participants to set the investigative agenda and research foci, and its concern that the conclusions drawn will be disseminated clearly should allow the subjects to participate equally and make their voices heard by becoming practical theorists. Moreover, as emancipatory research is concerned with reforming existing power structures and inequalities within the education system, it must be equally concerned that it does not reproduce or legitimize, through non-collaborative methodologies, any such dominant power structures within the research group. Thus the fear of muffling "the voices of the voiceless" can be subjugated. Yet while I agreed with the ideals and aims of emancipatory research, I felt its primary weakness lay in the fact that there is no actual mechanism contained within, or indeed no evidence to suggest that it does achieve its aims or indeed ensure policy or discourse change. This is ironic in that such research claims to be strongly committed to making a direct contribution to practice. Yet I am not convinced it can do this. My doubts as to the effectiveness of any research process carried out on somebody else's behalf nurtured my reluctance to label my study emancipatory or overly stress its collaborative elements. Thus while I emphasized that such ideals shaped my ideology and in turn my rationale, I felt the broader label of critical research was more appropriate. Therefore, I claim my research fell naturally within the critical research tradition based as it was on postmodern ideologies. While I agree with criticisms of critical research that it is good on critique but weak on strategies for change or indeed radical transformation, I still believe critical research is the best possible and most appropriate approach for my study.

My rationale for locating the research within this broad concept of critical research lies in its attempts to redefine the power relations inherent in any research process. I felt that such attempts could solve somewhat my dilemma of providing a forum for the prison students' voices. It would thus help develop "a deeper understanding of experience from the perspectives of the participants" (Maykut & Morehouse, 1994, p. 44). By being reflexive and working in close collaboration with a subgroup of the research cohort, I was hoping a dialogical process would develop through which the students' voices could be heard. Smith and Deemer (2000) suggest that "to speak at all must always and inevitability be to speak for someone else" (p. 891). They go on to opine that the issue of voice and validity is a moral and practical issue rather than an epistemological one (Smith & Deemer, 2000). This is similar to Scott's (1996) assertion that ethics and epistemology are two sides of the same coin because the ways researchers chose to manage the collected data and interact with the participants determines the epistemological status of that data. Thus I felt a qualitative stance and critical research approach was the most applicable to my research project, because I saw myself as a positioned insider attempting to produce a narrative. Such a narrative according to Ely et al. (1997) is in itself a method of inquiry and a way of knowing; it is equally a discovery and an analysis. After all, what more could one realistically ask of one's research?

The ultimate premise behind my choice of critical research paradigm is my belief that social investigation is not a neutral process. This belief questions the power relations inherent in any research process and compels me to return to the aforementioned dilemma. For me, this dilemma is further compounded by the fact that academic status bestows public legitimacy on theory formulation. As Lynch (1999, p. 53) states, "it is only those who speak in the language and voice of the established paradigm who will be heard." Until prison students are credentialed and thus bestowed public legitimacy, rarely will their voices permeate through to the establishment. Of course, one way for prison students to attain public legitimacy is through the attainment of university degrees and other academic qualifications and for them to conduct and publish academic research. The irony of the situation was not lost on me.

Postmodernists, feminists and Marxists alike will testify readily to the supposition that one's identity is inextricably bound with one's educational status among other things. Hence the working class prisoner who gains a degree (and voice) is suddenly in danger of entering a strange twilight world. Generally he is not fully accepted by those who view him as a reformed ex-criminal or by those who view him as a genuine third-level student, while simultaneously being no longer accepted fully by his non-graduate criminal peers. This anomaly is best illustrated by the following quotation from one of the students interviewed as part of my research. On finishing a prison sentence he completed two years of a chemical engineering degree in Trinity College Dublin before returning to prison on a new sentence. Reflecting on this time at university he states:

> …there was a social element to not fitting in. The course I chose is essentially training to become a high-level management/ executive type person. I was never going to succeed at this level even if I was highly successful academically. Too much of a culture shock in leaving prison and starting at university, I suffered a lot because of this and felt no matter what, I would never shed the prison yard mentality.

What is interesting about his quotation is that it is the individual's self-perception rather than the perception of others that supports my supposition.

McMahon (1997), a mainstream mature student, echoes the perception of the prison student:

> ...certain areas of knowledge are regarded as more important than others. In Ireland, these are the areas that suit the middle-class ethos. As a consequence, people like myself who may have obtained access in a formal sense are still marginalized within the third-level institution. For me, this marginalization was more to do with my class background than with the fact that I was a mature student.

Such views support Schuller's (1998) contention that those who acquire educational qualifications not expected of them risk separation from the community. The view that one's social class identity is automatically changed through participation in higher education feeds into the irony mentioned earlier. If a working class prisoner who has gained a degree should carry out research similar to mine in the future, his or her perspective and vision can as easily be called into question as mine—the middle-class academic. It would be telling to see just how qualitatively different research conducted by a prisoner would be from my research.

Gergen and Gergen (2000) raise some interesting questions concerning identifying just who the author and the participant truly are in any research piece. Suggesting that while it may be evident each individual participant is polyvocal (speaks from multiple social positions, with different "voices"), the author of the research is the coordinator of the voices and thus the ultimate arbiter of what to write/speak. (This is what I meant when I suggested it might be futile to attempt to research on somebody else's behalf.) For them a new research relationship is the only way forward: A relationship that facilitates the participants as "cultural insiders" and replaces "re/search with re/presentation" (Gergen & Gergen, 2000). I agree with this conceptualization and would suggest that throughout my research I wanted to represent some form of situated knowledge that presents some sense of a truth located within a particular community at a particular time. While I accept that this raised once again the contentious issue of voice and validity, I felt this would lead to productive dialogue until such a time as prisoners are afforded the opportunity to carry out their own research. This position can be pitted against Scott and Usher's (1996, p. 29) proposition that there is "neither an originary point of knowledge nor a final interpretation." If we concur, then legitimately neither the prisoner nor the researcher can paint the complete picture. Indeed I would suggest that merely sketching the picture would suffice, with the readers' interpretations determining its truth and value. Pring (2000) suggests rather philosophically "...that the pursuit of truth makes sense without the guarantee of ever having attained it." At last, here was the get-out clause for which I searched. In the end I decided this was the best for which I could hope and concluded that the spoken texts of the participants in tandem with the written text of the researcher constructed a reflective academic text located in a particular context and at a particular time. After that, it was up to the reader to take it or leave it.

The Prison Education Service of Ireland provides a variety educational services to Irish inmates. These images are from a complete deck of inmate-created playing cards produced by the Education Service. (Original art is in full color.)

Visit http://www.pesireland.org for more information.

The Council of Europe's Recommendation No. R(89) 12 of the Committee of Ministers to Member States on Education in Prison, known as the *European Prison Rules (EPR)*, provides an illuminating contrast to the dominant U.S. corrections paradigm. To see the *Rules* in their entirety, visit the European Prison Education Association's website at http://www.epea.org

– Editor

CHAPTER XV

THE ECOLOGY OF IDENTITY

by Richard Ashcroft

Introduction

This chapter is a reflection upon identity and identity change. It includes a discussion of formative events and training that shaped my perspectives on the process of identity formation and change. It is my intention to describe and explain events that were influential in my own development of and understanding of identity, both personal and professional, as well as my understanding of the dynamics of this process as it relates to us all, and in particular, those of us whose career paths led us to alternative and institutional instructional settings.

A Fundamental Question of Identity: Who Are You?

A question I sometimes suggest my graduate students ask themselves during a class called "Effective Communication in Education" is, "Who am I?" The purpose of entertaining this question is the notion that one's "sense of self" is critical to effective communication. When people are most "at home inside their own skin," so to speak, they tend to communicate more clearly and effectively, and with less tentativeness. They "come from" a place of clarity, presence and spontaneity. Aspects of their identity are "transparent" enough that what emerges from them when they communicate from their "core self" can resonate with listeners' deeper selves. This clarity contrasts with the automaticity, guardedness, and defensiveness that colors much of our intended communicative behavior, our *conditioned* way of being-in-the-world, our automatic manner of social conduct of which we are largely unaware.

Of course, most of us think that we are quite self-aware. After all, don't we think rationally, make decisions based upon evidence, work at maintaining a "sameness" in reaction to varying stimuli? In other words, don't we expend energy to avoid being perceived as individuals who change in response to the stimulus conditions of the moment? Indeed, a "flip-flop" mantra was used in an attempt to discredit an American presidential candidate in a recent election. My assumption is that the viewpoint of the electorate, or at least what was being appealed to in the assumed viewpoint, was a common notion that one's identity should be fixed, secure, steady, in order for one to be perceived as psychologically strong, healthy and dependable. This perspective on identity, although it is widespread in Northern Europe, North America, Australia and New Zealand, especially among males, namely that one's identity is fixed and separate, bounded and entirely individual, is not a perspective held by everyone in the world. In fact, on a planetary scale, it may be a minority viewpoint. Among many cultures in Asia, Africa, Oceania, as well as the indigenous cultures of the Americas, one's identity is viewed as being mutable and interdependent (Kim, 2002). My reason for mentioning this difference is to point to the influence of culture upon identity. Many aspects of our identity have been culturally conditioned, and have become so much a part of who we perceive ourselves to be that we are entirely unaware of the degree of automaticity with which they function in us. For example, before you turn the page, prepare yourself to *not* read the single word that appears on the next page. Look at it, but don't read it. Ready? OK, turn the page.

BLUE

Were you able to look at it but not *read* it? Of course you weren't, because reading text is so automatic for you that you cannot *not* do it. And just like the acculturated skill of reading, we have many social behaviors: facial expressions; body postures; emotional reactions; ways of perceiving and attending, that are just as automatic. Because they are automatic, we are not conscious of them.

In response to the question "Who am I?" my students have produced lists that have included items like: teacher, parent, nice person, scholar, son or daughter, etc. The second part of the activity is to tease out any items that represent what you might "do" or "have" rather than what you "are." The lists then become much shorter and the discussions become more interesting regarding items like "nice person," for example. Is "nice" something one *is* or something one *does*? On items like this where a student might be having difficulty seeing the distinction between their *being* "nice" and *doing* "nice," I ask, "Would you still be you if this item were not on your list? Have there been moments in your life when you were not nice?" Because the answer to these questions usually produces a period of reflection and a "yes," I use it to illustrate an aspect of identity that we typically don't consider, namely, that much of what we hold to be our identity is actually a product of our cultural conditioning and socialization, features we *learned* for some reason related to our survival, and then *identified with* them. We incorporated (literally, "took into the body") these features, these schemas, these cognitive constructs, into the production of a self, and began to view that self as who we are. Yet we didn't always have these features, this particular self, this particular identity. We can recall being younger than the life events that influenced our production of some of these features we now identify with. Were we still *us* without those features? These are questions for reflection and are central to my own perspective on identity.

Identity Change: A Personal Reflection

Given by the editor of this volume the honor of relating an original narrative for my perspectives on identity, I would like to share with readers several experiences that I now see as critical in shaping my own identity as well as my current understanding of the process in general. An event relevant to identity change first entered my life during a time that was difficult for me. It was 1951, I was ten years old and my family had just decided we were going to move. We were going to move away from the only home, school, park, friends, railroad tracks, library, corner store; in short, the only world I had ever known. Although later in my life I would realize how upset I was over this impending loss, at the time I merely acted badly. I sabotaged friendships, quit sixth grade basketball, acted "weird" in school, got bad grades, was rude to grownups: an observing psychologist might have said that I was dismantling the structure of my life, my identity, in preparation for the move. There was no observing psychologist and the available observers, myself included, simply thought I was acting badly.

But move we did, and I and my citified brothers and sisters, six children at this point – I was fourth from the oldest in a clan of children who would eventually number nine—found ourselves living in a large farmhouse on 72 acres of land in Central Maryland. From urban East Orange, New Jersey, where from Eagle Rock summit one could see the New York City skyline, and make out the movement of cars on the George Washington Bridge, we were now in a large rural landscape, miles from the small hamlet of Taneytown (pronounced by locals, for some mysterious reason of dialect as "Tawnytown"), in a house from which we could see a single neighboring house almost a mile away on the road to Taneytown. In addition, we were outsiders, Yankees with Yankee accents, and where we had moved in 1951 was South of the Mason-Dixon line. We had entered a culture that had not forgotten the Civil War; its battlefields surrounded us and a lingering apartheid had bred a social climate quite foreign to us. Culture shock was felt collectively and by each member of the family and addressed differently by each of us depending upon our relative ages, level of development, sense of loss, family positioning, and ability to adapt. For myself, I became a child of the forest and took to following a creek that crossed our farmland and entered our woods and then continued deeper into an old hardwood forest. Each time I walked I would explore it farther, always knowing that I could follow the creek back to familiar landmarks. My world had shrunk in one sense but had opened more widely in another. Walking out one's door and following paths into what seemed a vast and eternal forest was endlessly fascinating, filled with sights and sounds and smells, plants and creatures that were all new to me. But newest of all was the sky.

The rural Maryland sky of the early 1950's was vast and stunning compared to what I had seen in New Jersey. Soon my forays into nature included night walks as well. My second storey bedroom window opened onto the roof of the one storey laundry room. In the middle of the night, I sometimes would climb quietly out my bedroom window, lower myself from the edge of the laundry room roof and drop to the ground for a walk in the dark. Over time, my night vision improved. Although I didn't know it then, our night vision is the older system of "rods" pushed mostly to the outer perimeter of our retina by the more recently emerging "cones." These newer cones provide color vision and work best in the field of vision directly in front of us because of their grouping in the central portion of our retinas. In contrast, the rods are not for color vision but for black and white and grey, and are highly sensitive to movement. They can provide vision at night if we train our awareness to the periphery of our field of vision, rather than the field of vision directly in front of us, which daylight trains us to do. Of course, I was not yet aware of any of this information, when one night near Taneytown, Maryland, on a starry moonless night, I lay on a grassy hill in an open area near where the creek entered the forest. A vast sea of stars was spread across the sky. And as I lay there, gazing at the night sky, my night vision gradually expanded my view of the sky until I reached a moment when simultaneously I was holding in my field of vision, the entire sky above me from horizon to horizon. Instantly I could see the slow movement of stars horizon to horizon. Unexpectedly my perspective changed. Suddenly, it was not the stars moving on the horizon that I was seeing, but I could perceive, almost feel, the earth itself slowly tumbling through space, through this vast sea of stars, and I was part of it. It's difficult to describe the experience, but if you have ever looked at one of those 3-D pictures and in order to see it you have to play with the focus of your eyes until your perception of the image suddenly shifts to three dimensions, it was like that only exponentially grander. As I lay there, seeing/feeling this journey through the cosmos, everything else seemed to fall away. Loss, loneliness, my whole "story" up to that point, all of my personal identity, my "me," disappeared and all that was left was the experience and my awareness of it.

I don't know how long I lay there. In a sense, part of me is still there in my preadolescent memory as a write this. Reflecting now upon the experience, I can say that it affected me in my relationship to, and my subsequent understanding of, identity formation in two ways that are important to me now. The first effect began to influence me immediately, and although I would only later learn to articulate it verbally, I developed a deep sense that experience is senior to understanding. At the time, I *understood* as a schoolboy that the earth "rolled" through space both in its journey around the sun and in the common journey of our solar system within our galaxy, and ultimately, within the universe. I *knew* this from books and school. And then I *experienced* it that night when I saw in real time the slow movement of earth's journey through the stars and subsequently I held this *knowing* in a profoundly different way. An illustration I use as an adult to illustrate the difference between my notion of *experiencing* versus *understanding* is the example of how jokes work. When we *get* the joke we have an *experience*. When we *don't get* the joke we can have someone *explain* it to us and then we *understand* why it would have been funny if we had only *gotten* it.

The second thing I got from this experience developed over time. I've come to realize that each of us has a sense of who we are, a way of responding to the question, "Who am I?" But much of the "self" we have become is a product of our conditioning. During this "star" experience from my early adolescence, one thing that occurred was that during it, my entire preadolescent identity seemed to disappear. All that I "was" during the event was awareness; there was only awareness, no point of view, no attitude toward the event, no judgment or evaluation, no thoughts, no story, no sense of "me." There was only the flow of experience and awareness of it. That was all. When it was over I returned to my "normal" way of being-in-the-world; I behaved in ways that were both thoughtless and kind, defensive and open, fearful and brave, honest and deceiving, in short, I did all of the things I always had done, things we all do. Over time, and through other experiences and education, I've learned to hold one aspect of that event under the stars as being highly relevant to identity and identity formation, and it's this: When all is stripped away of who we think we are; when we disidentify with the roles with which we have identified; when we become clear in our response to the question *who am I*, all that we are at the core of our being is awareness, simple awareness, the rest is structure we have built, artifacts of our interaction with our life experience. The only thing that makes the vast collection of cognitive structures, of schemata, or roles we have learned, come to be considered by us as *who* we are, is our habitual way of *identifying with* them. In short, we truly are creatures of habit, we *are* our habits, or at least, we behave that way.

As a young man in the 1960's, I had other experiences of my identity being reduced to a single point of awareness, and since that time I regularly have practiced meditation, a daily silent visit to a simple level of non-representational awareness. The continuing flow of the experience of my life is continually touched by the realization that I am not my identity; and that my identity is something that I *have*.

My formal education included preparation for teaching high school, and graduate study in philosophy, linguistics, psychology, and special education. This final area of professional focus, teaching individuals with disabilities, involved the largest portion of my pre-university teaching career. Eventually I focused on teaching individuals with emotional disturbance, discovering that my preference was to work with individuals who could recover from the condition that placed them in a "special" category, and those conditions that are defined as emotional and behavioral disorders can sometimes be overcome. Teaching individuals with emotional disturbance and behavioral disorders introduced me to institutional teaching, because many school-aged individuals so identified have been institutionalized by their families in treatment centers. Still others are in protective custody from abusive environments, while others have been adjudicated by the juvenile courts for acting out in their communities. It was during this period that I began to see that many of the ways that these children and youth differed from me were differences of degree rather than kind. To clarify, many of the labels used to identify specific pathologies can define and objectify the individual in a way that can cause them to be seen as very different from those in professional relationships with them. I noticed that a significant number of professionals providing educational or custodial care seemed to invest their own identities with how different they were from those they treated. This seemed to constrain communication; the professional communicating from the role of professional, seemingly calling forth from the one being "treated" the role of client, ward, patient, inmate or subject. I also noted that the power relationships often were maintained by an aversive tone of using actual punishments or the threat of punishment.

While I was working in an institution for adjudicated wards of the juvenile courts I began my doctoral studies. My doctoral research was experimental, investigating the effects of non-aversive interventions on the incidence of serious problem social behavior, testing the pragmatics' theoretical assertion that all behavior has a communicative function. When I completed my doctorate I accepted a position with California State University, San Bernardino, because those who interviewed me there expressed the clearest commitment to provide support for projects related to the education of at-risk and adjudicated youth. In that role I developed a number of training projects, two of which were conducted within the eleven youth prisons of the California Youth Authority (CYA, now called the Department of Juvenile Justice) from 1993 until 2003.

California Youth Authority as a Total Institution

What is immediately apparent working within the context of a youth prison is that it meets the criteria set forward by Erving Goffman (1961) as being a "total" institution. Briefly stated, a total institution is a social microcosm dictated by hegemony and clear hierarchy, with examples that include boarding schools, concentration camps, prisons, mental institutions and boot camps. They are established so that identified groups of individuals live and conduct all of life's activities entirely within its walls.

> The recruit comes into the establishment with a conception of himself made possible by certain stable social arrangements in his home world. Upon entrance, he is immediately stripped of the support provided by these arrangements. In the accurate language of some of the oldest *total institutions*, he begins a series of abasements, degradations, humiliations, and profanations of the self. His self is systematically, if often unintentionally, mortified. He begins some radical shifts in his moral career, a career composed of the progressive changes that occur in the beliefs that he has concerning himself and the significance of others. (Goffman, 1961, p. 14)

According to Goffman's words, one of the primary functions of the institution is to attempt to bring about change in the self-structure or identity-structure of "recruits," who are, in this case, the wards. Each institution derives its own identity from the characteristics of its members in establishing the identity of this self-contained world. Institutional identity is symbolized by the barriers to social contact with "the outside" that are built into the physical plant. At CYA some of the main elements are locked doors, clear delineation of traffic patterns for group movement and fences topped with razor wire. Of Goffman's five categories of "total institution" it is clear that CYA is "organized to protect the community against what are felt to be intentional dangers to it, with the welfare of the persons thus sequestered not the immediate issue: ..." (Goffman, 1961).

Also in keeping with Goffman's characterization of life in a "total institution," a central feature of CYA can be described as a breakdown of the barriers ordinarily separating the spheres of life, sleep, play and work. In the total institution, all aspects of life are conducted in the same place and under the same central authority. Each phase of daily activity is carried on in the immediate company of a number of others, all of whom are treated alike and required to do the same thing together. All phases of the day's activities are scheduled, one activity leads at prearranged times into the next; the entire sequence of activities directed from "above" by a system of explicit formal rulings and a body of officials. The various enforced activities are brought together into a single plan purportedly designed to fulfill the official aims of the institution (Goffman, 1961).

Goffman was not the first to contribute to the development of this view of institutional life. Baltard (in Foucault, 1979) described the "complete and austere" institution as one that assumes every aspect of the everyday lives of its clients, including their conduct, work, waking, sleeping, recreation and maintains an uninterrupted control over every aspect of lives by maintaining mechanisms to repress and punish. In part, Goffman's more elaborated "total institution" is one where all aspects of life occur under one roof; where all activity is in groups and strictly scheduled; and all activities are planned to suit rational goals. Among these goals are: maintaining a social distance between inmate and staff populations; suppression of individual self expression favoring collective identities such as "guard" and "ward;" and, maintaining a maximum degree of authority. In addition, there is typically a set of rules specific to the institution that contribute to an interior "world view" with its own provincial vocabulary, jargon or lingo, sometimes contextualized by wards into their own "code," so as to retain some sense of controlled separateness from the official institutional vocabulary. Depending upon identity orientation, school personnel use a greater or lesser amount of institutional jargon depending upon what seemed to me to be two major factors. One is the length of time they had been working within the institution, a reflection of their having been "socialized" over time into a partially "institutionalized" identity. The second seemed more a matter of choice. Some educators seemed to naturally "identify with" institutional staff and adopted more of the institutional jargon, especially that of its most visible and ubiquitous representatives, the guards.

Of the groups who provide an institution with its identity, some groups are more essential to this identity. The institution suffers or ceases to exist without the presence of the individuals who make up essential groups. A prison is not a prison without prisoners, or, as in the case in CYA, wards (the term used in CYA for youthful offenders who are now "wards" of the state). Wards are an essential group. Also essential to CYA's identity as a prison are guards. Without guards CYA would not be a prison. Because these two groups are essential they will always be present simultaneously within the institution. Imprisonment requires that there be "the imprisoned" and those who maintain and monitor their imprisonment. These two groups (at least) are essential. They are also easy to identify. Each has a "uniformed" appearance. Once identified by the state as either guard or prisoner, they are identified in the institutional context by what they wear. It is clear that what these individuals from both groups wear within the institutional context differs from dress they might choose on the "outside."

You Shall Know Them by Their Clothing

"Do not wear denim," was a serious caution I gave to my San Jose State University graduate students when we visited youth prisons in California. Denim clothing *could* have identified them as wards. In these total institutions denim is the "uniform" of the imprisoned. Prison guards wear uniforms that are similar in style to those worn by others in the "policing" professions. These uniforms clearly serve as "identifiers" of them and their role within the institutional context. The uniform signifies parameters, especially regarding communication. The communicative tone or register used when communicating "from" the role of uniformed guard "to" uniformed ward, is dramatically different from the reverse: the tone or register used when communicating "from" the role of uniformed ward "to" uniformed guard. Much of the institutional context is produced by this difference in vocal register. These observations on deferential behavior reflect an earlier view expressed by Goffman (1967) in his essays on "Face Work" and "The Nature of Deference and Demeanor," which also reference institutional life, though of a different type. In Goffman's day there were asylums, mental hospitals and psychiatric institutions. A recent PBS documentary (Navasky & O'Connor, 2005) identified prisons as the "new asylums," noting that of the approximately 2 million individuals incarcerated in the United States, approximately half a million, or close to 25%, have been diagnosed as mentally ill. In the 1950s and 1960s when Goffman studied identity in institutional contexts, he was focusing upon large state psychiatric institutions. Few of these exist today, and in their place, prisons house these individuals.

The wards who are considered "on program" have learned to adopt a deferential vocal register in communicating with guards or others they may perceive to be in agreement with, or a part of, the institutional power structure. I have seen examples of "shifts" from this register when I answer questions from wards I am meeting by telling them I'm a teacher (their first impression of an outsider dressed in a "professional uniform"—a jacket and tie— tends to produce their "vocal register" response to parole officer). When they realize I'm not a member of the "policing" profession, and I'm not "their" teacher they often appear confused as if searching for an appropriate communication register. I do my best to project assertive, non-threatening calmness, which produces from them a vocal register I call "being nice." The reason I mention this here is that it illustrates questions that arise regarding being an educator in a "total" institution. What communication "register" is the appropriate one for wards when addressing their own teacher, who is not "uniformed," indeed, who wears clothing that would also be worn "on the outside." Does their presence "call up" the vocal register used for teachers in regular neighborhood schools? Perhaps not, because some aspects of teaching in the institution are idiosyncratic in relation to how one might have learned to address teachers on the "outside."

For example, teachers who witness improper conduct in their classrooms do not directly apply negative sanctions, as would be more typical in an "outside" school. This difference is likely to be noted by wards at some level of awareness and also have some influence upon their means of relating to their institutional teachers. This single difference can alter the type of relationship that can exist between ward and teacher and will mutually affect respective role identities. In spite of this role difference, or maybe because of it, some teachers feel (perhaps out of fear) that they must maintain a degree of coercive dominance over their wards. But another peculiarity of the institutional educator role is that they are obliged to render a service to wards, which in the institutional context can communicate a kind of deference to the needs of wards. This is especially true for the significant proportion of teachers offering "compensatory" educational services such as speech therapy, bilingual instruction, special education or other specialized remedial instruction. In the prison setting, such acts can be seen as slightly out of place when contrasted with the role of guard or of custodial staff in living units (called "counselors" in CYA), which is not intended to be perceived by wards as deferential to their needs.

In contrast with this view of the teacher role as deferential to the needs of wards, in CYA, because security of the ward is a top priority, in some limited respects the teacher is also a member of the security team. Members of the educational staff are requested to report changes in wards' behavior and appearance, to inventory property and tools, and to maintain a routine of alertness for any "contraband." Teachers have varying degrees of acceptance of this aspect of the role, some resisting it a bit, others embracing it, both stances a function of the degree to which a teacher has "identified with" the institution in order to belong, and the degree to which they have "institutionalized" at least a portion of their professional identity.

Identity and Selfhood in General: Contrasting Viewpoints

Puzzling over identity and selfhood and their overall place in the human relationship to the cosmos have been essential questions of people for millennia. According to Kim (2002, p. 8), "The self, then, is an organized locus of the various, sometimes competing, understandings of how to be a person, and it functions as an individualized orienting, mediating, interpretive framework, giving shape to what a person notices and thinks about, what she is motivated to do, and how she communicates with others." Concepts about selfhood include information about the self in various temporal and situational contexts, as well as internal states, such as mood, and interrelationships among these features (Neidenthal & Beike, 1997).

How concepts of self and identity are acquired and built can be explained in reference to two contrasting philosophical positions regarding the link between identity concepts and social relationships. One position is that relations with others constitutes identity. A contrasting view is that separation from primary relationships, combined with experiences and features that are unique, make up identity (Kim, 2002). This latter viewpoint is decidedly Western, more typically male, and has developed from processes activated during the historical periods in European history referred to as the Renaissance and the Enlightenment. In the dominant Western cultural framework, self identity has come to be equated with being an independent and autonomous bounded individual who is seperate from others.

A contrasting view is common to East Asian cultures who define identity primarily in terms of interdependence rather than uniqueness or distinctiveness. A heightened awareness of the other and one's relationship to others is carefully nurtured and crafted culturally until it becomes automatic and spontaneous (Kitayama & Markus, 1999).

According to a number of Western scholars, teachers' professional identity is the key concept in finding out teachers' relationship of self (Ashmore & Jussim, 1997; Baumeister, 1986; Deaux, 1992, 1993; Stryker, 1987) within a certain context of practice. In this respect, professional identity is the result of an interaction between the personal experiences of teachers and the social, cultural, and institutional environment in which they function on a daily basis (Van den Berg, 2002). It would be impossible to consider the whole complexity of this relationship in this chapter (for a wider perspective see, e.g., Ashcroft, 1999; Halpin & Moore, 2000; Nelson, 2002; Van den Berg, 2002). For our purposes here, it is enough to consider identity in relation to change, because one of the purposes of the projects I directed in CYA, especially for the paraprofessional participants, was to effect a change in identity, to develop a professional identity.

While the existence of a "true" or immutable self or identity has been the topic of much debate in the literature (e.g., Markus & Kunda, 1986), and theoretical traditions differ in whether they posit the existence of an internal feeling of personal identity that is distinguished from mere outward appearance, a large literature in social psychology, for example, has found consistent support for self-verification, defined as our tendency to seek evaluations and interaction partners who confirm our self-views (Swann, 1987). According to this view, we more easily "identify with" others who verify, or display agreement with, the sense of personal self we have "identified with." This suggests that much of our identity is produced by us in the social context of our lives, and once we have achieved "identification with" this produced sense of self, we like to have it recognized and reinforced by others.

Swann (1987) noted that career transitions are times in which people are more prone to modifying their self-conceptions, but these changes are primarily based on their treatment by others. This is an important contribution of social psychology, namely, demonstrating the socially constructed nature of identity. Contrary to common notions of the self in Western culture, which view the self as consisting of cultural, political and interpersonal sensibilities and styles that are permanent and non-negotiable, the self is multiple and socially situated. Few doubt that the self is socially shaped in the early stages of life. However, common sense notions of the self view this as an early developmental stage through which all selves pass on the way to a more stable adult form. Cooley's (1998) conceptualization, "The social self is simply any idea, or system of ideas, drawn from the communicative life, that the mind cherishes as its own" (p. 17), may be useful here. Also consider Mead's words (1998), "The self, as that which can be an object to itself, is essentially a social structure, and it arises in social experience..." (p. 22). With even greater emphasis, Cooley acknowledges a fixity of the adult self. "After a self has arisen, it in a certain sense provides for itself its social experiences... (p. 22). After primary socialization has led to a self, this self may undergo radical transformation, through a process of re-socialization. The radical nature of such re-socialization is emphasized by noting that it requires "[d]ismantling, disintegrating the preceding nomic structure of subjective reality" (p. 157). Such transformations do not easily occur. "It takes severe biographical shocks to disintegrate the massive reality internalized in early childhood" (p. 142).

Internal Identity Change and Maintenance: From Compliance to Belonging

I would like to offer an original conceptualization to address this issue of resistance to change in adult self-identity. Much of an individual's identity is a function of beliefs about oneself that have been internalized. One way to change these beliefs is to be supported through a difficult process that can lead to new beliefs but this process includes cognitive dissonance. When an individual's identity and internalized beliefs are inconsistent with newly learned conduct that is part of a new role they are beginning to perform in a given setting (however tentatively), the individual might not be able to meet the social behavioral expectations of that setting and role without external support. A system of external support for behavior change can transition to a system of internal support, if the individual's attitudes and beliefs change in such a way that they become consistent with those newly expressed and displayed through the new role in the setting. When there is a discrepancy between an individual's internalized beliefs and identity and the behavior they perform to comply with requirements of a new role, the individual may experience a psychologically painful state called "cognitive dissonance."

Cognitive dissonance can occur under a variety of conditions. One example is when an individual is coerced by a set of contingencies to behave in ways that are inconsistent with the beliefs and attitudes that they already have internalized. Beliefs and attitudes that have become internalized are difficult to change. They seem to the person to be a crucial part of his or her identity. This is evident from the fact that people usually protect and defend acquired attitudes and beliefs as if they were a part of their person—even erecting defenses as a kind of "early warning" system for incoming data that might be threatening to these identity structures (see figure 1 for a graphic display of how I am conceptualizing these defenses). Their survival feels threatened if their beliefs are threatened. The cognitive dissonance literature tells us that the state of dissonance is so stressful and unpleasant that an individual will either escape from the setting or change their attitudes and beliefs to adapt to it.

But if the individual is *beginning* to adjust to new beliefs and attitudes expressed by a particular group in a particular setting it can be observed by any changes in grooming, dress, verbal behavior, body language, etc., that indicate approach toward the standards of the setting and new role. "Identification with" the new role can occur when an individual has been supported in internal belief and attitude change through a willingness to comply behaviorally with new standards and a willingness to experience the anxiety of cognitive dissonance. At this level, the individual is not entirely dependent upon the support of an external system of support but is partially reinforced from within through vicarious experiences of anticipated group membership, belonging

176

and acceptance. However, identifications can shift, and so these changes can be temporary.

Figure 1

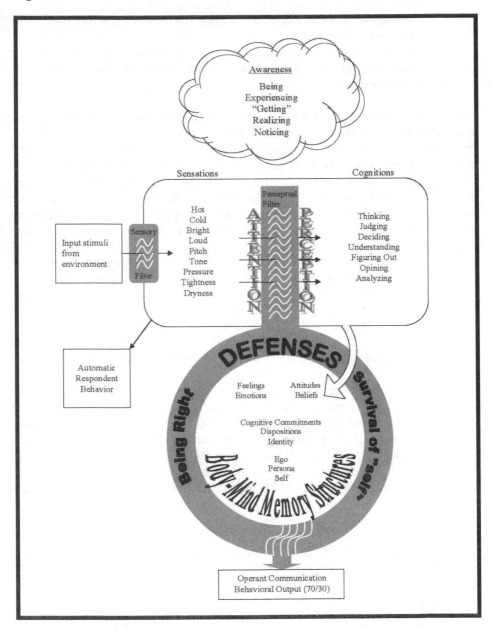

Internalization has occurred when an individual has incorporated the new beliefs and attitudes displayed in conformity to the new role being performed in the setting into their own set of beliefs and attitudes. The individual's social behavior is no longer maintained by external contingencies but by an internal sense of cognitive consistency ("being right"), and the potential for internal reinforcement from shared beliefs and belonging. Behaviors maintained by these internal contingencies are very stable and are difficult to change.

Jean Piaget (1973) has described the process of incorporating new material into our self-system in his stage independent theory. According to Piaget it involves two processes. One he called *assimilation*, the registering of new material within already existing cognitive structures of our self-system. The term applies to the assimilation of new material that is somewhat congruent with material already held in structure. The second process he called *accommodation*. This term describes a process whereby an individual encounters material that is very different from prior experience and so calls upon the individual to break down and reconfigure existing structures. According to Piaget, we are continually engaged in both processes throughout the life span because each new experience we encounter will be somewhat different from each of our prior experiences. Some require more or less assimilation or accommodation. When we encounter new experiences that could be perceived as threatening or dangerous to existing self-systems, we could ignore the stimulus (see the functioning of "defenses" as illustrated in Figure 1). Another possibility is that we could face the internal disruption (cognitive dissonance) caused by intentionally "allowing in" material that is threatening to the cognitive structures of existing self-systems, thereby allowing a restructuring of our "selves." The accompanying shift from automatically using defenses to protect self-structures has been termed "deautomatization" by Deikman (1987).

External Factors of Self-Identity Change and Maintenance

Adler and Adler (1998) reported on changes in self-concept that take place with athletes who are glorified by the media and their fans. Despite efforts by the basketball players who were studied to resist the redefinition of themselves and even despite their coach's urging such resistance, their self concepts changed. As the Adler's write, "...[i]t highlights the ascendence of an unintended self-identity in the face of considerable resistance" (p. 89). The interactions of this "gloried" self are far different from that described by either Cooley or Mead. According to Adler and Adler, the "gloried" self becomes "a powerful part of their new, reflected identity." Media play a new role in this process becoming a new mirror into which these individuals may gaze to learn of themselves. The Adler's also offer a new dimension to the transformation of self: Goffman's impression management. As the athletes deliberately transformed their behavior into that of their media selves they increasingly believed these self-concepts.

Another example of this type of "identifying with" one's "media self" is represented by an anecdote that Clint Eastwood has related in several interviews I've watched regarding the early years of his career. One of Mr. Eastwood's "breaks" came when he accepted a role that had been turned down by John Wayne. The part called for the main character to shoot an adversary from behind. "John Wayne does not shoot people in the back," said the late star as he refused the role. This example serves to support the Adler and Adler view that quantity of interaction is an important aspect of the changeable self: "The more individuals interacted with others through this [media] self, the more it developed a life and a destiny of its own" (p. 96).

Conclusion

In conclusion, the identity ˙one has constructed is a reflection of how that individual interacted with his or her own life experience. This identity can range from being a "gloried" one as described above, to being one to which one has been *harshly* socialized. A brief example emerges from gender studies. Each of us is "socialized" into our gender identities. Typically, young males are socialized more harshly into identity where gender is concerned and young females are allowed to be more playful with identity. As adults, females tend to be more flexible with identity; males tend to be more rigid. There's only one rule to be a stereotypical male—*don't be female*. This means no emotional displays or other behavior that might appear to be female to a stereotypically socialized male. This aspect of male culture can be harsh. Males who have been socialized into a stereotypical male identity and test high on attitudinal and behavioral traits associated with this stereotype are at much greater risk for substance abuse, behavioral problems and suicide than males who test lower on these scales. Many of our inmates and wards reflect this profile, especially regarding harsh socialization into the identities they currently wear. The intent of prison has always been to demean what is viewed as a dysfunctional self or identity. It can be fairly effective at doing that. Even boot camp can accomplish this. The problem is the recontextualizing of the anticipated new identity. History provides us with stories of individuals who experienced sudden transformations of their existing identity into a new one. Paul on the road to Damascus; Siddhartha under the Bho tree, serve as examples. The dissolution of their former identities is not as important as how their new identities formed. The harsh conditions of prison can support transformation into a more troubling identity.

Currently, the only relief comes from educators who truly internalize the "educere" in education. Not only are we conduits of information, but we also must become capable of "bringing forth" or "leading out" the humanity of each ward or prisoner. This requires that we work on ourselves, for we too, can be ground down by institutional life and lose our compassion in the process. There is a kind of "ruthless compassion" that treats others as if they already were the capable beings we already see them as, even if no one else does. It's the only way I know to recontextualize a life.

Conclusion

Metaphors of Experience—The Prison Teacher as Stranger

by Randall Wright

Introduction

Most of us working in prison education "recognize that our training did not prepare us for the realities of prison teaching" (Eggleston, 1991, p. 16). This situation is dangerous, frustrating and isolating; teachers often experience feelings of rejection. Often "out of context" in a "strange environment" prison teachers look to related fields "for identity and leadership" (Eggleston & Gehring, 1986, p. 87), sometimes to no avail. Teachers become strangers in a strange land.

The metaphor of the prison teacher as a stranger helps us consider and reconstruct, partially at least, teacher experience on the inside. The figure of the stranger haunts the domains of sociology, philosophy and education as a metaphor for personal experience and social interaction. As a personal experience metaphor, the stranger speaks to feelings of dissociation, dislocation and dissonance. As a metaphor of social interaction, the stranger helps us understand the relational tensions of "nearness" and "farness," or social distance, from other groups (teachers on the outside, prisoners, guards, community members) that teachers experience. And so, for prison educators, it is a particularly rich metaphor for reflection on our practice.

Extending our metaphoric framework, we might ask: How is it that teachers become strangers? The answer lies in the experience of "going inside" that is akin to traveling to a strange or foreign country—even if we are going just next door. Solzhenitsyn (1973) reminds us of this fact:

> How do people get to this clandestine Archipelago? Hour by hour planes fly there, ships steer their course there, and trains thunder off to it—but all with nary a mark on them to tell of their destination. And at ticket windows or at travel bureaus for Soviet or foreign tourists the employees would be astounded if you were to ask for a ticket to go there. They know nothing and they've never heard of the Archipelago as a whole or any one of its innumerable islands…the Gulag country begins, right next to us, two yards away from us. (p. 3)

The cover of Mark Dow's (2004) recent book, *American Gulag: Inside U.S. Immigration Prisons,* similarly reminds us there are some prisons, such as those operated by Immigration and Naturalization services, that are a world apart, not only from American society but also from what we consider to be penal business-as-usual, because prisoners seem to have no rights, no voice, and guards exercise unbridled power with little censure or public accountability. The Gulag country begins right next to us....

The Prison Teacher as Sociological Stranger

When teachers go to prison, they become strangers. "The discovery that things in his new surroundings look quite different from what he expected them to be at home is frequently the first shock to the stranger's confidence in the validity of his habitual 'thinking as usual'" (Schutz, 1964, p. 99). There is an interruption in the "flow of habit" that "gives rise to changed conditions of consciousness and practice" (p. 96). In other words, the stranger appears as a figure in a novel culture or situation.

Park and Burgess (1928/1967) employ the figure of the stranger to conceptualize intercultural contact and its social forms such as assimilation, hybridization, competition, accommodation and so on. "Travelers" experience forms of personal disintegration and reassembly of self in cultural contact with different "Others." The stranger is not an empty or hollow figure that is simply absorbed into the new culture. In the figure of the stranger they find an explanation for broad social change and cultural transformation because strangers combine their knowledge from elsewhere with local knowledge(s). This hybridization results in new and often vibrant, cultural and social forms. The writers in this book help us appreciate the hybrid pedagogy we create to meet the unique, often practical needs of prisoners. This is what Jane Penwell discovers, for example, when she tries to teach the three R's and fails—until she understands that her curriculum must be relevant to the lives of the incarcerated women she teaches.

Strangers are persons who change residences, who leave home— whatever and wherever that may be. This is a physical and psychological process that brings about personality changes because leaving home—even metaphorically—frees or individuates the person from the social ties that kept them safely within the group. The person who teaches in these non-conventional settings becomes "in a certain sense and to a certain degree a cosmopolitan" (Park, 1928/1967, p. 201). This new, cosmopolitan "location" is often characterized by an expanded and inclusive or universalistic perspective that authors like Kohlberg describe as the final stages of moral development. So teachers attuned to these processes may be catalytic because they shift the center of gravity from the good boy-bad boy cognitive/moral orientation of prison reasoning to a higher level.

In the personal stories contained in this volume it is clear, too, that many teachers realize they must learn about and from their students if they are to reach them. Their departure from their world empowers and liberates them as they confront another world—the rich and complex world of their students—and reflect on their differences.

Transformative learning occurs when taken-for-granted assumptions are called into question. It is also this critical sentiment that infuses the European authors in this collection who challenge the "natural" link between rehabilitation, narrowly defined, and education. Teachers as strangers are closely aligned in orientation and because of their travels, with transformative teaching and learning.

Jary and Jary (1995) describe the sociological stranger as "any person who is within a group or society, but not entirely of that group of society" (p. 656). This is the state of "in-betweeness" that Susan Yantz and others explore as they "position" themselves (their identities) and their pedagogy in the borderlands. For Anne Costello, this becomes a methodological problem as she strives to appropriately re-present in her research the lives of her students. Resolving the status of persons who are both inside and outside has been the focus of ethnographic and anthropological research for the past two decades, especially after the publication of works by authors like Clifford and Marcus (1986). Becoming a stranger in order to do research reflexively presents us with a "crisis of representation" when, as researchers, we struggle to write about the lives of others through the filters of gender, race, class (which are possibly, positions of power and privilege). It also raises ethical questions about the rights of the researcher to speak for others. Being a stranger in order to do research raises questions of research validity and reliability as well.

Jary and Jary identify three aspects of the stranger that make the concept of sociological interest:

(a) the position of the individual on the margin, part inside and part outside the group;

(b) a particular combination of remoteness and proximity (or social distance) between the stranger and the group members; and,

(c) various further implications of the role of the stranger and his or her interactions with the group which make this position of particular sociological interest. (1995, pp. 656-657)

The sociological stranger is a figure that explicates the personal and social dimensions of non-conventional teachers, who often must manage the social distances or the relationships of affiliation and difference between self and other. Simmel elaborates on this phenomenon:

The unity of nearness and remoteness involved in every human relation is organized in the phenomena of the stranger, in a way which may be most briefly formulated by saying that in the relationship to him, distance means that he, who is close by, is far, and strangeness means that he, who also is far, is actually near... to be a stranger is naturally a very positive relation; it is a specific form of interaction. (Simmel, 1951, p. 402)

Paul Ropp's essay reminds us that teachers who fail to manage social distances, who become too close to students, cross professional boundaries, get set up, and lose their jobs. This is a fluid interpersonal dynamic, not one rigidly fixed, but locally negotiated by teachers who must struggle to find the "relational mean." This relational dynamic is evident in Bill Muth's contradictory and ambiguous feelings of hostility and affection, closeness and farness with his students. It is a dynamic experienced in multiple situations, fleetingly, that often places the teacher and student on the borders of inclusion/exclusion.

The stranger experiences feelings or relations of "aloofness and unapproachability," especially between members of different social strata. Conceptions of social distance are formally institutionalized in extreme situations of social stratification, such as apartheid and caste, but informally they exist is all societies. (Jary & Jary, 1995, p. 608)

The caste-like nature of prison life (the ceaseless struggle for status on the part of guards, inmates and teachers) cannot be overlooked, and neither can the relations of exclusion that leave the teacher and prison teaching cultures on the margins between the keepers and the kept. As a result of this stratification (where teachers are not members of the guard "caste") and because of sheer physical proximity (spatial closeness), teachers and inmates are often more closely aligned than teachers and prison officers (especially if teachers are paid by school districts outside the prison walls). This, too, may contribute to the phenomena of groupthink that Paul Ropp describes.

The departure from home (broadly speaking) is never quite complete, so that the teacher as stranger is caught in the time/space relations of places left and a time past, while living in the here and now. Park describes the marginal person as a cultural hybrid who is:

...living and sharing intimately in the cultural life and traditions of two distinct peoples; never quite willing to break, even if he were permitted to do so, with his past and his traditions, and not quite accepted...in the new society in which he now sought to find a place. He was a man [person] on the margin of two cultures and two societies, which are never completely interpenetrated and fused. (p. 205)

The stranger as a phenomenological figure also underscores the "hybrid" nature of our practice.

The Prison Teacher as Phenomenological Stranger

For phenomenologists, the stranger is a "cultural hybrid on the verge of two different patterns of group life, not knowing to which of them he belongs" (Schutz, 1964, p. 104). The metaphor of the teacher as phenomenological stranger alludes to experiences of crisis, dissonance and even more profound shifts in consciousness because phenomenological strangers learn to "bracket" (call into serious question) their world in order to deeply appreciate their consciousness of it. Phenomenological strangers acutely become aware that the social or cultural "recipes" they typically use to make sense of their world no longer seem to apply. Teachers on the inside must make sense of their novel professional location by searching for new "recipes" for their world. In these stories teachers frequently become students, so they can appreciate the world they have entered, and they develop new recipes that they know work in prisons and alternative settings; recipes that involve negotiations or bracketing teacher power, authority and identity. Inevitably their professional identifications as teachers, students and, potentially, prison guards "cross-cut, compliment and trouble each other" (Clifford in Vila, 2003, p. xvi).

As phenomenological strangers, teachers are potentially critical, transformative intellectuals. The average person, writes Alfred Schutz (1964), ordinarily "accepts the ready-made standardized scheme of cultural pattern" handed to him or her. The "trustworthy recipes" serve as "schemes of interpretation" for thought, feeling and behavior. When a crisis arises, the "cultural pattern no longer functions as a system of tested recipes at hand; it reveals that its applicability is restricted to a specific historical situation" (p. 96). Teaching in prisons and alternative settings may create both a personal and professional crisis that places "into question nearly everything that seems to be unquestionable to the members of the approached group" (p, 96).

Looking homeward while immersed in new institutional cultures, teachers encounter translation problems: They encounter new institutional recipes with the old cultural patterns imported from their home world and must struggle to make sense of their connections. Teachers as strangers recognize and struggle as translators between worlds. Teaching behind bars enhances teachers' interpretive arts and contributes to their wisdom—they appreciate the relative values and nuances of social, historical and institutional contexts, awakening as it were, from their slumbers.

As strangers, teachers may question the taken-for-granted carceral intervention strategies that focus on deficits and criminogenic factors. Implicitly, they take a stand that education, aligned with principles of restoration, contributes to the shaping of new worlds for their students. A narrow focus on criminogenic factors has become the recipe for carceral interventions worldwide. Our work as teachers calls into question these prevalent cultural patterns and challenges them with educative models based on seeing inmates as a citizens with rights, multi-dimensional human beings not narrowly defined one-dimensionally in terms of their deficits. The ever-increasing numbers of prisoners in prisons worldwide that signals a hardening of the lines between the prisoner and society has contributed to the "hollowing out" of prison education programs. As strangers between two worlds, who come to know prisoners as subjects rather than objects, we begin to understand how we construct prisoner and "Others" within the state; this experience inspires us to question and respond critically to the Othering process.

The social distance that teachers feel from the prison staff and operations is embodied in their understanding of school as an "oasis," a "third" or "free space" where other ways of interacting and being are possible. As I noted in the Introduction, schools within prisons often appear as "back regions" where social actors are permitted relatively autonomous forms of interaction and behaviors that would not be permitted in front of other socially or operationally demanding audiences—like prison officers. Back regions are locales of different meanings, norms and status not under surveillance by others who set the normative standards; these are zones where social actors "recover forms of autonomy which are compromises...in frontal contexts" (Giddens, 1984, p. 127). In the hotel business, for example, back regions would be the kitchens, the spaces behind the buffet lines where the waiters fill the trays, the stall that separates the kitchen staff eating a meal from the paying customers who are eating theirs and so on (Goffman, 1959).

Teachers seem to solve the problem of being in a school within a prison by actively working to create a definition of the situation where more authentic, closer social and educative relationships between student and teacher are permitted. Many schools become "spheres of civility," (Wright, 2005; Wright & Gehring, 2008) where mutual respect and dialogue between students and teachers are apparent. Similar to the tension between prison and community, the tension between the school and the prison is never quite resolved. Nor is it always possible for teachers to define the school as a different place—despite their intentions. Again, this is a question of status and power; and it is this lack of control over their workplace that contributes to teacher alienation and burnout (Wright, 2005). Again, the stranger as metaphor of teachers' experience is helpful:

> ...the stranger has to face the fact that he lacks any status as a member of the social group he is about to join and is therefore unable to get a starting-point to take his bearings. He finds himself a *border case* [emphasis mine] outside the territory covered by the scheme of orientation current within the group. He is, therefore, no longer permitted to consider himself as the center of his social environment, and this fact causes a *dislocation* [emphasis mine] of his contour lines of relevance. (Schutz, 1964, p. 99)

The Teacher as Existential Stranger

Influenced by Schutz, Maxine Greene (1973) considers the metaphor of the teacher as stranger as a positive pedagogical identity. Infused by their sense of colliding schema of interpretation, teachers gain a heightened sense of relativism. They appreciate more thoroughly the existential choices they and their students make. They bump up against ethical and philosophical issues of choice, responsibility, freedom and the ideal of the good life. The existential themes of sorrow, homesickness, pain, remorse, loss, trust, anger and anxiety create a halo that surrounds prison teaching, like it or not, so that many teachers experience an intensified self-consciousness that arises from the messiness of the human condition.

> To take a stranger's vantage point on everyday reality is to look inquiringly and wonderingly on the world in which one lives. It is like returning home from a long stay in some other place. The homecomer notices details and patterns in his environment he never saw before. He finds that he has to think about local rituals and customs to make sense of them once more. For a time he feels quite separate from the person who is wholly at home in his in-group and takes the familiar world for granted. (Greene, 1973, p. 267)

Their students' lives call out to teachers—insisting they look beyond matters of "delivering content" to them; they are called upon to care:

> We must consider Heidegger's deepest sense of care. As human beings, we care what happens to us. We wonder whether there is a life after death, whether there is a deity who cares about us, whether we are loved by those we love, whether we belong anywhere; we wonder what we will become, who we are, how much control we have over our fate. For adolescents these are among the most pressing questions: Who am I? Who will love me? How do others see me? Yet schools spend more time on the quadratic formula than on any of these existential questions. (Noddings in Webb, Metha & Jordan 2003, p. 109)

The prison truly is an "existential village" that insists upon educational practices that are concerned primarily with people over content (Thom Gehring's chapter makes this clear). To take up existentialist theory in practice transforms our role as teachers from "sages on stage" to facilitators who face the same human conditions as our students (humanity is our common bond). Taken seriously, prison teaching restores also our sense of humanity.

In some ways, however, teachers in prisons and alternative settings never leave home. Like strangers, teachers try to create schools "inside" that mimic those on the outside—in the "real" world—with regard to programs, accreditation, schedules, professional development and ceremonies that signal changes in status (such as graduations). These outside practices authenticate those on the inside. The ontological priority of the outside world exerts its influence in the curricular decisions of teachers, who import programs from the community that have the status of being "real" programs. To prepare their students for life on the outside (and to compensate for the stripping process, boredom and ennui inside), teachers often try to mimic life outside through holistic approaches and integrated curricula. In this regard, programs from the community have epistemic authority (they represent "real" knowledge and "real education"), which is why teachers become strong advocates for importing these programs.

These centripetal and centrifugal forces on prison education create advantages for teachers who sometimes experience more autonomy than they would in traditional schools under public scrutiny (after all, who cares—they're just teaching prisoners). In the borderlands teachers often feel empowered as they seem to escape some of the oppressive bureaucracy of the public school. Sometimes they are entrusted with curricular decision-making authority and are able to sculpt their programs to suit their personal philosophies and meet their students' needs. On the other hand, prisons often have an anti-educational bias that creates a hostile working environment and of course, teachers encounter constraints, rules and norms necessary for the good order of the institution.

Caught in these forces, teachers as existential strangers realize the importance of dialogue as a means of evoking and offering students a meaningful curriculum. Most teachers implicitly strive to create a significant, existential place for prisoners in the world. Teaching in alternative settings is an existential effort because teachers recognize they must attend to the complicated nature of being at all times in their pedagogical encounters with students. Teaching in prisons and alternative settings is also an ontological effort that says to anyone that cares to listen: This person behind bars exists, and must have a place in the world. Teaching in alternative settings must address this homesickness that incarcerated students experience.

Women as Strangers

Immersed in male systems of hierarchy and power, women teachers become strangers because they see the world from the standpoint of their socially determined, gendered roles. Historically and currently, prisons are male-driven institutions where issues of power, status and control are embedded and reproduced in gendered interactions (Wright, 2004). Women communicate differently. They offset interactions based on strategic forms of communication oriented to gaining compliance and establishing dominance because they typically show concern for a "variety of interests, their own and others" and they act out of a spirit of "cooperation and not mastery" (Lengermann & Niebrugge-Brantley, 1983, p. 321). They partake in "role merging" or "role balancing" rather than role conflict because they "may be socialized to experience that life-world as a place in which one balances a variety of actor's interests" (p. 320).

Tannen (1990) has noted how women are predisposed to communication styles—relationship talk, based on equality and community—rather than status and hierarchy (male talk). Many of the essays here reflect gendered, connected ways of knowing the world inside. Women tend to "step into, not back from situations, to see and respond to others in their own particular situations and contexts rather than to challenge them" (Lyons, 1990, p. 169). They are relationally connected knowers "who look for connections between events, considering motives, intentions and believability" rather than separate knowers, who approach their task with "traditionally known, objective, rule-seeking ways of evaluating, proving, and disproving truth" (p. 170). It might be that the strangeness of women in prison contributes to the positive atmosphere of the classroom, the school and the institution because they know and speak as Gilligan would say, in a different voice. For these reasons they also may be doubly alienated.

Women prison teachers may become strangers to themselves (remember that they must not look too much like women) as their role-taking is complicated by their,

> ...intense awareness that they must learn the expectations of an Other who by virtue of differences in power is alien. Two, they must relate not to a generalized other but to many generalized others, many subcultures, both the subculture of the powerful and the various subcultures of the less empowered and the dis-empowered. Three, they do not experience themselves as purposive social actors who can chart their own course through life–although they may be constantly told that they can do so, especially within the American ethos. And finally, and most pervasively, they live daily with a bifurcated consciousness, a sense of the line of fault between their own lived experiences and what the dominant culture tells them is social reality. (Lengermann & Niebrugge-Brantley, 1983, p. 321)

Conclusion: Identity Politics

Once we go inside the walls, we are engaged in identity politics:

> Increasingly important from the 1970s onwards, identity politics is based on upon the contention that collectivities and individuals defined by criteria of ethnicity, religion, gender or sexual orientation have interests that are not or cannot be promoted or defended by broader agencies such as class or a constitution state. Identity politics takes the form of a demand for the right to be different, and for that difference to be recognized as legitimate. (Macey, 2000, p. 197)

Often we hear prison teachers complain about being left out in prisons. They idealize the move from the margins to the center. They feel it would overcome their de-centeredness, legitamize their identity, knowledge and practice. Understanding the positive positioning of the teacher as a stranger makes these assumptions questionable. Perhaps as teachers we would be better to live in the borderlands, resisting assimilation, continuing to travel pedagogically, socially and psychologically. As strangers, teachers might be wise to enjoy unpacking knowledge from different places, negotiating new identities, seeking out novel relationships and exploring new meanings and practices in different landscapes; remaining forever strangers in a strange land. As I've written previously:

> This, it seems to me, is the "place" of correctional education, the view from somewhere that our practice offers—located as it is at the juncture of state, education and society. It is a curious place of cultural, social, political and educational mutations and hybridizations. If this is true, then the issues surrounding the lack of professional and epistemological...authority that plagues correctional education [and prison educators, I might add], should be reconsidered from the perspective, not what correctional education "is" but what it "does," as a (sub)culture of translation and mutation. The teacher's voices heard in this essay point to the connections and unexpected openings (translations and hybridizations) that appear within the practice of correctional education. For teachers, the question of identity is de-centered...as we move away from descriptions of essential characteristics and skills into subject positions realized through creative connections with others. (Wright, 2001, p. 38)

This anthology has provided readers with firsthand accounts of teaching so as to prepare novice prison teachers for a teaching career in alternative settings such as prisons and juvenile halls. Hopefully seasoned prison teachers will feel supported and validated as well by these essays. If this work has contributed to genuine professional and personal development for novice and veteran teachers, then the effort certainly has been worthwhile.

Afterword

Standing on the Shoulders of Giants

By Scott Rennie

"We are like dwarfs sitting on the shoulders of giants. We see more, and things that are more distant, than they did, not because our sight is superior or because we are taller than they, but because they raise us up, and by their great stature add to ours." John of Salisbury, 1159

The invention of writing raised the human condition. When the famous explorers Lewis and Clark crossed the North American continent and reached the Pacific Ocean after almost three years of travel through pure, unknown wilderness, they had exhausted nearly all of their original stores. The only items remaining were ammunition and pen and paper. Lewis had kept meticulous records of the geography, plants and animals new to science and spawned years of further study. Because of Lewis' ability to write and share information, those who came after him benefitted from his work, even years after his death. Lewis and Clark were giants.

Correctional education is not without its own giants, some of whom have contributed chapters to this volume. Unfortunately, many of those who educate in the wilderness of prisons and alternative settings remain unaware of the major contributors to the field. Called the "Hidden Heritage," correctional education literature is often long out of print and inaccessible to most practitioners (Gehring, 2005, p. 1). Most educators have received no direct preparation in correctional education and attempt to apply whatever specific educational instruction they have received to the prison environment (Eggleston, 1991, p. 16). The result is a disparate patchwork of isolated educators, each doing the best they can to change inmate's lives. Often seen as less of an educator then their local school counterparts, correctional educators work with the most forgotten members of society in the most brutal of environments. It would be a mistake to apply local school methodologies in prison settings precisely because such approaches obviously did not work for this population before. Inmates have fallen through the cracks of traditional education and correctional educators often represent the final opportunity for them to turn their lives around. The stakes of correctional education really are life or death for the students we teach.

For me, the main benefit of having access to the correctional education literature is not about specific knowledge gained, although the importance of that should not be understated; it is about the deep and profound meaning that underlies our work. It is about the *whys?* of correctional education. Our history is full of men and women who dedicated their lives to improving the human condition, often at great personal and professional risk. Correctional education has long been closely tied to the prison reform movement—any separation of the two is but a recent wrinkle in our history. My sense of social justice, about what is right and what is wrong, finds correctional education to be perhaps the most powerful form of education. By elevating the status of the most oppressed members of society we elevate the status of us all. In a materialistic world and in a low status, low paying field, I am certainly not the only educator who feels this way. Few who become correctional educators enter the field for the prestige or the money.

The first North American correctional educators were clergy, concerned primarily with spiritual redemption. They often entered the prisons for little or no pay, and only after their weekly duties on the outside had been completed. The earliest documented instance of North American correctional education involved a loaded cannon aimed directly at the inmates, as the warden was fearful of a riot. Later, under the Pennsylvania system of solitary confinement, inmates were taught to read using only the Bible, often through the bars of their cell doors with barely enough light to see. These intrepid correctional educators braved deplorable conditions and fearful wardens to deliver the slightest services to those unfortunate souls who populated the early American penitentiaries.

> When it was first proposed to teach them to read...the reply was, we have no convenient room...where they can be assembled for instruction. The answer to the objection was, teach them through the grated iron doors of their cells, so long as you are subject to the evil of having no room. The next objection was, we have no spelling books. The answer to this objection was, it is possible that you can learn them to read quicker without spelling books. (Gehring & Eggleston, 2006, p. 32)

May I be so bold as to say similar sentiments exist still today?

These early educators were giants. Anyone today who enters a California prison and signs a form acknowledging the State's no hostage rule follows in their footsteps. These men and women laid a foundation of care for their fellow human beings that continues to the present day (Wright, 2004). They established precedent by advocating for salaried jailers, who had previously eked out a living by wrangling from the convicts whatever they could. Men, women, and children were often incarcerated together in conditions of "universal riot and debauchery" (Freedman, 1981, p. 47). The environment in early penitentiaries was often "so dark, damp, and cold, that the prisoners can scarcely be seen themselves" (Gehring & Eggleston, 2006, p. 39). So began the field of correctional education.

There are many people who have worked to give individuals a chance to reform. They all share an unwritten underlying principle—a profound faith in the intrinsic decency of the human spirit, and the ability of individuals to be transformed. This puts the aims of education squarely at odds with the aims of confinement institutions. Prisons exist to punish, education exists to transform. To borrow from Cormac Behan (see chapter XI), "prison damages people," it is "alien to the human condition."

When I first read of Thomas Mott Osborne's voluntary incarceration in New York's Auburn Prison, any self-imposed limits I had on the power of educators were promptly lifted. While chairman of the New York State Commission on Prison Reform, he spent seven days inside Auburn as inmate Tom Brown, including a 14 hour stay in solitary confinement. Osborne's time inside garnered national attention, with most newspaper stories blasting him for his efforts. One article went so far as to say it is "not necessary to wallow in a mud hole to know how a pig feels" (Tannenbaum, 1933, p. 69). But the atmosphere inside the prison had changed. Osborne gained the confidence of the prisoners, "no such experience had ever before touched their lives" (p. 71). He left the prison with "an idea that men might be given responsibility of some sort—that certain privileges might be granted to them, and that perhaps certain powers of discipline for their own enforcement might be extended to them" (p. 74). His idea grew into the Mutual Welfare League, a democratic movement Osborne implemented in three separate institutions, New York's Auburn and Sing Sing Prisons, and the U.S. Naval Prison in Portsmouth, New Hampshire.

Prison inmates are generally not allowed to make even the smallest choices or decisions—certainly not beyond the color of their toothbrush. But if people are sent to prison for having made poor choices, and they eventually leave prison without ever having the chance to practice making decisions, how can we ever expect them to have developed that ability? "It is liberty alone that fits men for liberty" (Osborne in George, 1911, p. 7). This was the beauty of the Mutual Welfare League. With the consent of the warden, multiple aspects of the day to day operations of the prison were transferred to the inmates. Disciplinary measures became their responsibility. On February 12, 1914, the first meeting of Auburn's Mutual Welfare League took place. All 1,400 inmates marched from their cells to the chapel and, after listening to speeches and music, marched back to their cells without a whisper. "Such perfect discipline had never been seen before at Auburn Prison; and one of the guards was heard to remark 'why the hell can't they do that for us?'" (Osborne, 1924, p. 78). What is remarkable is the transformation the inmates underwent simply because they were given a bit of responsibility. One Sing Sing inmate explained why discipline was better under the League:

> Take, for instance, the mess hall…. Under the old system they had forty guards along the wall at mealtime. If any fight happened in the middle of the hall, none of the prisoners would try and stop it—it was the business of the guards to do that, and to arrest the fighters. But it was very dangerous for the guards to go into the midst of the prisoners…for there was lots of crockery handy and we each had our favorite guard.

192

Now under the League it's different. If there should be a fight, the men around would stop it, for it would be bad for them—it would endanger League privileges. The Sergeant-at-Arms and his deputies would go right in—because they were prisoners like the rest. They can handle any such trouble without starting a riot—but the guards can't. (p. 75)

Osborne, in his slim and potent tome, *Prisons and Common Sense*, wrote "prisoners are human beings; for the most part remarkably like the rest of us.... They can be clubbed into submission...but they cannot be reformed by that process" (pp. 7-8). Reading Osborne's books produced a kind of epiphany. Prisoners may not be trusted individually, but they can be trusted in groups. Osborne built upon the work of William George, who managed his Junior Republics democratically, in addition to being a remarkable individual himself. But they were not the only correctional education giants to do this. There have been at least 22 documented instances of democratic movements inside prisons over the last 200 years, in seven different countries. This is the value of the hidden heritage, it provides access to what has worked in the past; it has connected me to the great personalities that compose an inspiring trail of reform and improving conditions across time and national boundaries.

The literature is replete with similar stories. Anton Makarenko, who was charged with reforming street thugs after the Bolshevik revolution, applied similar approaches. William George built a boxing ring in Manhattan's Lower East Side, took on any and all opponents from the local gang, became their leader and transformed the kids from law breakers into law enforcers. Kenyon Scudder, the first warden of the California Institute for Men, expressed to the inmates that he should be disappointed in any of them who would be unable to escape their prison without walls. The inmates went on to break records for labor related to the war effort during World War II. Alexander Maconochie defied authority when he instituted what became the basis for modern penal practice on Norfolk Island in the South Pacific. Elizabeth Fry gave blankets to the women in London's Newgate prison, whose clothes were literally rotting away from their bodies. These stories of giants are not mere historic artifacts, they are active in the present day, inspiring and uplifting me while providing a profound rationale for my daily work. I read them with my eyes, process the information and wisdom they contain with my mind, but I feel them in my heart.

At the Center for the Study of Correctional Education at California State University, San Bernardino we are trying to change this lack of access to the correctional education literature. Through teacher inservice, college courses, our Center website, and our book series published by the University, educators finally have a path to awareness of the grand correctional education tradition. I hold a unique position; I do not directly teach inmates, but I provide needed services to those who do. I am often in contact with other educators, through Correctional Education Association conferences and Center activities, both "inside" and "outside" and I have found that these teachers often are in need of a sympathetic ear and benefit from a connection to the larger struggle. These educators need all the support they can get.

People who teach in prisons and alternative settings would benefit greatly from access to the correctional education literature, as I most definitely have. On its value I share the sentiment of Bill Muth who wrote, "This newly discovered history of correctional education and prison reform was not shelved in a musty alcove; it became my intellectual and professional home" (in Gehring & Rennie, 2008, foreword). And so, if we are not to live historically, temporally, in the borderlands between an unknown past and an uncertain future, we must return to our intellectual and professional home, to better prepare for future departures.

CALIFORNIA STATE UNIVERSITY, SAN BERNARDINO
CENTER FOR THE STUDY OF CORRECTIONAL EDUCATION

C S C E

Transform Professional Communities   Transcend Traditional Contraints

The Center for the Study of Correctional Education at California State University is one of the few organizations of its kind working to support correctional educators.

Visit their website for more information.

http://www.csusb.edu/coe/cg/csce/index.html

REFERENCES

INTRODUCTION

Arlin, P. K. (1990). Teaching as conversation. *Educational Leadership, 48*, 82-84.

Arlin, P. K. (1999). The wise teacher: A developmental model of teaching. *Theory into Practice, 38*(1), 12-17.

Bennett deMarrais, K. & LeCompte, M. D. (1999). *The way schools work: A sociological analysis of education* (3rd ed.). New York: Longman.

California State University. (2000). *College of Education institutional standards— Conceptual framework.* San Bernardino: Author.

Eggleston, C. R. (1991). Correctional education professional development. *The Journal of Correctional Education, 42*(1), 16-22.

Foucault, M. (1977/1995). *Discipline and punish: The birth of the prison.* (Alan Sheridan, Trans.). New York: Vintage. (Original work in French, 1975).

Foucault, M. (1980). *The history of sexuality: Volume one.* New York: Vintage Books.

Freire, P. (1970). *Pedagogy of the oppressed.* New York: The Continuum International Publishing Group.

Gehring, T. & Wright, R. (2006). The case for reflective practice in alternative and correctional education. *The Journal of Juvenile Court, Community, and Alternative School Administrators of California, 19*, 40-45.

Geraci, P. (2002). *Teaching on the inside: A survival handbook for the new correctional educator.* Scandia, Minnesota: Greystone Educational Materials.

Giroux, H. A. (1997). *Pedagogy and the politics of hope: Theory, culture, and schooling.* Boulder, Colorado and United Kingdom: Westview Press.

Giroux, H. A. (2004). Teachers as transformative intellectuals. In A. S. Canestri & B. A. Marlowe (Eds.), *Educational foundations: An anthology of critical readings* (pp. 205-212). Thousand Oaks: Sage Publications.

Goffman, E. (1961/1997). Hospital underlife: Places. In K. Gelder & S. Thornton (Eds.), *The subcultures reader.* London and New York: Routledge.

Goffman, E. (1970). On the characteristics of total institutions. In E. Goffman (Ed.), *Asylums: Essay on the social situation of mental patients and other inmates* (pp. 1-125). Chicago: Adline Publishing Co.

Macey, D. (2000). *The Penguin dictionary of critical theory*. New York: Penguin Putnam, Inc.

Wright, R. (2002). *Frictions in the machine: Teacher practical knowledge in a correctional setting*. (Ph.D. diss., University of Calgary.)

Wright, R. (2004). You were hired to teach: Ideological struggle, education and teacher burnout at the New Prison for Women. *The Qualitative Report, 9*(4), 30-651.

Wright, R. (2005). Going to teach in prison: Culture shock. *The Journal of Correctional Education, 56*(1), 19-39.

Wright, R. (2005b). Teacher burnout and toxic cultures in alternative school/ prison settings. *The Journal of Juvenile Court, Community and Alternative School Administrators of California, 18*, 44-53.

Wright, R. & Gehring, T. (2008, in press). From spheres of civility to critical public spheres: Democracy and citizenship in the big house (Part I). Accepted for publication in *The Journal of Correctional Education*, March, 2008.

$\mathcal{U}\cap$

CHAPTER I

Burke, P. J. & Reitzes, D. C. (1981). The link between identity and role performance. *Social Psychology Quarterly, 44*, 83-92.

Castro, A. B. (2004). Emotional vs. physical labor: The demand of using emotions as a job duty. *American Journal of Nursing, 104*(3). Available at: http:// nursingworld.org/ajn/2004/ mar/health.htm

Evans, K. (2002). *Negotiating the self: Identity, sexuality, and emotion in learning to teach*. New York: Routledge Falmer.

Geraci, P. (2001). *Teaching on the inside*. Scandia, Minnesota: Greystone Educational Materials.

Gergen, K. (1991). *The saturated self: Dilemmas of identity in modern life*. New York: Basic Books.

Goodson, I. & Cole, A. (1994). Using personal histories in teacher education. *Teacher Education Quarterly, 21*(1), Available at: http://www. teqjournal. org/backvols/ 1994/ 21_1/volume_21,_number_1.htm

Hochschild, A. R. (1983). *The managed heart: Commercialization of human feelings*. Berkeley: University of California Press.

Lamb, R. & Davidson, E. (2002). *Social scientists: Managing identity in socio-technical networks*. (Proceedings of the 35th Hawaii International Conference on System Sciences.)

Magala, S. (2003). Unhealthy paradoxes of healthy identities. In *ERASMUS: Research institute of management report series research in management* (pp. 5-6). ERS-2003-054-ORG.

Marsh, M. (2003). *The social fashioning of teacher identities*. New York: Peter Lanz.

Riley, J. (1998). Sensemaking and the stereotype of the brutal guard. *Alaska Justice Forum, 14*(Winter), 2.

Seifert, K. (2004). *How can we be ourselves when teaching?* Available at: http://home.cc.umanitoba.ca/~seifert/

Tracy, S. J. (2001). *Emotion labor and correctional officers: A study of emotion norms, performances and unintended consequences in a total institution* (Ph.D. diss., University of Colorado).

Wink, J. & Wink, D. (2004). *Teaching passionately: What's love got to do with it?* Boston: Allyn & Bacon.

Wright, R. (2004). Care as the "heart" of prison teaching. *The Journal of Correctional Education, 55*(3), 191-210.

CHAPTER IV

Kegan, R. (1994). *In over our heads: The mental demands of everyday life*. Cambridge: Harvard University Press.

Maslow, A. (1970). *Motivation and personality* (2nd ed.). New York: Harper & Row.

Redl, F. & Wineman, D. (1952). *Controls from within: Techniques for the treatment of the aggressive child*. New York: The Free Press.

Ryan, T. A. (1975). *Education for adults in correctional settings*. Honolulu: University of Hawaii.

Wilson, A. (2003). Researching in the third space: Locating, claiming and valuing the research domain. In S. Goodman, T. Lillis, J. Maybin & N. Mercer (Eds.), *Language, literacy and education: A reader*. Trenham Books/Open University.

Wright, R. (2005). Going to teach in prison: Culture shock. *The Journal of Correctional Education, 56*(1), 19-39

CHAPTER VI

Chaddock, G. R. (n.d.). *U.S. notches world's highest incarceration rate.* Available at: http://www.freepublic.com/focus/f-news/966172/posts

Gendreau, P. & Cullen, F. (1999). *The effects of prison sentences on recidivism.* Ottawa: Solicitor General Canada. Available at: http://www.psepc.gov.ca/publications/ corrections/1999/2

Snell, M. B. (2002). Profile: Law and nature's order. *Sierra Magazine.* Retrieved April 5, 2006, from: http://www.sierraclub.org/sierra/ 200211/profile.asp

Wright, R. (1998). Teacher's voices, teacher's knowledge: Reflection on The (new) Journal of Correctional Education. *The Journal of Correctional Education, 49*(2), 45-58.

CHAPTER VII

Allen, B. & Bosta, D. (1981). *Games criminals play: How you can profit by knowing them* (1st ed.). Susanville, California: Rae John Publishers.

Barber, K., (Ed.) (1998). *The Canadian Oxford dictionary.* Ontario, Canada: Oxford University Press.

Bezeau, L. M. (2002). *Educational administration for Canadian teachers* (3rd ed.). Available at: http://www.unb.ca/education/bezeau/eact/eact21.html

British Columbia College of Teachers. (2004). *Standards for the education, competence and professional conduct of educators in British Columbia* (2nd ed.). Available at: http://www.bcct.ca/documents/edu_stds.pdf

Brownfield, Charles. (1972). *The brain benders: A study of the effects of isolation.* New York: Exposition Press.

Correctional Service Canada. (1994). Code of discipline. *Commissioner's directive 060.* Available at: http://www.csc-scc/text/plcy/cdshtm/060-cde_e.shtml

Harrison, A. A. & Connors, M. M. (1984). Groups in exotic environments. In L. Z. Berkowitz (Ed.), *Advances in experimental social psychology* (Vol. 189). New York: Academic Press, Inc.

Haythorn, W. W. (1973). The miniworld of isolation: Laboratory studies. In J. E. Rasmussen (Ed.), *Man in isolation and confinement*. Chicago: Alpine Publishing Company.

Langone, M. (1996). Clinical update on cults. *Psychiatric Times, 8*(7). Available at: http://www.psychiatrictimes.com/p960714.html

CHAPTER VIIII

American Prison Association. (1930). *Proceedings of the sixtieth annual congress of the American Prison Association*. Louisville, Kentucky: American Prison Association.

Barry, J. (1958). *Alexander Maconochie of Norfolk Island: A study of a pioneer in penal reform*. Melbourne: Oxford University Press.

Brockway, Z. (1969/1912). *Fifty years of prison service: An autobiography*. Montclair, New Jersey: Patterson Smith.

Carpenter, J. E. (1974/1881). *The life and work of Mary Carpenter*. Montclair, New Jersey: Patterson Smith.

Carpenter, M. (1864/1969). *Our convicts*. Montclair, New Jersey: Patterson Smith.

Deutscher, I. (2003). *The prophet armed: Trotsky, 1879-1921*. London: Verso.

Gehring, T. (1981).The correctional education professional identity issue. *The Journal of Correctional Education, 33*(1), 9-10.

Gehring, T. (1981).The correctional education professional identity issue [Part II]. *The Journal of Correctional Education, 32*(3), 20-23.

Gehring, T. (1982). An identified need: The development of a CEA rationale statement. *The Journal of Correctional Education, 32*(4), 4-8.

Gehring, T. (1983). Our future is in our own hands: Recognizing common goals to develop a CEA 'core program.' *The Journal of Correctional Education, 34*(1), 15-17.

Gehring, T. (1984). CEA Executive Board approves Resolutions, begins implementation. *The Journal of Correctional Education, 34*(4), 137-141.

Gehring, T. (1988). Five principles of correctional education. *The Journal of Correctional Education, 39*(4), 164-169.

Gehring, T. (1993). Five more principles of correctional education. *The Journal of Correctional Education, 44*(1), 4-8.

Gehring, T. (1989). A change in our way of thinking. *The Journal of Correctional Education, 40*(4), 167-173.

Gehring, T. & Hollingsworth, T. (2002). Coping and beyond: Practical suggestions for correctional educators. *The Journal of Correctional Education, 53*(3), 89-95.

Goswami, A. (2001). Reconciling science and spirituality: Quantum yoga. *IONS Noetic Sciences Review, 56* (June-August), 26-31.

Holl, J. M. (1971). *Juvenile reform in the Progressive era: William R. George and the Junior Republic movement*. Ithaca, New York: Cornell University Press.

Holy Bible: Containing the Old and New Testaments in the King James version. Nashville, Tennessee: Thomas Nelson.

Knowles, M. (1970). *The modern practice of adult education: Andragogy versus pedagogy*. New York: Association Press.

Osborne, T. M. (1924). *Prisons and common sense*. Philadelphia: J. B. Lippincott.

Osborne, T. M. (1975/1916). *Society and prisons: Some suggestions for a new penology*. Montclair, New Jersey: Patterson Smith.

Quick, R. H. (1916). *Essays on educational reformers*. New York: D. Appleton.

Rogers, R. & Hammerstein, O. (2000/1958) Lyrics. "Happy Talk." South Pacific: Original Soundtrack. New York: RCA Records.

Wilber, K. (1999). *One taste: The journals of Ken Wilber*. Boston: Shambhala.

Wilber, K. (2000). *A theory of everything: An integral vision for business, politics, science, and spirituality*. Boston: Shambhala.

Wines, E. C. (Ed.). (1871). *Transactions of the National Congress on Penitentiary and Reformatory Discipline*. Albany, New York: Argus.

Abramson, A. (1991). *Theoretical conceptions of curriculum: Implications for juvenile correctional education.* (Ph.D. diss., Drake University.)

California Commission on Teacher Credentialing. (1997). *California standards for the teaching profession.* Sacramento, California: California Department of Education.

California Commission on Teacher Credentialing. (2001). California formative assessment and support system for teachers guidebook: Beginning teacher support and assessment.

Drakeford, W. (2002). The impact of an intensive program to increase the literacy skills of youth confined to juvenile corrections. *The Journal of Correctional Education, 53*(4), 139-146.

Foley, R. M. & Gao, J. (2002). Correctional education program serving incarcerated juveniles: A status report. *The Journal of Correctional Education, 53*(4), 131-138.

Gehring, T. & Hollingsworth, T. (2002). Coping and beyond: Practical suggestions for correctional educators. *The Journal of Correctional Education, 53*(3), 89-95.

Holl, J. M. (1971). *Juvenile reform in the progressive era: William R. George and the Junior Republic movement.* Ithaca, New York: Cornell University Press.

Kilgore, D. & Meade, S. (2004). Look what boot camp's done for me: Teaching and learning at Lakeview Academy. *The Journal of Correctional Education, 55*(2), 170-185.

Marland, P. (1998). Teachers' practical theories: Implications for pre-service teacher education. *Asia-Pacific Journal of Teacher Education & Development, 1*(2), 15-23. Retrieved October 29, 2004, from: www.ied.edu.hk / cric/ apjed / index.htm

McKibbin, M. (1999). Alternative certification in action: California's teaching internships. *Kappa Delta Pi Record, 36*(1), 8-11. Retrieved November 5, 2004, from: http:// mercury.claremont.edu:2096 / hww / results / results_ single.jhtm

Moody, B. A. (2003). Juvenile corrections educators: Their knowledge and understanding of special education. *The Journal of Correctional Education, 54*(3), 105-107.

Osborne, T. M. (1975). *Society and prisons: Some suggestions for a new penology.* Montclair, New Jersey: Patterson Smith. (Reprinted from 1916. Yale University Press.)

Preliminary Report on Teacher Retention in California. (2002). Retrieved December 30, 2004 from: http://www.ctc.ca.gov/reports PrelimRptOnTeacherRetInCA.pdf

Stigler, J. W. & Heibert, J. (1999). *The teaching gap: Best ideas from the world's teachers for improving education in the classroom.* New York: The Free Press.

Steurer, S. J. & Smith, L. G. (2003). *Education reduces crime: Three-state recidivism study executive summary.* Lanham, Maryland and Centerville, Utah: Correctional Education Association and Management and Training Corporation.

Thomas, M. T. (Ed.). (1990). *International comparative education: Practices, issues, & prospects.* New York: Pergamon Press Inc.

Wolford, B., Purnell, B., & Brooks, C. C. (1998). *Educating youth in the juvenile justice system: Results of a national survey on state juvenile justice education standards.* Richmond, Kentucky: National Juvenile Detention Association. Eastern Kentucky University.

Wright, R. (2004). Care as the "heart" of prison teaching. *The Journal of Correctional Education, 55*(3), 191-210.

Chapter X

Duguid, S. (1983). Democratic praxis and origins and development of university education at Matsqui Institution. *Canadian Journal of Criminology, 25*(3), 295-308.

Duguid, S. & Pawson, R. (1998a). Education, change and transformation: The prison experience. *Evaluation Review, 22*(4), 470-495.

Duguid, S. & Pawson, R. (1998b). Final report, British Columbia prison education research.

Chapter XI

Boggs, C. (1976). *Gramsci's Marxism.* London: Pluto.

Brookfield, S. (1987). *Developing critical thinkers: Challenging adults to explore alternative ways of thinking and acting*. Milton Keynes: Open University Press.

Brookfield, S. (2001). Repositioning ideology critique in a critical theory of adult education. *Adult Education Quarterly, 52*(1), 7-22.

Council of Europe. (1987). *European Prison Rules. Recommendation No. R (87) 3*. Strasbourg: Council of Europe.

Council of Europe. (1990). *Education in prison: Recommendation No. R (89) 12*. Strasbourg: Council of Europe.

Davidson, H. (1995). Possibilities for critical pedagogy in a 'Total Institution': An introduction to critical perspective on prison education," In H. Davidson (Ed.), *Schooling in a 'Total Institution.'* Westport, Connecticut: Bergen and Garvey.

Department of Justice. (1985). *Report of the Committee of Inquiry into the penal system* [The Whitaker Report]. Dublin: Government Publications.

Department of Justice. (1994). *The management of offenders: A five year plan*. Dublin: Government Publications.

Duguid, S. (2000). *Can prisons work?: The Prisoner as object and subject in modern corrections*. Toronto: University of Toronto Press.

Foucault, M. (1977). *Discipline and punish: The birth of the prison*. London: Penguin.

Fleming, T. (1998). The role of adult education in Ireland. *Institute of Guidance Counselors Journal, 22*, 58-61.

Fleming, T. (2002). Habermas on civil society, lifeworld and system: Unearthing the social in transformation theory. *Teachers College Record*, Available at: http://www.tcrecord.org./Content.asp? Content ID=10877

Freire, P. (1970). *Pedagogy of the oppressed*. London: Penguin.

Freire, P. & Shor, I. (1987). *A pedagogy for liberation: Dialogues on transforming education*. London: Macmillan.

Germanotta, D. (1995). Prison education: A contextual analysis. In H. Davidson (Ed.), *Schooling in a 'Total Institution.'* Westport, Connecticut: Bergin & Garvey.

Glancey, J. (2001). Within these walls. *The Guardian Supplement*, (February 1), 3-4

Goffman, E. (1961). *Asylums*. London: Penguin.

Goffman, E. (1997). *The Goffman Reader*, ed. C. Lambert & A. Branaman. Oxford: Blackwell Publishers

Haulard, E. (2001). Adult education: A must for our incarcerated population. *The Journal of Correctional Education, 52*(4), 157-59.

Irish Prison Education Service. (2004). *Strategy statement of the Prison Education Service, 2003-2007*. Dublin: Prison Education Service.

Irish Prison Education Service. (2004). *Prison statistics 2003*. Available from: http://www.irishprisons.ie/stats.asp.table1

James, E. (2001). Does prison work? *The Guardian Supplement*, (January 29), 2-4.

Joll, J. (1977). *Gramsci*. London: Fontana.

Kolb, D. (1993). The process of experiential learning. In Thorp et al. (Eds.), *Adulthood and learning*. London: Routledge.

Mayo, P. (1999). *Gramsci, Freire and adult education: Possibilities for transformative learning*. London: Zed Books.

Mezirow, J. (1996). Adult education and empowerment for individual and community development. In B. Connolly, T. Fleming, D. McCormack & A. Ryan (Eds.), *Radical Learning for Liberation*. Maynooth Adult and Community Education Occasional Series, No. 1.

Mezirow, J. (1999). *Transformation theory: Post-modern issues*. Available at: http://www.edst.ubc.ca/aerc/1999/ 99.mezirow.htm.

Mezirow, J. & Associates. (2000). *Learning as transformation*. San Francisco: Jossey Bass.

Morgan, R., ed. (1997). *The Oxford book of criminology*. Oxford and New York: Oxford University Press.

Morris, N. (2004). Jails crisis as Britain's prison population reaches all time high. *The Independent*, (February 18), 1.

National Economic and social forum. (2002). *Reintegration of prisoners: Forum report, no. 22*. Dublin: Government Publications.

O'Mahony, P. (1997). Punishing poverty and personal adversity. *Irish Criminal Law Journal, 7*, 152-70.

O'Mahony, P. (2000). *Prison policy in Ireland: Criminal justice versus social justice.* Cork: Cork University Press.

Sbarbaro, E. (1995). A note on prison activism and social justice. In H. Davidson (Ed.), *Schooling in a 'Total Institution.'* Westport, Connecticut: Bergen and Garvey.

Thomas, J. (1995). The ironies of prison education. In H. Davidson (Ed.), *Schooling in a 'Total Institution.'* Westport, Connecticut: Bergen and Garvey.

Thompson, J. (1996). Really useful knowledge: Linking theory and practice. In B. Connolly (Ed.), *Radical learning for liberation.* Maynooth Adult and Community Education Occasional Series, No. 1.

U.S. Department of Justice, Bureau of Statistics. (2003). *Number of persons under correctional supervision, 2002.* Available at: http://www.ojp.usdoj.gov/bjs/glance/tables/corr2tab.htm

Warner, K. (1998).The 'prisoners are people' perspective: And the problems of promoting learning where this outlook is rejected. *The Journal of Correctional Education, 49*(3), 118-132.

Warner, K. (2002b). Widening and deepening the education we offer those in prison: Reflections from Irish and European experience. *The Journal of Correctional Education, 53*(1), 32.

CHAPTER XII

Behan, C. (2006). From outside to inside: Pedagogy within prison walls. In R. Wright (Ed.), *In the borderlands: Learning to teach in prisons and alternative settings.* Elkridge, Maryland: Correctional Education Association.

Brookfield, S. (2001). Repositioning ideology critique in critical theory of adult learning. *Adult Education Quarterly, 52*(1), 7-22.

Brookfield, S. (1987). *Developing critical thinkers: Challenging adults to explore alternative ways of thinking and acting.* Buckingham: The Open University Press.

Caffarrella, R. & Merriam, S. (1999). Perspectives on adult learning: Framing our research. In A. Rose. (Ed.), *Proceedings of 40th Annual Adult Education Research Conference.* DeKalb: LEPS Press.

Council of Europe. (1990). *Education in prison.* Strasbourg: Council of Europe.

Council of Europe. (1987). *European Prison Rules*. Strasbourg: Council of Europe.

Costelloe, A. (2003). Third level education in Irish prisons: Who participates and why? (Doctoral thesis, The Open University).

Duguid, S. (2000). *Can prisons work? The prisoner as object and subject in modern corrections*. Toronto: University of Toronto Press.

Foucault, M. (1972). *The archaeology of knowledge*. New York: Pantheon.

Freire, P. (1972). *Pedagogy of the oppressed*. Hammondsworth, England: Penguin Educational.

Habermas, J. (1987). *The theory of communicative action: Volume two, lifeworld and system – a critique of functionalist reason*. Boston: Beacon.

Irwin, J. & Austin, J. (1993). *It's about time: America's imprisonment binge*. Belmont, California: A. Wadsworth Publishing Company.

MacCormick, A. (1931). *The education of adult prisoners*. New York: The National Society of Penal Information.

Mayo, P. (1999). *Gramsci, Freire and adult education: Possibilities for transformative action*. London: Zed Books.

Mezirow, J., (Ed.). (2000). *Learning as transformation: Critical perspectives on a theory in progress*. San Francisco: Jossey-Bass.

Morin, L., (Ed.). (1981). *On prison education*. Ottawa: Canadian Government Publishing Centre.

National Adult Literacy Agency. (2005). *Guidelines for good adult literacy work*. Dublin: National Adult Literacy Agency.

Nordic Council of Ministers. (2005). *Nordic prison education: A lifelong education approach*. Copenhagen: Nordic Council of Ministers.

Prison Education Service. (2002). *Guidelines for quality literacy work in prisons*. Dublin: Prison Education Service.

Prison Education Service. (2003). *Strategy statement, 2003-2007*. Dublin: Prison Education Service.

Prison Education Service. (2004). *Prison education in Ireland: A review of the curriculum*. Dublin: Prison Education Service.

Thompson, J. (1997). Really useful knowledge: Linking theory and practice. In T. Fleming (Ed.), *Radical learning for liberation*. Maynooth Adult and Community Education Occasional Series No. 1.

Tulkens, H. (1988). The concept of treatment in the European Prison Rules. In *Prison Information Bulletin No. 11*, June 1988. Strasbourg: Council of Europe.

Warner, K. (2002). Widening and deepening the education we offer those in prison: Reflections from Irish and European experience. *The Journal of Correctional Education, 53*(1), 32-37.

✺

CHAPTER XIII

Alberti, J. (1997). A fantasy of belonging? In L. Stanley (Ed.), *Knowing feminisms: On academic borders, territories and tribes* (pp. 144-153). Thousand Oaks, California: Sage Publications.

Anzaldua, G. (1987). *Borderlands/la frontera: The new Mestiza*. San Francisco: Spinsters/Aunt Lute.

Brown, C. (1997). Dancing between hemispheres: Negotiating routes for the dancer-academic. In L. Stanley (Ed.), *Knowing feminisms: On academic borders, territories and tribes* (pp. 132-143). Thousand Oaks, California: Sage Publications.

Butler, J. (1992). Contingent foundations: Feminism and the question of "postmodernism." In J. Butler & J. Scott (Eds.), *Feminists theorize the political* (pp. 3-21). New York: Routledge.

Carlson, D. & Apple, M., (Eds.). (1998). *Power/knowledge/pedagogy: The meaning of democratic education in unsettling times*. Boulder, Colorado: Westview Press.

Collins, M. (1988b). Towards a distinctive vocation for prison educators: Some key concerns and relevant strategies. *The Journal of Correctional Education, 39*(1), 24-28.

Collins, M. (1995c). Shades of the prison house: Adult literacy and the correctional ethos. In H. Davidson (Ed.), *Schooling in a 'Total Institution': Critical perspectives on prison education* (pp. 49-64). Westport, Connecticut: Bergin & Garvey.

Collins, M. (1998). *Critical crosscurrents in education*. Malabar, Florida: Krieger Publishing Company.

Craig, C. (1995). Dilemmas in crossing the boundaries on the professional knowledge landscape. In D. Clandinin & F. Connelly (Eds.), *Teachers' professional knowledge landscapes* (pp. 16-24). New York: Teachers College Press.

Eagleton, T. (1983). *Literary theory: An introduction*. Minneapolis: University of Minnesota Press.

Kothari, U. (1997). Identity and representation: Experiences of teaching a neo-colonial discipline. In L. Stanley (Ed.), *Knowing feminisms: On academic borders, territories and tribes* (pp. 154-165). Thousand Oaks, California: Sage Publications Inc.

Lather, P. (1991). *Getting smart: Feminist research and pedagogy with/in the postmodern*. New York: Routledge.

McLaren, P. (1995). *Critical pedagogy and predatory culture: Oppositional politics in a postmodern era*. New York: Routledge.

Overall, C. (1998). *A feminist I: Reflections from academia*. Peterborough, ON: Broadview Press.

Schick, C. (1998). *"By virtue of being white:" Racialized identity formation and the implications for anti-racist pedagogy*. (Ph.D. diss., Ontario Institute for Studies in Education of the University of Toronto, Ontario.

Stanley, L., (Ed.). (1997). *Knowing feminisms: On academic borders, territories and tribes*. Thousand Oaks, California: Sage Publications Inc.

Weiler, K. (1995). Freire and a feminist pedagogy of difference. In J. Holland, M. Blair, & S. Sheldon (Eds.), *Debates and issues in feminist research and pedagogy* (pp. 23-44). Philadelphia & Clevedon, England: Multilingual Matters Ltd., Open University.

Wright, R. (1998). Teacher's voices, teacher's knowledge: Reflection on The (new) Journal of Correctional Education. *The Journal of Correctional Education, 49*(2), 45-58.

ᘒ

CHAPTER XIV

Carr, W. (1993). What is an educational practice? In M. Hammersley (Ed.) *Educational Research: Current Issues* (pp. 160-174). London: The Open University.

Costelloe, A. (2003). Third level education in Irish prisons: Who participates and why? (Doctoral thesis, The Open University).

Denzin, N. & Lincoln, Y. (2000). The discipline and practice of qualitative research. In N. Denzin & Y. Lincoln (Eds.), *Handbook of Qualitative Research* (2nd ed.) (pp. 1-28). Thousands Oaks, California: Sage Publications Inc.

Ely, M., Vinz, R., Downing, M. & Anzul, M. (1997). *On writing qualitative research: Living by words*. London: The Falmer Press.

Freire, P. (1972). *Pedagogy of the oppressed*. Harmondsworth: Penguin.

Freire, P. (1993). *Pedagogy of the city*. New York: Continuum.

Freire, P. & Shor, I. (1987). *A pedagogy for liberation: Dialogue on transforming education*. London: Macmillan.

Gergen, M. & Gergen, K. (2000). Qualitative inquiry: Tensions and transformations. In N. Denzin & Y. Lincoln (Eds.), *Handbook of Qualitative Research* (2nd ed.) (pp. 1025-1046). Thousands Oaks, California: Sage Publications Inc.

Hammersley, M. (1993). On the teacher as researcher. In M. Hammersley (Ed.), *Educational Research: Current issues* (pp. 211-227). London: The Open University.

Hitchcock, G. & Hughes, D. (1995). *Research and the teacher: A qualitative Introduction to school-based research*. London: Routledge.

Kemmis, S. (1993). Action research. In M. Hammersley (Ed.), *Educational Research: Current issues* (pp. 177-189). London: The Open University.

Lynch, K. (1999). *Equality in education*. Dublin: Gill & Macmillan.

Maykut, P. & Morehouse, R. (1994). *Beginning qualitative Research: A philosophical and practical guide*. London: Falmer.

Mezirow, J. (1997). Transformative theory out of context. *Adult Education Quarterly, 48*(1), 60-63.

Mezirow, J. (1998a). Postmodern critique of transformative theory: A response to Pietrykowski. *Adult Education Quarterly, 49*(1), 65-68.

Mezirow, J. (1998b). Transformative learning and social action: A response to Inglis. *Adult Education Quarterly, 49*(1), 70-73.

Mezirow, J. (2000). Learning to think like an adult: Core concepts of transformation theory. In J. Mezirow (Ed.), *Learning as transformation: Critical perspectives on a theory in progress* (pp. 3-33). San Francisco: Jossey-Bass.

McMahon, B. (1997). The meaning and relevance of education for working-class mature students: A personal view. In R. Morris (Ed.), *Mature students in higher education. proceedings of conference in Athlone Regional Technical College on 29 March, 1996* (pp. 3-33). Cork: Higher Education Equality Unit. Retrieved January 5, 2001 from: http://www.ucc.ie/ publications/ heeu/Mature/mature.htm

McNiff, J., Lomax, P. & Whitehead, J. (1996). *You and your action research project.* London: Routledge.

Oppenheim, A. (1992). *Questionnaire design, interviewing and attitude measurement.* London: Pinter Publishers.

Pietrykowski, B. (1998). Modern and postmodern tensions in adult education theory: A response to Jack Mezirow. *Adult Education Quarterly, 49*(1), 65-68.

Pring, R. (2000). *Philosophy of educational research.* London and New York: Continuum.

Schon, D. (1987). *Educating the reflective practitioner.* San Francisco: Jossey-Bass.

Schuller, T. (1998). Three steps towards a learning society. *Studies in the Education of Adults, 30*(1),11-20.

Scott, D. (1996). Ethnography and education. In D. Scott & R. Usher (Eds.), *Understanding educational research.* London and New York: Routledge.

Scott, D. & Usher, R. (1996). *Understanding Educational Research.* London and New York: Routledge.

Smith, J., & Deemer, D. (2000). The problem of criteria in the age of relativism. In N. Denzin & Y. Lincoln (Eds.), *Handbook of Qualitative Research* (2nd Edition) (pp. 877-896). Thousands Oaks, California: Sage Publications Inc.

CHAPTER XV

Adler, P. & Adler, P. (1998). The gloried self. In Cahill, S. (Ed.), *Inside social life: Readings in sociological psychology and microsociology* (89-97). Los Angeles: Roxbury.

Ashmore, R. D. & Jussim, L. (Eds.). (1997). *Self and identity: Fundamental issues.* New York : Oxford University Press.

Ashcroft, R., Price, T. & Sweeney, D. (1998). Special training for teachers in alternative and correctional education. *The Journal of Correctional Education, 49*(3), 110-116.

Ashcroft, R. (1999). Professional identity for teachers in alternative education. *The Clearing House, 73,* 2.

Baumeister, R. F. (1986). *Identity: Cultural change and the struggle for self.* New York: Oxford University Press.

Berg, R. V. D. (2002). Teachers' meanings regarding educational practice. *Review of Educational Research, 72*(4), 577-625.

Cooley, C. H. (1998). The self as sentiment and reflection. In Cahill, S. (Ed). *Inside social life: Readings in sociological psychology and microsociology,* (16-20). Los Angeles: Roxbury.

Deaux, K. (1992). Personalizing identity and socializing self. In Breakwell, G. M. (Ed.), *Social psychology of identity and the self-concept.* San Diego, CA: Surrey University Press.

Deaux, K. (1993). Reconstructing social identity. *Personality and Social Psychology Bulletin, 19*(1), 4-12.

Deikman, A. (1982). *The observing self.* Boston: Beacon Press.

Foucault, M. (1979) *Discipline and punish: The birth of the prison.* Vantage Books, New York.

Goffman, E. (1961). *Asylums: Essays on the social situations of mental patients and other inmates.* New York: Anchor Books.

Goffman, E (1967). *Interaction ritual: Essays on face-to-face behavior.* New York, Pantheon Books.

Howarth, C. (2002). Identity in whose eyes? The role of representations in identity construction. *Journal for the Theory of Social Behavior, 32*(2), 145-162.

Kim, M. (2002). *Non-Western perspectives on human communication: Implications for theory and practice.* Sage: Thousand Oaks, CA.

Kitayama, S. & Markus, H. (1999). Yin and yang of the Japanese self: The cultural psychology of personality coherence. In Cervone, D. & Shoda, Y. (Eds.), *The coherence of personality; Social-cognitive bases of consistency, variability and organization* (pp. 242-302). New York: Guilford Press.

Kitayama, S., Markus, H., Matsumoto, H. & Norasakkunkit, V. (1997). Individual and collective processes in the construction of the self: Self-enhancement in the united states and self-criticism in Japan. *Journal of Personality & Social Psychology, 72,* 1245-1267.

Markus, H. & Kunda, Z. (1986). Stability and malleability of the self-concept. *Journal of Personality and Social Psychology, 42,* 38-50.

Mead, G. H. (1998). The self as social structure. In S. Cahill, (Ed). *Inside social life: Readings in sociological psychology and microsociology* (21-25). Los Angeles: Roxbury.

Navasky, M. & O'Connor K. (2005). *Frontline: The new asylums.* Public Broadcasting Service Documentary.

Neidenthal, P. M. & Beike, D. R. (1997). Interrelated and isolated self-concepts. *Personality and Social Psychology Review, 1,* 106-128.

Nelson, C. (2002). Between anonymity and celebrity: the zero degree of professional identity. *College English, 64*(6), 710-719.

Nick O. v. Terhune. Case No. CIV S-89-0755-RAR-JFM (Stipulation and Order filed Feb. 16, 1990).

Piaget, J. (1973). *To understand is to invent.* New York: Grossman.

Presser, L. (2004). Violent offenders, moral selves: Constructing identities and accounts in the research interview. *Social Problems, 51*(1), 82.

Presser, L. (1992). The construction of the self: An evolutionary view. Current Psychology: *Research and Reviews, 11,* 110-121.

Stryker, S. (1987). The vitalization of symbolic interactionism. *Social Psychology Quarterly, 50,* 83-94.

Swann, W. B. (1987). Identity negotiations: Where two roads meet. *Journal of Personality and Social Psychology, 53,* 1038-1051.

Conclusion

Clifford, J. & Marcus, G. (1986). *Writing culture: The poetics and politics of ethnography.* Berkeley: University of California Press.

Eggleston, C. R. & Gehring, T. (1986). Correctional education paradigms in the United States and Canada. *The Journal of Correctional Education, 37*(2), 87-89.

Eggleston, C. R. (1991). Correctional education professional development. *The Journal of Correctional Education, 42*(1), 16-22.

Giddens, A. (1984). *The constitution of society.* Los Angeles: University of California Press.

Goffman, E. (1959). *The presentation of self in everyday life.* New York: Doubleday Anchor Books.

Greene, M. (1973). Teacher as stranger. In M. Greene (Ed.), *Teacher as stranger: Educational philosophy for the modern age* (pp. 267-302). California: Wadsworth Publishing Company.

Jary, D. & Jary, J. (1995). *Collin's dictionary of sociology* (2ⁿᵈ ed.). Glasgow: Harper Collins Publishers.

Lengermann, P. M. & Newbridge-Barnsley, J. (1983). Contemporary feminist theory. In G. Riser (Ed.), *Contemporary sociological theory,* (2ⁿᵈ ed.) (pp. 282-325). New York: Knopf.

Lyons, N. (1990). Dilemmas of knowing: Ethical and epistemological dimensions of teacher's work and development. *Howard Educational Review, 60*(May), 159-180.

Park, R. & Burgess, E. (1928/1969). Human migration and the marginal man. In R. H. Turner (Ed.), *On social control and collective behavior: Selected papers* (pp. 194-206). Chicago: The University of Chicago Press.

Schutz, A. (1964). The stranger: An essay in social psychology. In A. Broderson (Ed.), *Alfred Schutz: Collected papers II: Studies in social theory* (pp. 91-134). The Hague: Martinus Nijhoff

Simmel, G. (1950). The stranger. In K. Wolff (Ed.), *The Sociology of Georg Simmel* (pp. 402-408). Glencoe, Illinois: Free Press.

Solzhenitsyn, A. I. (1973). *The gulag archipelago.* New York: Harper & Row, Publishers

Tannen, D. (1990). *You just don't understand: Women and men in conversation.* New York: William Morrow.

Vila, P. (2003). *Ethnography at the border.* Minneapolis: University of Minnesota Press.

Webb, D. L., Metha, A., & Jordan, F. K. (2003). *Foundations of American education.* Columbus, Ohio: Merrill Prentice Hall.

Wright, R. (2001). Justice with her eyes wide open: Situated knowledges, diversity and correctional education in the post-modern era (part II), *The Journal of Correctional Education, 52*(1), 33-38.

Wright, R. (2004). You were hired to teach: Ideological struggle, education and teacher burnout at the New Prison for Women. *The Qualitative Report,* December 9(4), 630-651.

Wright, R. (2005). Teacher burnout and toxic cultures in alternative school/ prison settings. *The Journal of Juvenile Court, Community and Alternative School Administrators of California, 18,* 44-53.

AFTERWORD

Eggleston, C. (1991). Correctional education professional development. *The Journal of Correctional Education, 42*(1), 16 - 22.

Freedman, E. (1981). *Their sister's keepers: Women's prison reform in America, 1830-1930.* Ann Arbor: University of Michigan Press.

John of Salisbury. (1159). Retrieved December 30, 2007, from http://timelines. ws/1100_1199.HTML

Gehring, T. (2005). *Elements of the CSUSB Correctional and Alternative Education Program.* San Bernardino: California State University (unpublished document).

Gehring, T. & Eggleston, C. (2006). *Correctional education chronology.* San Bernardino: California State University Press.

Gehring, T. & Rennie, S. (2008). *Correctional education history from A to Z.* San Bernardino: California State University Press.

George, W. (1911). *The Junior Republic: Its history and ideals.* New York: D. Appleton.

Osborne, T. M. (1924). *Prisons and common sense.* Philadelphia and London: J. B. Lippincott Company.

Tannenbaum, F. (1933). *Osborne of Sing Sing.* Chapel Hill: University of North Carolina Press.

Wright, R. (2004). Care as the "heart" of prison teaching. *The Journal of Correctional Education, 55*(3), 191-209.

LIST OF IMAGES